We hope you enjoy this b
renew it b   date.

Berlitz

THAILAND

POCKET GUIDE

ARTS & CULTURE

Space disco ho[...]
featuring the[...]

Music   Arts & C[...]

A Z INFO

SHOPPIN[...]

Shopping in [...]
around the [...]
be fo[...]

Chancel Brother
STEAKS
♀100 m

...RPOT

DIAMANT
Restaurant

BROOKLANN

JOE'S BURGERS
Restaurant

...ATE BRIDGE   ♀100 m

♀ MAP   ⤴ SHARE

♡ LIKE

Sailing under the Golden Gate Bridge today, it is interesting to consider that engineers once thought it impossible to span the Golden Gate Strait at this point; because of the depth of the water (318ft/ 97 meters, at its deepest point) and the powerful tidal rush.

The city authorized studies for a bridge in 1917, but it was 1933 before the first shovel turned under the gaze of master engineer Joseph B. Strauss (no relation to the famous waltz composer). Four years later the bridge opened, at a cost of $35 million and the lives of 11 construction workers. Today the bridge

🔍

INSIGHT ⊙ GUIDES

SPAIN

☰   📄 INTRODUCTION

🔲 EXPLORE P[...]

🗺 EX[...]

...LE   ₩ $8.00

...LORIDA   ₩ $8.00

This new edition of Insight Guide
Florida is comprehensive, with inspiration
travel and all-in-it everything
and visiting features on everything
from Channel Surf Wars and

FRANCE   ₩ $8.00

This brand new edition Insight Guide
full colour features outstanding
edition, packed with 250 illustrated
infographics, stunning
exploration of all the places to go.

FRANCE

ST LUCIA Pocket Guide   ₩ $8.00

St Lucia is one of the most popular
first class destinations from dramatic
plantations houses to a lively
explores dedicated to a wide
edition ideal this Pocket Guide St

⊙ Walking Eye
mobile app

Discover the world's best destinations with the Insight Guides Walking Eye app, available to download for free in the App Store and Google Play.

The container app provides easy access to fantastic free content on events and activities taking place in your current location or chosen destination, with the possibility of booking, as well as the regularly-updated Insight Guides travel blog: Inspire Me. In addition, you can purchase curated, premium destination guides through the app, which feature local highlights, hotel, bar, restaurant and shopping listings, an A to Z of practical information and more. On purchase and download Insight Guide eBooks straight to your device.

Download on the App Store **GET IT ON Google Play**

INSIGHT ⊙ GUIDES

Walking Eye

⊙ DESTINATIONS

⊘ INSPIRE ME

⊟ EBOOKS

▦ EVENTS

TOP 10 ATTRACTIONS

KWAI RIVER BRIDGE
Pay homage to the thousands of prisoners who died during the bridge's construction in World War II. See page 41.

MAE HONG SON
This north-eastern town lies in a serene forested valley. See page 73.

BANGKOK'S WAT PHRA KAEW AND GRAND PALACE COMPLEX
Highlights include the chapel of the Emerald Buddha and a golden *chedi* (stupa). See page 27.

CHIANG MAI
For Thai silks visit the bustling Night Bazaar. See page 64.

PHANG NGA BAY
Paddle around a landscape filled with oddly shaped islands and hidden caves. See page 79.

PHANOM RUNG
This spectacular sanctuary is one of the highlights of the Khmer Culture Trail. See page 49.

AYUTTHAYA
A national treasure, this ruined city gives an insight into the ancient history of Thailand. See page 43.

HILL TRIBES
Trek by Jeep or on foot to see these followers of ancient rituals. See page 67.

KO SAMUI
The place to swim, snorkel, windsurf, dine on the sand or just people-watch. See page 81.

CHAO PHRAYA
Take a boat on Bangkok's majestic river. See page 36.

A PERFECT DAY

9.00am

Breakfast
Drop in for a leisurely breakfast at The Verandah, on the Mandarin Oriental's riverside terrace. The luxurious surroundings provide a fine start to the day, and the Oriental boat pier is next door, with boats waiting to whisk you on to the next leg of the day's journey.

12 noon

Gold and dragons
Grab a taxi to Chinatown, which has some of the most historic shopping alleys in Bangkok. Along with gold, dragon dresses and Chinese lanterns, these lanes are full of cheap food stalls that make it an ideal stop for lunch. At Wat Traimit see the world's biggest solid gold Buddha.

2.00pm

Shopping
A taxi to Pathumwan brings you to the heart of the city's mall district. As well as offering local and international fashions, Siam Paragon hosts Sea Life Ocean World, home to penguins, sharks, stingrays and other creatures of the deep.

10.00am

Lying down
Take a Chao Phraya river boat to Tha Tien pier where, just beyond a market and Chinese shop houses, the grounds of Wat Pho host the Reclining Buddha. Afterwards, get pampered at the temple's traditional massage school.

IN **BANGKOK**

6.00pm

River sunset
Hop on the Skytrain to Saphan Taksin station, from where it is a 10-minute walk to the 200m (656ft) -high, al fresco rooftop restaurant Sirocco. Have a sunset cocktail at the rooftop bar with stunning views along the Chao Phraya River.

10.30pm

Bars and clubs
Take the Skytrain to Nana Station and stroll down Sukhumvit Soi 11, the location of some of Bangkok's best clubs. Levels Club & Lounge (formerly Q Bar) has one of the city's best stocked bars and good views out over the city. For dirt-cheap drinks, try Cheap Charlie's.

4.00pm

Culture
A 10-minute walk away, the Bangkok Art and Culture Centre has regular performances and exhibitions by local and international artists, restaurants and a café. A further 10 minutes' walk away is the Jim Thompson House and Museum, a traditional Thai house full of art and antiques. There is a restaurant here, too.

8.30pm

Night market
Ten minutes in a taxi brings you to the infamous Patpong red light district, which has a bustling night market. The stalls are full of funky T-shirts, watches, jewellery, trinkets and handbags. Bargain hard. There is a good choice of restaurants and bars in the surrounding streets, with and without the ignoble pole dancers and ping pong acrobatics.

CONTENTS

INTRODUCTION

As the only country in Southeast Asia that was never colonised, Thailand explodes with the boundless energy and self-confidence of its people. Literally translated, Thailand means 'Land of the Free', although it is most often referred to as 'Land of Smiles'. The Thais are easy going and proud of their country. And they are always smiling. They value *jai yen* or a 'cool heart' and dislike hot tempers and loud voices. They are warm and welcoming to foreigners. Even on Bangkok's impossibly crowded streets, a visitor will feel quite safe asking a stranger for directions. There is a sense of calm and tolerance that prevails throughout the country.

THAILAND AND ITS ATTRACTIONS

Roughly the size of Texas or France, Thailand offers a vast variety of holiday possibilities. You'll find thick jungles, bustling cities and sparkling beach resorts. In the northern city of Chiang Mai, there is one of the world's most fascinating night markets. Those interested in purchasing silk, woven baskets and lacquered wood will want to shop here; it is also an excellent place to buy imitation designer-wear at incredibly low prices. In the lush valleys north of Chiang Mai you will see the many orchid farms and elephant training camps that contribute towards Thailand's unique identity.

Going deeper into the northern regions, to Chiang Rai and the Golden Triangle, hill-tribes follow rituals established thousands of years ago. Do not miss the opportunity to take a boat-trip down the Mekong, one of the world's great rivers. It runs down from Tibet, irrigating the rice fields in the north of Thailand, Laos and Cambodia before it empties out in the Mekong Delta of South Vietnam. If trekking in the jungles is an experience you are after, head further north-west to the town of Mae Hong Son. Here, deep in the jungle, jeep tours and overnight camping trips can be arranged.

In the centre of the country there are tranquil rice fields stretching as far as the eye can see, and the magnificent ruins of Sukhothai and Ayutthaya. If you prefer more natural attractions, head for one of the vast national parks, which now constitute a huge

Boat navigating at a floating market

34,500 sq km (23,479 sq mile) of Thailand. Of particular note is Khao Yai National Park where iridescent kingfishers and orange-breasted, red-headed trogons flit beneath the shade of the leafy canopy. Gibbons and flying squirrels, elephants, black bears and possibly tigers dwell in these vast stretches of dense evergreen. You might catch a glimpse of any one of over 900 different species.

In the south, in the Gulf of Thailand, and off the sandy shores of the Andaman Sea you will find spectacular tropical islands jutting out of the shimmering blue water. The resorts of Phuket, Ko Phi Phi and Ko Samui attract sun-worshippers from around the world. Here, the beach is the main attraction and there are many world-class hotels and resorts to suit every taste and budget.

Many visitors begin their visit in Bangkok where direct flights from around the world arrive at the Bangkok International Airport. Thailand's capital is one of the most crowded cities

Khao Yai National Park contains mostly tropical forest

in Asia. It has the majestic Chao Phraya (River of the Kings) and many criss-crossing canals. The old way of life still exists along the waterways and floating markets are still a sight to behold, but these days there are also endless traffic jams and scores of high-rise buildings. After the initial shock of Bangkok's polluted and chaotic streets, you will begin to discover the city's many splendid sights. From the glorious Temple of Dawn to the magnificent reclining Buddha and the impressive Grand Palace, Bangkok is rich in royal, religious and historical monuments. It has excellent shopping in its many malls and endless shop-lined streets.

With its diverse range of restaurants, the city is also a food-lover's paradise. Fresh, delicious and inexpensive food is found practically everywhere in this urban agglomeration of more than 14 million residents. But there are upmarket options, too. From simple street-side eateries to elegant dining rooms overlooking the Chao Phraya river, you will definitely eat well in Bangkok. Thai cooking is based on balancing foods between spicy, sour, hot and sweet; the success of any meal relies on creating delightful contrasts, which ensure that the palate never becomes jaded. Popular delicacies such as prawns in coconut, or succulent chicken wrapped in a banana leaf take their place among an array of hotter culinary specialities. With so much variety you could enjoy a different dish every day of your visit and leave with plenty of fine dishes still unsampled.

WHEN TO GO

Thailand's weather can appear to be hot, hotter and hottest. The hottest months are April and May when the country is at its driest before the rains arrive. June to October is the less hot monsoon season, when the rains come in heavy downpours, usually in the afternoons, but only lasting for an hour or two. November to February is the least hot period and inevitably forms the high tourist season in Thailand. Cool northern winds blow down from China, making Bangkok more tolerable for visitors. Northern regions can be chilly.

Although many travellers avoid the country during the monsoon months, this can actually be a very pleasant time to visit. Domestic flights are virtually empty, and temples and beaches are not as crowded. If you don't mind the occasional rain, then you'll be rewarded with reduced hotel rates and restaurants eager to please the adventurous off-season traveller.

A WARM WELCOME

Thailand's people often afford the most memorable experiences. From friendly northerners who may sell you sweet honey pineapple by the side of the road to the smiling fishermen of the southern beaches, the philosophy underlying every aspect of life is, simply, *mai pen rai* ('no worries').

Thai customs

On being introduced, Thais will place both palms of their hands together under their chin in a traditional Wai greeting. The head is considered sacred in Buddhism; try not to touch anyone, even children, there.

A BRIEF HISTORY

Archaeological finds in Ban Chiang, northeast Thailand, date back over 5,000 years, proving the country was home to one of the world's first Bronze Age civilisations. What happened to those prehistoric people is unknown.

As for the Thais today, they are descended from many ethnic groups. The Mon Dvaravati kingdom flourished in the west from the 6th to the 11th centuries, with Nakhon Pathom and Lopburi as major settlements. East of the Chao Phraya valley, the Khmer empire of Angkor, strongly influenced by Indian culture, and forerunner of present-day Cambodia, ruled as far north as Laos.

However, the group who gave their name to present day Thailand were the Tai, who migrated in several tribes from China's Yunnan region, probably starting in the 10th century.

Around AD1259, the kingdom of Lanna ('Land of a Million Rice Fields') was established in what is now northern Thailand. Chiang Rai was chosen as capital until King Mengrai spotted five white mice, two white *sambars* and two white barking deer beside the Ping River, and relocated to Chiang Mai.

Mengrai ruled prosperously until the age of 80, when he was struck by lightning.

KING RAMKAMHAENG

The first great chapter of Thai history began with King Ramkamhaeng the Great, ruler of Sukhothai (founded in the 1230s) around 1280 to 1317. King Ramkamhaeng – renowned for legendary war exploits on elephants – nurtured a powerful kingdom that was a thriving centre for the arts. In its heyday, the kingdom stretched from Lampang in the north of Thailand to Vientiane, now part of Laos, and south towards the Malay

Sukhothai, centre of a once powerful kingdom

Peninsula. Sukhothai contributed some of the finest examples of Thai sculpture, many of which can still be viewed in parts of the old city today.

After the death of King Ramkamhaeng, the kingdom's power declined. By the 15th century the city of Sukhothai was little more than a provincial town, and shortly afterwards it was abandoned altogether.

AYUTTHAYA

Established in 1350, Ayutthaya continued for over 400 years and earned a place as one of the East's greatest civilisations. Under King U-Thong and a succession of legendary monarchs, the kingdom expanded rapidly. Towards the end of the 14th century, the Khmers were driven out of vast areas of central and northern Thailand, and the people of Sukhothai were finally vanquished. In 1431 the capital at Angkor in Cambodia was sacked, and

Ayutthaya's pre-eminence was established beyond question. It became a centre for trade between China, India and Europe.

Despite the loss of several kings – some of whom were either cudgelled to death or poisoned – the people of Ayutthaya were, by all accounts, a happy lot, 'much given to pleasure and ryot' according to the observations of one 17th-century traveller. Opium was in quite abundant supply, and cohabitation and wife-swapping found many enthusiastic supporters.

Many foreign travellers who visited Ayutthaya during the 17th century were impressed by the size and opulence of the Siamese capital. Directors of the East India Company compared it favourably with London, estimating its population to be anything from 300,000 to 1 million. With palaces, canals and temples, the city acquired a justified reputation for being the most beautiful in Southeast Asia.

European influence reached its zenith during the reign of King Narai (1656–88), when Siam was visited by ambassadors from as far away as the court of Louis XIV, along with explorers, zealous Jesuit missionaries and traders. One Greek adventurer, named Geraki Constantine Phaulkon, was even

⊘ ABSOLUTE RULE

When it came to rhetorical flourishes, the monarchs of Ayutthaya in the 17th century took the biscuit. Any mortal who was so bold as to address the king was obliged to start as follows: 'High and mighty Lord of me, thy slave, I desire to take thy royal word and put it in my brain and on the top of my head.' Some who failed to follow this code of conduct were summarily chastised with bamboos. Others were buried alive in the cement walls surrounding the city.

Riding round the Unesco World Heritage Site of Ayutthaya

appointed the king's first minister, and acted as the principal go-between when diplomatic exchanges were held. But his apparent influence sparked jealousy. Shortly before the king died in 1688, at the time of a bloody revolt, Phaulkon was arrested and then executed. Following this incident, Thailand had almost no contact with the West for a period of 150 years.

Between the 15th and 18th centuries, the Thais fought innumerable battles against the neighbouring Burmese. In April 1767, the Burmese succeeded in capturing Ayutthaya, after a 14-month-long siege. They pillaged the city and vandalised every aspect of Thai culture and art. The sack of Ayutthaya, a great tragedy in Thai history, still casts a shadow over the national consciousness of the Thai people.

One survivor, a young general from Tak province, rallied the remnants of the Thai army and managed to expel the Burmese garrison. Ayutthaya had been almost totally destroyed, however, so Taksin – as he was known – founded a new capital at Thonburi, directly across the Chao Phraya river from what has since become Bangkok. Though his father was Chinese – and a commoner at that – Taksin was crowned King of Thailand. He ruled until 1782, at which point he was dethroned on the grounds that he had gone mad.

FROM THONBURI TO BANGKOK

The death of Taksin saw the rise to power of the Chakri Dynasty, the greatest in Thai history, and the one that still occupies the throne today. Rama I, the first Chakri-dynasty king, immediately moved his capital from Thonburi to Bangkok – on the east bank of the river – saying that the new city would be larger and easier to defend. He then went on to defeat a number of marauding Burmese expeditions.

His son, Rama II, devoted himself to preserving Thai literature, and produced a classic version of the Thai *Ramakien*, based on the epic Sanskrit poem, *Ramayana*. He also re-established relations with the West, and still found time to sire 73 children by 38 mothers.

Although no less influential, Rama III (1824–51) is largely overlooked by historians. As a devout Buddhist he renovated some of Bangkok's finest temples, including Wat Arun and parts of Wat Pho. He also went on to introduce Western medicine to his country – including smallpox vaccinations – as well as arranging for American missionaries to visit the country; one of them brought the first printing press with Thai type.

PROGRESSIVE MONARCHS

King Rama IV (1851–68), also known as King Mongkut, is loosely represented in the Hollywood film *The King and I*, which is deemed disrespectful and banned in Thailand. Thais worship

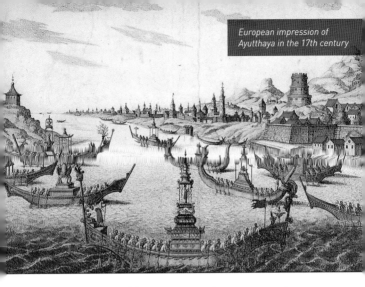

Mongkut as one of their greatest and most progressive monarchs. He was a modern-minded scholar of languages and sciences, and was a monk for 27 years before taking the throne. During his reign commoners were allowed for the first time to set eyes on the King. Waterways and roads were built and laws were passed to improve the rights of women and children.

Mongkut was succeeded by Rama V, who became known as Chulalongkorn, or Lord of the White Elephant, and was one of the most popular and enlightened of the Chakri kings. During his 42-year reign, he abolished slavery and established a schooling system, the first post office and a national library. He led his country literally as well as symbolically into the 20th century.

THE WORLD WARS

The effect of World War I was to propel Thailand out of isolation. In 1918, King Vajiravudh (Rama VI) dispatched troops to France

Wat Arun, which was renovated by Rama III

to support the Allied cause. A likely explanation for his sympathies is that he was Cambridge-educated and had served for a time in the British army. Once the war was over, Siam became a member of the League of Nations.

One legacy of Rama VI was the use of surnames by the Thai people. Prior to the war, family names were not used in Siam, but the king decreed that all his subjects should adopt one. Women were also encouraged to grow their hair long, and the game of football was even introduced, with a royal team.

The genteel world of Siam was rocked once more in 1932, when a group of army officers staged a bloodless revolution, which brought the monarchy's absolute supremacy to an end. The authorities of Siam (by then renamed Thailand) signed friendship agreements with the Japanese in 1940. The following year, the Japanese invaded Thailand, and the Thais – seeing further resistance as hopeless – entered World War II soon afterwards on the side of the Axis. It was at this time that the notorious Death Railway was built, with its bridge over the River Kwai. Despite the fact that Thailand ended the war on the losing side, it was later allowed to join the United Nations due to a legal loophole in the original declaration of war.

Since its first military coup in 1932, continual political turbulence has beset Thailand. It has endured 12 successful coups and had over 60 prime ministers, although some have served several (shorter) terms. Only one has lasted the full term of five years. Ironically though, Thailand is deemed one of the most stable countries in the region. It sided with the US during the Vietnam War, and throughout its history it has remained resolutely monarchist and equally resolutely anti-communist.

MODERN-DAY THAILAND

Three anti-government uprisings, in 1973, 1976 and 1992, resulted in many civilian deaths. Following the king's intervention to calm the last crisis, stable, democratically elected governments endured for the next 14 years. Thailand saw rapid economic growth during the 1980s and 1990s, until a market crash in 1997 caused currency devaluation.

In 2001, Thaksin Shinawatra won a landslide election victory but proved controversial. He defended corruption charges, but

⊘ SANDWICHES FOR DEMOCRACY

Thai history teems with military coups. The most recent one on 22 May 2014 was the first in the social media age. With the current regime taking a very tough stance on the opposition, even liking an anti-coup page on Facebook constituted a criminal offence. As a symbol of resistance, the anti-coup protest movement used a three-finger salute. Once the military government announced that it would arrest anyone who used it, the protesters adopted a new sign of rebellion – a sandwich. 'Sandwiches for democracy' were handed out in the streets, until this too was banned. All social media contact with three outspoken critics of Thailand's government was also prohibited in 2017.

was condemned for suppressing the media and for hundreds of deaths in his War on Drugs. In 2005, anti-Thaksin demonstrators adopted the colour yellow to show allegiance to the monarchy, becoming known as the Yellow Shirts. The movement intensified after Thaksin sold his telecommunications company and paid no tax. In 2006, he was ousted in a military coup.

A Thaksin proxy, the People Power Party (PPP) won the 2007 general election, but was disbanded by the courts. Democrat Abhisit Vejjajiva became prime minister. Thaksin's followers, the Red Shirts, clashed with the army in 2010. 91 people died.

2011 saw the general election victory of the pro-Thaksin Pheu Thai party, with Thaksin's sister Yingluck Shinawatra becoming prime minister. But in 2013, massive anti-government rallies were held and the house of representatives was dissolved. New elections were declared invalid by the Constitutional Court, which also removed Shinawatra from office over nepotism allegations.

Amidst political turmoil, in May 2014, the army seized power in a coup. The new regime took control of the media, while martial law and curfews were imposed nationwide (the latter were soon lifted). The coup leader, General Prayuth Chanocha, was made prime minister and King Bhumibol Adulyadej soon endorsed his rule. Immensely popular in Thailand, King Bhumibol Adulyadej died on 13 October 2016, aged 88. He was succeeded by his only son Maha Vajiralongkorn, who became Rama X, the tenth monarch of the Chakri Dynasty.

Meanwhile the post-coup military regime (which remains in power at the time of writing) has employed stringent measures to crack down on any dissent. In August 2016 the Thai people voted for a military-drafted constitution which was signed by King Maha Vajiralongkorn in April 2017. It is the country's 20th constitution since 1932.

HISTORICAL LANDMARKS

1st–11th century AD The Dvavarati culture flourishes.

1238 Sukhothai kingdom is established.

1351 The kingdom of Ayutthaya is founded on the central plains.

1431 Ayutthaya conquers the Khmer empire centred on Angkor.

1767 Ayutthaya is invaded by the old enemy, Burma. General Taksin escapes and is crowned king the following year in Thonburi.

1902 in the new capital of Bangkok. General Chao Phaya Chakri proclaims himself Rama I, the first king of the Chakri dynasty.

1851–68 King Mongkut (Rama IV) ascends the throne.

1910–25 Rama VI (Vajiravudh) concentrates on political reform.

1932 After a military coup Siam becomes a constitutional monarchy.

1939 The country's name is changed to Thailand.

1973–92 Internal politics are dominated by power struggles between the generals and civilian politicians.

1992 Demonstrations following the election of General Suchinda are violently suppressed. The king intervenes, forcing Suchinda to resign.

2001 Thaksin Shinawatra becomes prime minister.

2004 The Asian tsunami strikes southern Thailand.

2006 A coup unseats Thaksin.

2007 A Thaksin proxy party wins election.

2008 Mass anti-government rallies. Opposition leader Abhisit Vejjajiva becomes prime minister.

2010 91 people killed as pro-Thaksin supporters clash with the army.

2011 Pro-Thaksin party wins election. Yingluck Shinawatra, sister of Thaksin, becomes head of government.

2014 Amidst political turmoil, the army seizes power in a coup led by General Prayuth Chan-ocha.

2016 King Bhumibol Adulyadej dies, having reigned for 70 years. His son Maha Vajiralongkorn ascends to the throne.

2017 King Maha Vajiralongkorn (Rama X) signs a new, military-drafted constitution.

2018 Prayuth Chan-ocha's rule as prime minister enters its fifth year.

Gold statues at the Temple of the Emerald Buddha

WHERE TO GO

BANGKOK

Thailand's capital might well come as a shock to the senses, but there is plenty to see for anyone prepared to put up with the haul and confusion. King Rama I modelled **Bangkok ❶** after Ayutthaya, with canals that ringed the city and many magnificent temples. The temples are still beautiful attractions, along with palaces and historic buildings, but today the city has expanded beyond the old town into a bursting metropolis. It is a mix of huge shopping malls, bustling markets, sleepy canals, and, of course, the city's notorious nightlife.

The heat and the urban sprawl make it one of the world's least walkable cities, and aimless sauntering may result in nothing but a twisted ankle, for the pavement is chronically torn up. Three preferable options are to find yourself a taxi, a *tuk-tuk* (a three-wheeled passenger-carrying motor scooter) or a coach tour, which can be arranged in any hotel. There are also two mass transit systems – called the Metro or subway (an underground network) and Skytrain (an elevated service) – which enable you to circumnavigate the city in air-conditioned comfort. Both operate frequently between key points such as Hualamphong Station, Silom Road, Sukhumvit Road and the hotels by the river (see page 131).

CITY DISTRICTS

The city's sights are widely spread, with several major neighbourhoods vying for attention. Start your tour with the area called **Ko Rattanakosin**, which has the greatest monuments and is situated just a stone's throw from the Chao Phraya River.

Food stall in bustling Chinatown

This is the original royal centre of the old city, and is home to the Wat Phra Kaew and Grand Palace complex (see page 27), as well as Wat Pho. North, within the old city, **Banglamphu** contains the famous backpacker area of Khao San Road, and beyond is **Dusit**, which developed as a royal enclave from the time of King Chulalongkorn. It has wide boulevards, European-influenced palace buildings and Dusit Zoo.

East of the old city, lively **Chinatown** has a profusion of entrepreneurs along Charoen Krung and Yaowarat Roads and the small lanes (sois) that cross between them. Walk along Sampeng Lane (Soi Wanit 1), the original 19th-century market, or **Soi Itsaranuphap A** for shops that sell everything from Chinese lanterns and wigs to gold necklaces and street food.

Charoen Krung (also known as New Road) was the first paved road in Thailand. It leads south to **Bangrak**, one of the city's original centres for Western businesses. Several churches and embassies are situated between Charoen Krung and the river, as are now-faded examples of 19th century architecture and the Oriental Hotel, once the haunt of such luminaries as Joseph Conrad, Noel Coward and Somerset Maugham. The area is well supplied with gift shops and 'instant' tailors.

Running east from Charoen Krung, Silom Road contains the modern tourist collection and **Patpong ⑬**, the most famous of the city's red-light strips.

To the north, cinemas, restaurants and giant shopping malls populate **Pathumwan**, where **Siam Square**, a low-rise grid of streets, houses the boutique designers fashionable with the young. Look out for the 30,000 marine creatures at **Sea Life Ocean World** (www.sealifebangkok.com/en) in Siam Paragon shopping centre (www.siamparagon.co.th), and Bangkok's branch of **Madame Tussaud's** (www.madame tussauds.com/bangkok). **Erawan Shrine**, the city's most important spirit house, is on the corner of Ratchadamri Road and Ploenchit Road. It was built by the owners of the former Erawan Hotel following various mishaps. There have been no further incidents, and today, a steady stream of the faithful arrive to offer flowers and carved wooden elephants to the resident spirits.

Further east, Ploenchit Road becomes **Sukhumvit Road**, a busy shopping, entertainment and residential area. It has cheap beer bars aplenty, red light districts at Soi Nana and Soi Cowboy and several of Bangkok's best clubs.

WAT PHRA KAEW AND GRAND PALACE COMPLEX

If you have time for only one sight in Bangkok, make it the Wat Phra Kaew and Grand Palace complex (tel: 0 2224 3273; www. palaces.thai.net; daily 8.30am–3.30pm), near Tha Chang pier. No temple so typifies Thai aesthetics as **Wat Phra Kaew ⓒ**, the Temple of the Emerald Buddha. Its glittering surfaces and wealth of art make it one of Asia's architectural wonders.

Wat Phra Kaew was the first major complex to be built in Bangkok. As you enter the compound, you will encounter an imposing trio of structures to your left – the huge golden **Phra Si Rattana Chedi**, the **Phra Mondop** (Library of Buddhist Scriptures), and the **Prasat Phra Thep Bidom** (Royal Pantheon). Behind the Phra Mondop is a large sandstone model of Angkor Wat. Along the northern edge of the model, you will also find **Vihan Yot** (Prayer Hall), flanked by **Ho Phra Nak** (Royal Mausoleum) on the left and **Ho Phra Montien Tham** (Auxillary Library) on the right.

Next you will come to the **Chapel of the Emerald Buddha**, which was specially constructed to house the kingdom's most sacred image, the Emerald Buddha. Sitting high on a pedestal, the 66cm (26in) -tall jadeite image is surprisingly small, but the belief in its power is apparent from the pilgrims who prostrate themselves before it.

> ### Visiting tips
>
> If visiting the Wat Phra Kaew and Grand Palace, make sure you allow at least a couple of hours and don't forget that respectful dress (no sleeveless T-shirts, low-cut tops, short skirts, shorts or flip-flops) is required and the guards at the main entrance vigorously enforce this dress code. For a small fee you can hire more modest clothing.

From Wat Phra Kaew, turn left into the adjacent **Grand Palace**, where the first building of note is the **Amarin Vinitchai Throne Hall**, which served as a royal residence for the first three kings of the Chakri dynasty: Rama I, II and III. Built during the reign of Rama I, the hall contains two thrones, the upper in the shape of a boat, the lower covered by a magnificent nine-tiered white canopy.

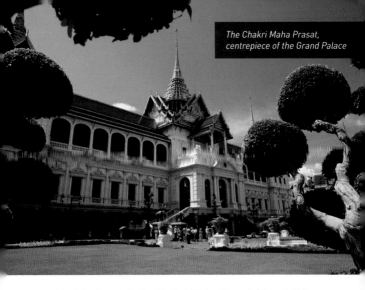

Next is the majestic **Chakri Maha Prasat** (Grand Palace Hall). It was built in 1882 by the internationally minded Rama V, and blends Asian and Italian Renaissance styles. The approach stairway and central balcony are of particular note. These are topped by a traditional roof, which rises in stages to three seven-tiered spires. Below the central spire stands a golden urn containing the ashes of most of the Chakri kings, including those of King Bhumibol.

Further on the left, a pair of 200-year-old stone lions stand guard at the entrance to the **Dusit Maha Prasat** (Dusit Hall), where kings used to conduct state business. It is now the final resting place for deceased kings before they are cremated in the nearby Sanam Luang field.

On the edge of the square, near Dusit Hall, you will see a white marble building known as the **Arporn Phimok Prasat** (Disrobing Pavilion). Built to the height of the king's palanquin, this was where the king would alight from his carriage and adjust his ceremonial hat before entering the throne hall.

Opposite is the **Wat Phra Kaew Museum**, which has a collection of exquisite Buddha images made of crystal, silver, ivory and gold as well as some beautiful lacquer screens.

On the way out, you can also visit the **Coins and Decorations Museum**. Displayed in glass cases in two jail-like enclaves are gold coins, swords and crown jewels, dating from the 11th century.

SIX GREAT WATS

Visit six of Bangkok's *wats* – monasteries or temples – as part of your tour of its greatest architectural wonders. It is advisable to tackle these in two or more trips, as distances between them are considerable.

⊘ WHAT'S A WAT?

You will see wats, or Buddhist temples, everywhere in Thailand. To help you find your way around, here's a brief rundown of the most common architectural terms:

bot: the main sanctuary of a temple, where religious rites are held

viharn: a replica of the bot that is used to keep Buddha images

prang: an ellipse-shaped stupa based on the corner tower of a Khmer temple and also housing images of the Buddha

chedi (stupa): the most venerated structure, a bell-like dome that originally enshrined relics of the Buddha, later of holy men and kings

mondop: wood or brick structure with pyramidal roof, built as a repository for a holy object

One of the best-known Thai landmarks, **Wat Arun**  (Temple of Dawn; across from Tha Tien Pier; tel: 0 2891 2185; www.watarun.org; daily 0.00am–5.00pm), stands on the opposite bank of the Chao Phraya River in Thonburi, but is only a minute or two away by ferry. The temple was renovated during the first half of the 19th century by Rama II and Rama III, and is decorated with millions of fragments of porcelain arranged in the shape of flowers. The central tower affords stunning views across the river. For quintessential sunset views, photographers should perch themselves at the riverside bar on the opposite bank.

Reclining Buddha in Wat Pho, Bangkok's oldest temple

Wat Pho (tel: 0 2226 0335; www.watpho.com; daily 8am–6.30pm), Bangkok's oldest temple, houses an incredible 19th-century gilt reclining Buddha in its vast white enclosure. Almost 15m (49ft) high and 46m (151ft) long, it reaches right up to the roof of the temple. On the feet, inlaid with mother-of-pearl, are the 108 auspicious characteristics of the Buddha.

Wat Suthat (Bamrung Muang Road; tel: 0 2221 4026, 0 2221 4331; daily 8.30am–9pm) was started by Rama I in 1807, but took three reigns to complete. Its 8-metre (26ft) -tall Buddha is one of the largest surviving from Sukhothai. Rama II himself is said to have carved the bot's teakwood doors. In the square outside, the Giant Swing is where young men at Brahmin New Year swung to

The Buddha at Wat Traimit, Thailand's largest gold image

great heights in a gondola to catch purses of gold hanging from poles. The ceremony was banned in 1931 after several accidents.

The **Golden Mount** ⑥ (tel: 0 2621 2280; daily 8am–5.30pm), accessed via Wat Saket (Boriphat Road; daily 5am–9pm), can be seen long before you reach it. It sits atop Bangkok's only hill – and an artificial one at that – surmounted by a big gold *chedi* (stupa). Spiral steps up the mount's reinforced sides lead to a viewing platform. Take a map with you to identify the palaces and temples spread out below the summit. The faithful make the climb for the shrine containing relics of the Buddha. These were given to King Rama V in 1897 by Lord Curzon, Viceroy of India.

The best time to visit **Wat Benchamabophit**, the Marble Temple (Rama V Road; tel: 0 2281 3277; www.watbenchama.com; daily 7am–6pm), is at dawn, when the graceful marble is still tinged with orange and the monks are lining up for their daily alms. Built at the turn of the 20th century, it is one of the finest examples of recent temple architecture in the city. It is a haven of calm, with its inner courtyard surrounded by Buddha statues, and its ponds filled with fish and turtles, fed daily by the monks. Outside and past the canal are the monks' quarters, set among lawns.

The impressive Buddha at **Wat Traimit** (Charoenkrung Road; tel: 0 2623 1227; www.wattraimitr-withayaram.com; daily

8am–5pm) might have remained concealed forever had it not been for workmen extending the port of Bangkok, who dropped the then stucco-covered statue from a crane, revealing the vast Buddha inside. This is Thailand's largest gold image, weighing 4.5 metric tonnes (5 tons) and dating from the Sukhothai period, when it was probably disguised to keep it out of the hands of the warring Burmese.

MUSEUMS AND PALACES

On Na Phra That Road, a short walk from the Grand Palace, stands the **National Museum G** (tel: 0 2224 1333; Wed–Sun 9am–4pm). The museum houses Thailand's finest collection of antiquities. The sculpture, ceramics and jewellery exhibited offer an insight into the country's unique synthesis of different cultures – as well as the sheer variety of the kingdom's artefacts. Try to be there for a tour (ask at Tourism Authority offices for times) so as not to be overwhelmed by the museum's size and scope.

The exhibition divides Thai culture into several periods, starting off with the Dvaravati (6th–11th century AD), then tracing the development of political power to Lanna, Sukhothai, Ayutthaya and ultimately Bangkok. The rooms are arranged in a chronological fashion, and you can see the changes in the portrayal of the Buddha, the overriding theme of Thai art, as you walk through.

The museum offers a range of other things to see, from an 18-metric tonne

Museum highlight

The earliest works in the National Museum – from excavations at Ban Chiang in Northeast Thailand – are the most interesting: pots and jars with bold designs in the shape of fingerprints. The haunting patterns are curiously modern, and yet the pottery is probably 5,000 years old.

(20-ton) royal funeral chariot – which needed over 290 people to push it – to thrones, litters, 19th-century Thai typewriters, and even a full-sized model elephant fitted out for battle.

A different sort of museum is situated in the tasteful **Jim Thompson House** Ⓗ, located to the east of the city (Soi Kasemsan 2, off Rama I Road; tel: 0 2216 7368; www.jim thompsonhouse.com; daily 9am–6pm, guided tours only). Bringing a sense of calm to even the most frenetic of days, the cool timber rooms of this teak house are packed with priceless artefacts, sculptures and ceramics.

The story of Jim Thompson is as intriguing as his taste in art. A New York architect, he came to Southeast Asia as a secret agent in World War II. Settling in Bangkok after the war, he converted the Thai silk industry from a primitive craft into an international big business. In 1967 he vanished while on holiday in neighbouring Malaysia. The mystery of his disappearance is still unsolved. No trace of Thompson has ever been found, but this monument, 'the house on the *khlong*' (canal), is exactly as he left it.

Slightly south of the Thompson House, on the corner of Rama I and Phaya Thai roads, is **Bangkok Art and Culture Centre** (tel: 0 2214 6630; www.bacc.or.th; Tue–Sun 10am–9pm). Opened in 2008 in a state-of-the-art building with nine floors set around a circular atrium, it is home to various exhibitions, an auditorium, café and restaurants.

One final building not to be missed is the **Suan Pakkad Palace** on Sri Ayutthaya Road (tel: 0 2245 4934; www.suan pakkad.com; daily 9am–4pm, guided tours only), near the Phaya Thai skytrain station. Suan Pakkad literally translates as 'lettuce garden', and this superb building is owned by Princess Chumbot and surrounded by leafy gardens. In the garden stands the delightful **Lacquer Pavilion**, which is believed to be the only house of its type to survive the sack of Ayutthaya in

1767. Bought in 1959, the pavilion was rebuilt here as a gift to the princess from her late husband. Some of the inside walls are covered with exquisite paintings in gold leaf on black lacquer – which illustrate scenes in the life of the Buddha and episodes from the national legend, the *Ramakien*.

BANGKOK FROM THE WATER

The most popular way of exploring the fascinating *khlong* (canals), which are so central to Bangkok's character, is to take either a tour from Tha Chang pier near the Grand Palace, or a similar trip arranged by any of the hotels. A one-hour tour is quite expensive, but will take you to sections of old Thonburi that you would hardly dream still existed – past floating restaurants, floating petrol stations, old wooden houses and temples.

Suan Pakkad Palace

River taxis await passengers on the khlongs

Most river tours leave early in the morning and include a visit to the **National Museum of Royal Barges** (tel: 0 2424 0004; daily 9am–5pm) in a shed by Khlong Bangkok Noi. The otherworldly ceremonial craft are trimmed with fanciful prows and elaborate red and gold decorations. The king's own boat is propelled by 50 oarsmen.

You can explore the canals on your own by means of the local boats, called hang yao. These long, narrow craft, powered by noisy truck engines, carry the propeller on the end of a long drive shaft – hence their name, which means 'long-tailed' boats. You can also hire your own *hang yao* by the hour, but be sure to agree on a price in advance.

Down Khlong Bangkok Noi (Small Canal) and Khlong Yai (Big Canal), handsome houses with gardens and fountains are squeezed cheek by jowl with old, wooden houses on stilts, shaded by palm trees. Nearby you will see rubber tyre factories next to temples, floating markets and snack bars.

If you prefer slower and cheaper transport, although it doesn't travel the *khlongs*, take the **Chao Phraya Tourist Boat** (tel: 0 2866 3163-4; www.chaophrayatouristboat.com; daily 9.30am–5.30pm), which costs B180 *for a one-day river pass*. The route begins at Tha Sathorn and travels upriver to Tha Phra Athit, stopping at seven major piers in between. Boats

leave every 30 minutes; you can get off at any pier and pick up another boat later.

The Chao Phraya River Express Boat is run by the same company and travels between Tha Nonthaburi pier in the north and Tha Wat Rajsingkorn in the south, and between Pakkret, Nonthaburi and Sathorn. Tickets on this boat are cheaper, but there is no narration of the stop names in English so it is best to know how many stops you need to go in advance.

OTHER SIGHTS

The **Queen Saovabha Memorial Institute** (tel: 0 2252 01614; www.saovabha.com; Mon–Fri 8.30am–4.30pm, Sat–Sun and holidays 8.30am–12pm), more popularly known as the **Snake Farm**, is operated by the Red Cross. Its primary function is to produce

Chao Praya river boat

See traditional dancing at Rose Garden Riverside Resort

anti-venom serum to be used on snakebite victims. Tourists may view the venom milking sessions, which take place from Mondays to Fridays at 11am. Snake handling demonstrations are Mon–Fri at 2.30pm, and on Saturdays and Sundays at 11am.

Lumphini Park (daily 5am–9pm) is a haven of peace in the city centre. Thais come here to picnic, work out and practise tai chi. There is a lake with boats for hire, food stalls and a bar and restaurant at the park's northern exit from where you can watch the sun set. There are Sunday evening outdoor classical or jazz concerts from December to February.

Dusit Zoo (tel: 0 2282 71113; www.zoothailand.org; daily 8am–6pm) was originally King Chulalongkorn's private botanical gardens. As well as 300 animal species, many of which are located around the edges of the grounds, the zoo has a lake, where you can hire pedalos, and several places to eat. Thais come here to escape the city heat as much as to see the wildlife.

Off the centre, **Chatuchak Weekend Market** is a mind-boggling collection of stalls where anything is available, from snakes to potted plants and herbal cures for insomnia. Chatuchak is open for sale of miscellaneous goods only on Saturdays and Sundays, Wed–Thu are dedicated to plants and flowers and Friday is a wholesale day (www.chatuchak.org; 6am–6pm).

Further north from the market is the **Museum of Contemporary Art** (tel: 0 2016 56667; www.mocabangkok.com; Tue–Fri 10am–5pm, Sat–Sun 11am–6pm). Opened in 2012 and privately owned, it boasts an impressive collection of Thai modern art. It is well worth the trip.

EXCURSIONS FROM BANGKOK

The following excursions are all easily reached from Bangkok. Each one would make for a rewarding side trip or useful stepping stone on the way north or south.

BUDDHIST PARK AND NAKHON PATHOM

Less than an hour's drive to the west of Bangkok lies **Phutthamonthon** ❷ (tel: 0 2441 9013; http://bbc.onab.go.th), a laid-back Buddhist park. The park's centrepiece is the 15.87m (52ft)-high free-standing Buddha statue, around which large, well-manicured gardens and ponds attract many Thais looking to feed the numerous fish and escape the bustle of the city. The

Sanam Chan Palace

Also at Nakhon Pathom is the Sanam Chan Palace. This early 20th-century structure is in traditional Thai style, with the exception of one English Tudor building, which was once used as a setting for performances of Shakespeare plays.

Traders at a floating market

best time to go is in the morning before it gets too hot as there is not much shade.

From Phutthamonthon, continue 35km (22 miles) west to **Nakhon Pathom** (widely believed to be Thailand's oldest town). This is home to **Phra Pathom Chedi** (tel: 0 3424 2143; daily 8am–5pm), the largest *chedi* (stupa) in the country, built by King Mongkut in the middle of the 19th century on top of the ruins of an ancient temple. During the 1970s, this new *chedi* almost collapsed, but the Fine Arts Department took prompt action and fortunately saved the day, so that it can still be seen in all its glory.

FLOATING MARKET

You won't need a guide to show you the way to the Floating Market at **Damnoen Saduak ❸** (daily 7am–11am), as everyone runs tours there nowadays. Even so, the diminutive boats, which are piled high with coconuts, bananas and durian, remain – almost – as authentic as ever. Try to get there quite early, while the women in broad-brimmed hats are still out in full force, paddling along the narrow canals and haggling over wares. Photographers might want to walk along the edge of the canal, or stop on the wooden bridges, which make excellent spots for observation. For a few hundred *baht*, a boat ●●● ●●●● ●●●●●●●●●●● ●● ●●●● ●●●●●●●●●●● ●●●●●●●●● ●●●●●●● ●●●●●●●●●●●●● fray. At another tourist market onshore you can buy Burmese carpets, wood carvings and other such things. However, the goods are expensive and you will often find that identical goods are sold at keener prices in shops in Bangkok or in Chiang Mai's Night Market.

KANCHANABURI

Its calm, lush setting on the banks of the **Kwai River** belies the history of **Kanchanaburi ❹**, for it was here during World War II that thousands of prisoners of war died building the famous **Bridge on the River Kwai**, as recounted in Pierre Boulle's novel and the film based on it. The current structure was rebuilt after the war, and only the eight curved sections on it are original. Two trains cross the bridge every day on their way to the town of **Nam Tok** (Waterfall), a pleasant hour's journey further to the west. You can walk across the bridge or view it from the long-tailed boats that hurtle up and down the river, stopping off at the cemetery and nearby caves.

To get an idea of the horrors of building the bridge, visit the two cemeteries, which contain graves and memorials to over 8,000 British, Dutch, Australian, Malaysian, Indian, Canadian, New Zealand and Burmese prisoners and conscripts who died during the railway's construction, along with around 100,000 Asian civilians. The inscriptions on the gravestones are as simple and moving as tragic poems.

Elephant trekking

Afterwards, you can visit the **Thailand-Burma Railway Centre** (tel: 0 3451 2721; www.tbrconline.com; daily 9am–5pm), which is next door to the cemetery. It has exhibits on the history of the Death Railway and even a full-scale replica of the original bridge.

JEATH War Museum (tel: 0 3451 5203; daily 8.30am–4.30pm) sits on the riverbank. Housed in a type of bamboo hut used in the prison camps, the exhibition documents Japanese atrocities in photographs, paintings and relics. It also reveals the prisoners' ingenuity in surviving great hardships, as well as the sympathy and help secretly offered to the inmates by local people.

SANGKHLABURI

There are bases for travellers northwest of Kanchanaburi, making it easier to explore some of the most unspoilt scenery in the country. Some hotels pamper guests with air-conditioning and swimming pools, while a couple of others, slightly more spartan, are built on bamboo rafts floating in the stream. Jungle treks and excursions to waterfalls, caves, tribal villages and national parks, including **Erawan National Park** (tel: 0 3457 4222; www.dnp. go.th; daily 8am–4.30pm), can be arranged from these camps.

On the edge of Sai Yok National Park lies **Hellfire Pass**, christened by POWs who were forced to dig in this area by

torchlight. The road to **Sangkhlaburi** ❺ runs between the densely forested mountain slopes of the national parks, passing Khao Laem Reservoir, with the town situated at the northern tip of the lake. Sangkhlaburi is an ideal base for elephant trekking expeditions to nearby Mon and Karen villages. The **Three Pagodas Pass**, 12km (7.5 miles) further on, lies at an altitude of 1,400m (4,480ft). It owes its name to the three little white *chedis* erected here in the 18th century.

AYUTTHAYA

The most enjoyable way of visiting the ancient capital of Ayutthaya, 88km (55 miles) north of Bangkok, is by incorporating a trip on the Chao Phraya River. The River Sun Cruise (tel: 0 2266 9125; www.riversuncruise.co.th) organises daily trips to Ayutthaya, leaving at 8am by air-conditioned coach from the River City Shopping Complex and returning to the pier in front of it, on a converted rice barge. On the way you will see picturesque temples, rafts of floating logs bound for sawmills, and a countryside of rice fields and traditional stilt houses.

Before exploring the great historical site itself, most tours stop at the nearby royal estate of **Bang Pa-In** ❻ (tel: 0 3526 1044; daily 8am–4pm). This collection of palaces, set in gardens, was built by King Chulalongkorn in the late 19th century. The names of palaces like 'The Excellent and Shining Abode' and 'The Sage's Lookout' are as delightful as the structures themselves. Nothing beats the splendid **Aisawan Thipha-at** (The Divine Seat of Personal Freedom) in the middle of the lake by which King Chulalongkorn (Rama V) composed odes as the sun went down.

Back on the highway, continue 20km (12.5 miles) north to the town of **Ayutthaya**, former capital of Thailand and home to one of its greatest civilisations. In its heyday it was a fabulously wealthy, cosmopolitan city, until it was destroyed in 1767 by invading Burmese armies. Some sites are free to enter, others cost B30.

There are dozens of distinctive buildings, and you will be hard-pressed to visit the whole of the **Ayutthaya Historical Park ❼** (www.ayutthaya.go.th; daily 8am–6pm) in one day. For a tour of the ruins, you could start at **Wat Phra Sri Sanphet Ⓐ**, on Si Sanphet Road, near the tourist parking area. The temple was built in 1491 and once housed a 16m (52ft) Buddha image covered in gold. In 1767 the Burmese set fire to the statue in order to melt off the gold, destroying both temple and image. What you can see are restored *chedis* (stupas) which hold the ashes of King Borom Trai Lokanat and his two sons.

At **Wat Phra Ram ❽**, a graceful 14th-century building positioned amid reflecting pools, there is a beautiful cloister lined with stone Buddha images, as well as several elephant gates, and mythical creatures called *naga* and *garuda*. The temple was built in 1369 by King Ramesuan, on the site where his father was cremated.

Next, visit **Wat Phra Mahathat Ⓒ**, one of the most beautiful temple complexes in Ayutthaya. Once it held treasures of

⊙ FOUNDING A DYNASTY

According to one of several Thai legends, the founder of Ayutthaya was the illegitimate son of a princess, who was discovered to be pregnant after eating an aubergine on which a gardener had relieved himself! U-Thong, or Prince of the Golden Crib as the son was named, became the first of 33 ruling kings, while the kingdom became the largest and most beautiful in the East as well as the principal kingdom in Siam for over four centuries.

precious stones, gold and crystal, and a relic of the Lord Buddha in a gold casket, which is now housed in the National Museum in Bangkok (see page 33). Right to Wat Mahathat, **Wat Ratcha-burana**  was built in the 15th century around the tombs of Prince Ai and Prince Yo, brothers who slew each other in a tragic battle on elephant back. Rare frescoes remain in the crypt, but any portable antiquities were stolen or removed to museums years ago.

Wat Phra Mahathat

For an overview of Ayutthayan-style art, visit the **Chao Sam Phraya National Museum** (tel: 0 3524 1587; daily 9am–4pm), which holds well-preserved statues recovered from the ruins. There are beautiful bronze Buddhas dating from the 13th and 14th centuries, 17th- and 18th-century door panels with religious, traditional or floral carvings, and a hoard of 15th-century gold jewellery.

Finish off with a visit to the **elephant *kraal***, a few miles from town, where hunters used to drive large herds of up to 200 wild elephants into the stockade. Once captured, they were put into the king's service as fighters or, if they were the rare white type, as symbols of power. The last capture was in 1903 during the reign of King Chulalongkorn. If you want to learn more about elephants, visit non-profit organisation, **Elephantstay**, located in the village (www.elephantstay.com).

ANCIENT CITY

If your time is limited, there is no need to go to Sukhothai and Ayutthaya for ancient monuments. Loosely shaped like Thailand, the **Ancient City** ❽ or Muang Boran (tel: 0 2709 16448; www. ancientcitygroup.net; daily 9am–7pm), 33km (21 miles) southeast of Bangkok, has over 100 monuments, palaces, and other buildings placed approximately in their correct geographical location. Some are life-size reproductions of existing or lost structures, notably royal complexes from the ruins of Ayutthaya; others are relocated buildings that would otherwise have been demolished. The park also features exotic birds, monkeys and elephants. Travel agents run outings here, and there are daily buses from Bangkok.

CROCODILE FARM AND ZOO

Another 5km (3 miles) along the road from Ancient City is the **Samut Prakan Crocodile Farm & Zoo** (tel: 0 2703 4891; www. worldcrocodile.com; daily 8am–6pm). This huge enclosure is billed as the world's largest establishment of its kind, with the total 'croc' population touted at over 100,000. The farm preserves endangered species at the same time as it entertains and educates the public. There is also a zoo with exotic birds, tigers, ostriches and elephants, as well as a Dinosaur Museum.

KHAO YAI NATIONAL PARK

Khao Yai ❾ (www.dnp.go.th; daily 6am–6pm) rises from the Khorat plateau northeast of Bangkok, baked dry in summer and verdant after the rains. Khao Yai means 'big mountain', and the national park, located three hours' drive from Bangkok (200km/ 125 miles), is the oldest and one of the best in the land. The park can be reached by taking the bus from Bangkok to Pak Chong in Nakhon Ratchasima province, where there are pick-ups that leave for the main entrance.

Khao Yai National Park

The national park covers 2,100 sq km (837 sq miles). Within its boundaries are elephants and over 100 other species, including Asian wild dog, clouded leopard and black bear. Keep an eye out for some of Thailand's most significant bird concentrations, among which are some of the largest groups of hornbills in Southeast Asia, moustached barbets, orange-breasted and red-headed trogons and great slaty woodpeckers. Wildlife sightings are not consistently common or guaranteed, but the walks to waterfalls are pleasant. Night-time safaris employ spotlights to locate deer, tropical birds and – if you are lucky – tigers and bears.

Before being declared a national park in 1962, Khao Yai was known as a sanctuary not just for animals, but also as a popular hiding place for outlaws. This, of course, is no longer the case, and now the fringes of the park offer hotels, restaurants and 18-hole golf courses.

THAILAND'S 'KHMER CULTURE TRAIL'

About 250km (100 miles) from Bangkok is the provincial capital of Khorat, **Nakhon Ratchasima**. The richest and largest city in the northeast, it is a good jumping off point for excursions to the Khmer ruins of the Khorat Plateau, including Phimai, Phanom Rung and Prasat Muang Tam.

PHIMAI

Phimai ⑩, 60km (37 miles) north of Nakhon Ratchasima, is known for its ancient religious compound at the end of the long, dusty main street. Probably built during King Suriyavarman I's reign in the 11th century, and situated not too far from the Cambodian border, Phimai was designed by Khmer architects,

Khmer mythical lion guard

and predates Angkor Wat in Cambodia. Four gates dominate the ruins, the largest preceded by a bridge guarded by lions. Adorning the elegant arcades of the cloisters are intricate engravings of flowers, elephants and monkeys.

In the inner courtyard stand two small *prangs* (Prang Hin Daeng and Prang Phromathat), and in the centre there is an ornate dome with doors and a lintel, carved with scenes related to Mahayana Buddhism. In the gardens there is an open-air museum, with a collection of ancient friezes, statues and stone lintels showing Buddha, gods and monkeys.

PHANOM RUNG

Phimai may be the best-known and most easily accessible Khmer temple site in Northeast Thailand, but Buriram's **Prasat Hin Khao Phanom Rung** ⓫ (daily 8am–6pm) is better preserved, and set in more spectacular scenery atop an extinct volcano. Phanom Rung was constructed between the 10th and 13th centuries, but the greater part of the work was completed in the reign of King Suriyavarman II (1112–52), during the period when the architecture of Angkor reached its apogee. Today, after painstaking restoration, the sanctuary is the largest and best-preserved of all Thailand's Khmer monuments.

Phanom Rung was originally built as a Hindu temple honouring the deities Vishnu and Shiva. Beautifully carved representations of these two gods can be found in the lintels and pediments of the sanctuary. On the east portico of the antechamber to the main sanctuary you'll find a fine Nataraja, or Dancing Shiva figure.

PRASAT HIN MUANG TAM

About 8km (5 miles) south of Phanom Rung, in the dusty plain approaching the Cambodian frontier, stands the old Khmer

---

Banyan tree

A pleasant way to round off the trip to Phimai is to visit the banyan tree, which stands 2km (1 mile) from the temple. The banyan tree is said to be the biggest in Thailand. Delicious Isaan food is served in its shade, but only in the dry season – during the wet season, the nearby reservoir floods the picnic ground. If spirits live in trees – as many Thais believe – then this prodigious banyan is surely thronged with ghosts.

sanctuary of **Prasat Hin Muang Tam** (www.muangtam.com; daily 6am–6pm). Fifteen years ago, Muang Tam was a mass of stone walls and lintels, shrouded in dense vegetation. Today the temple complex has been splendidly restored by the Archaeological Commission of Thailand.

OTHER GEMS

Additional gems can be found in the neighbouring provinces of Surin and Si Saket. **Ban Pluang** (daily 7.30am–6pm), which dates from the second half of the 11th century and was once an important stop on the road between Angkor and Phimai, is a square sandstone tower built on a laterite platform. The surrounding moats and ponds have been turned into an attractive garden. Nearby **Sikhoraphum**

Prasat Hin Phimai

(daily 8am–6pm) consists of five brick *prangs* on a square laterite platform surrounded by lily-filled ponds. The lintel and pillars of the central *prang* are beautifully carved with heavenly dancing girls, or *apsaras*, and other scenes from Hindu mythology.

PRASAT KAMPHAENG YAI

The 'Khmer Culture Trail' ends with the laterite sanctuary of **Prasat Kamphaeng Yai** (daily 8am–5pm). Here the ancient Khmer ruins rub shoulders with a much more recent Thai temple, and saffron-robed monks may be seen eating, studying or contemplating in the shade of the massive, attenuated *prangs*. Although the Khmer sanctuary was originally dedicated to the Hindu god Vishnu, the overall effect is most pleasing, and the active Buddhist presence strangely at one.

CENTRAL THAILAND

The most striking feature of the central region is its sheer fertile abundance. This vast plain that starts at Bangkok's outskirts is called the country's 'rice bowl'. It is home to one-third of the population, and the source of one of the world's biggest rice crops. Centuries ago, this agricultural heartland was also home to some of the kingdom's greatest civilisations, among them those of Si Satchanalai, Sukhothai and Lopburi, ancient cities that are as enchanting in ruins as they must have been in their heyday. Also in Central Thailand are two of the country's most popular beach resorts – Pattaya and Hua Hin, located 147km (91 miles) southeast and 203km (126 miles) southwest of Bangkok respectively. Major towns to the north of Bangkok make good stopovers if you are en route to Thailand's northern region.

Nong Nooch Tropical Garden

PATTAYA

Visitors no longer come to **Pattaya** ⑫ for pristine beaches and tropical seas, for this infamous resort lost its original attractions to pollution and development many years ago.

It was in the 1960s that the provincial seaside town rose to prominence. This was when the first American servicemen arrived from Vietnam War duties for what was soon described as 'R & R' – rest and recreation. The Thais eventually realised Pattaya's commercial possibilities, and the area fast became a thriving international resort.

Today, Pattaya is notorious for its sex industry, but has an abundance of accommodation, bars, clubs, attractions and outdoor activities that draw a mixed crowd, including a surprising number of families. The sea around Pattaya Bay is not recommended, so if swimming is what you are after, take a boat trip to the outlying coral islands. Or catch a bus to the beach at

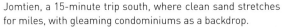

Jomtien, a 15-minute trip south, where clean sand stretches for miles, with gleaming condominiums as a backdrop.

The adventurous can try out parasailing, sailing, jet-skiing and water-skiing, while others may prefer a day's deep-sea fishing, relishing the opportunity to try catching delicious snapper and sizeable marlin. Excursion boats take tourists to islands in the surrounding area for swimming and snorkelling.

At **Ko Larn** (about 45 minutes from Pattaya in a converted trawler or half the time in a speedboat) you can explore the underwater world in a glass-bottomed boat, gazing at vivid tropical fish and coral – albeit now sadly depleted. Many scuba expeditions begin here before going on to a couple of wrecks further south near Sattahip.

Land tours are just as easy to arrange. To the east, **Nong Nooch Tropical Garden** (tel: 0 3823 8061; www.nongnooch tropicalgarden.com; daily 8am–6pm), 18km (11 miles) away, features Thai cultural performances and elephant shows, and a vast acreage of exotic palms, orchids and cacti. Alternatively, try the water theme park **Pattaya Park** (tel: 0 3825 12018; www.pattayapark.com; daily 10am–7pm), or **Pattaya Elephant Village** (tel: 0 3824 9818; www.elephant-village-pattaya.com; daily 8.30am–6pm), where you can ride an elephant or

Sculptures in the Sanctuary of Truth

The beach at Ko Samet

arrange an elephant trek. For a strange cultural experience, visit Naklua's fantastic wood-carved **Sanctuary of Truth** (tel: 0 3836 7229; www.sanctuaryoftruth.com; daily 8am–6pm), a 105m (340ft) -tall monument to Asian religions. It is made completely of hard woods with intricately hand-carved figures of gods and spirits. The sanctuary also offers activities such as speedboat rides on the adjacent lagoon, elephant trekking and horse riding, plus traditional dance and martial arts shows.

Pattaya offers abundant culinary delights. The restaurants serve first-rate seafood: there are plenty of simple waterfront restaurants that are rich in character but cheap in price. Those who prefer French fries and *bratwurst* are also catered for.

Pattaya's nightlife, too, has something to satisfy almost all tastes, from big stage productions at Alangkarn Theatre (www.alangkarnthailand.com) and transvestite shows, to nightclubs, beer bars and all other establishments that have earned this area its reputation as the international entertainment resort of Thailand.

THE EASTERN SEABOARD

Further east of Pattaya, the small idyllic island of **Ko Samet** ⓭ has become a firm weekend favourite for Bangkok residents. The white sand beaches and clear blue water are part of a national marine park so most accommodation is fairly low-key. The island is best avoided on public holidays, when visitors outnumber beds, and tents spring up everywhere.

Near the Cambodian border is Thailand's second-largest island, **Ko Chang** ⓮ (Elephant Island), the dominant isle of over 50 that make up the national marine park of the same name. A current development drive is gradually transforming the hilly island from a place of backpacker bungalows to one consisting of higher-end boutique resorts, but it is still one of the most pristine islands in the Gulf of Thailand.

HUA HIN

There are quieter charms at **Hua Hin** ⓯, 203km (126 miles) southwest of Bangkok on the opposite shore of the Gulf of Thailand. A slew of condominiums and retirement homes are changing this former fishing village, and its long, sweeping beaches are no longer as pleasant as they once were for swimming. They do, however, make fine strolling ground, with watersports, deckchairs to laze in, and pony-riding. The surrounding area has plentiful golf courses and luxury spa retreats, while the pier restaurants on Thanon Naresdamri grill excellent seafood.

LOPBURI

Lopburi ⓰ has superb stone temples built by the Khmers which dominate the city. These can be spotted even from the railway

Stone temple resident in Lopburi

station, as can the French-style architecture and several hundred monkeys that have become this town's other lasting claim to fame.

Originally one of the capitals of the Khmer people, Lopburi flourished under Thai rule in the 17th century. King Narai chose the town as an alternative capital, in case some unforeseen fate befell Ayutthaya. His caution was justified: Ayutthaya was sacked by the Burmese the following century.

Begin your tour at **King Narai's Palace** or Phra Narai Ratchaniwet (tel: 0 3641 1458; Wed–Sun 8.30am–4.30pm), which was constructed in the mid-17th century, and took more than 12 years to complete. Inside is the National Museum, housing exquisite examples of Khmer art. The palace also incorporates the old treasure houses, a banquet hall, an audience hall for high-ranking foreign visitors and stables.

After the palace, visit **Ban Vichayen** (daily 8.30am–4.30pm), which originally served as the residence of Chevalier de Chaumont, the first French ambassador to Thailand. Later it was the residence of Constantine Phaulkon (see page 16).

Near the railway station, **Wat Phra Si Rattana Mahathat** (daily 6.30am–6pm) is a fine example of 12th-century Khmer-style architecture, with its *chedis* built in Sukhothai style.

Lopburi's famous monkeys can be found by the railway in the Kala Shrine, as well as in nearby **Phra Prang Sam Yot** (Wed–Sun

6am–6pm), a magnificent 13th-century temple with three distinctive *prangs* from which they like to hang, begging food from visitors. Keep firm hold of your camera and other valuables, as monkeys clutching stolen goods are a not uncommon sight.

SUKHOTHAI

Sukhothai ⑫, the most striking of Thailand's various spectacular ruined cities, lies 427km (265 miles) north of Bangkok, surrounded by rice fields and distant hills. Built in the mid-13th and early-14th centuries under the legendary King Ramkam-haeng, Sukhothai flourished for almost 150 years until vanquished by Ayutthaya, and its people fled. Until around 40 years ago, the ancient capital was hidden by jungle, the outlines of the classical towers camouflaged by heavy undergrowth. The situation is now better, for in a huge renovation programme implemented by Unesco and Thailand's government, some 200 moats, kilns, images and temples have been partially restored to the glory of earlier days.

For a glimpse of some remarkable sculptures, start at the **Ramkamhaeng National Museum** (tel: 0 5561 2167; daily 9am–4pm), near the Kamphaeng Hek Gate. This houses a splendid 14th-century example of the Walking Buddha, which is, according to archaeologists, the finest of all Thai Buddhas. A replica of King Ramkamhaeng's famous inscription is also on show. This oft-repeated quotation is the earliest example of Thai script and includes

Reaching Sukhothai

The Sukhothai ruins lie within the boundaries of the historical park, 13km (8 miles) west of the new town of Sukhothai, and are reached easily by *songthaew*, pick-up trucks with seats in the back, which carry as many passengers as can be squeezed in.

the words: 'In the water there are fish, in the fields there is rice... those who choose to laugh, laugh, those who choose to cry, cry.'

A short walk across the **Sukhothai Historical Park** (tel: 0 5569 7241; daily 6.30am–7.30pm, tickets sold until 6pm) past the moat brings you to **Wat Mahathat**, the Temple of the Great Relic. This is Sukhothai's biggest and finest temple, dating from the 13th century and housing rows of the standing Buddha images known as Phra Attharot.

Continue by visiting beautiful **Wat Sa Si** (Temple of the Splendid Pond), with its graceful image of the walking Buddha and slender *chedi* shaped like a bell, and **Wat Trapang Ngoen**, situated around a large lake which floods occasionally during the rainy season. Carry on to the west outside the walled city and you reach **Wat Si Chum**, with its massive seated Buddha measuring 15m (49ft) from knee to knee, and each finger the size of a person. The sanctuary walls are 3m (10ft) thick and contain a secret passage off to the left just inside the entrance.

⊘ LOI KRATHONG

The best time of year to visit Sukhothai is on the full moon of the 12th lunar month (mid-November), when Thailand's most beautiful and serene festival, known as Loi Krathong, is celebrated. It is believed to have started here some 700 years ago, after one of the king's concubines fashioned a lantern from carved fruit and sent it floating down the river bearing a lighted candle. Now, thousands of people gather by water all over the country to launch boats made of banana leaves to celebrate the end of the rainy season. Sukhothai has colourful processions and a display of fireworks.

This passage was used by the king, though for what purpose is not clear.

The temple of **Wat Saphan Hin**, 2km (1 mile) west of the city, is known as the Temple of the Stone Bridge, after the slate pathway leading up the hill. It is a long haul to the summit, on which stands a Buddha statue more than 12m (40ft) tall. However, it is a trip that is well worth the effort.

The massive Buddha at Wat Si Chum, Sukhothai

SI SATCHANALAI

If you still have a craving for more temples, you may like to consider making an afternoon's excursion to the **Si Satchanalai Historical Park** (daily 7am–6pm), 55km (34 miles) to the north of Sukhothai. Si Satchanalai is the sister city of Sukhothai, but is wilder and less visited by tourists, with ramshackle temples and an air of faded grandeur. At the top of a steep flight of steps is the ruined **Wat Khao Suwan Khiri**, which is worth the climb for the views alone.

Hire a bicycle at the entrance to the historical park and explore what many regard as the city's most impressive temple, **Wat Chang Lom** (which translates literally as 'Temple Surrounded by Elephants'). The *chedi* is surrounded by 39 standing elephants and has a stairway representing a ladder to heaven. Real elephants can usually be found in front of the temple, and it is often possible to get rides around the park.

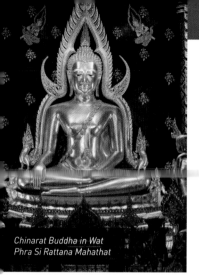

Chinarat Buddha in Wat Phra Si Rattana Mahathat

The Si Satchanalai area was the centre of a ceramics industry during the Sukhothai period. In nearby **Ban Ko Noi**, a village 4km (2.5 miles) to the north, archaeologists have discovered kilns that might revolutionise historical thinking by proving that the Thais began producing pottery 400 years earlier than the Chinese.

PHITSANULOK

A wide river cuts through the heart of Phitsanulok, about 390km (240 miles) to the north of Bangkok, separating the old part of town into two. Although the broad banks of the River Nan can make a pleasant spot to rest, the real attraction is **Wat Phra Si Rattana Mahathat** (temple daily 6.30am–6.30pm, antique museum Wed–Sun 9am–4pm).

Believers have been coming here for centuries, praying in front of the renowned golden Chinarat Buddha, famous for its curative powers. The temple, with lovely mother-of-pearl doors from King Boromkot, was built in 1357, and its shrine is so popular that Thai tourists swarm here every day. To meet this demand, a variety of shops in the complex stock pendants, relics and other souvenirs. Apart from Wat Phra Si Rattana Mahathat, there are few reminders of the town's great history. A giant fire destroyed most of the old town several years ago, and now it is best known for comfortable hotels and as a base for Sukhothai excursions.

NORTHERN THAILAND

Stretching up to the borders with Myanmar and Laos, and following the line of the great Mekong River, northern Thailand incorporates some of the most beautiful scenery in the country. This region was once divided into small principalities, which were isolated by the rugged terrain and accessible only by elephant. Even today, the people of the region speak a distinctive dialect – influenced by Burmese and Laotian – and retain their own culinary specialities.

Getting there for today's visitor, however, is a simpler process. Thai Airways International flies to Chiang Mai in less than an hour from Bangkok, while air-conditioned express buses make the run in about nine hours, and overnight express trains in 12 to 14 hours. On a five-day visit, it is easily possible to explore the area around Chiang Mai and Chiang Rai – and even take a trek among the northern hill tribes.

CHIANG MAI

The capital of the north, **Chiang Mai ⑱**, rises from the banks of the Ping River, bedecked with dazzling flowers, notably orchid

---

⊙ ORCHIDS

Some of Thailand's remote areas are happy breeding grounds for over 1,300 different varieties of orchid, ranging from the famous *Paphiopedium ascocenda* to the elegant 'Miss Udorn Sunshine'. The best place to see them is at the orchid farms in the area around Chiang Mai, although you only need to look in markets throughout the country to see and appreciate the kingdom's favourite flower.

blossoms, in the spring. Formerly no more than a hillside Shangri-la, the town has grown rapidly to become both a tourist magnet and a major city in its own right – with the traffic and pollution to match. Several thousand luxury rooms and cheap, cheerful guesthouses are available, as well as European-style bars and restaurants. Tour operators offer countless trips to colourful handicraft villages, hillside temples and mountain tribes.

After the oppressive heat of Bangkok, the more temperate climate of Chiang Mai comes as a relief. The cooler weather is immediately evident (remember to pack a jumper if you are here between October and January), and so too is the abundance of fruit, vegetables and flowers, which can be seen at almost any time of year.

Chiang Mai means 'New Town' and was founded by King Mengrai the Great at the end of the 13th century. According to one legend, the city wall – parts of which can still be seen – was built by 90,000 men working in shifts round-the-clock. Mengrai also built various temples and fine buildings, some of which remain and can be explored on foot or by hiring a bicycle or motorbike. Don't forget to go to the handicraft centres nearby for silk, painted umbrellas and lacquerware.

Inside the city

Start your tour at **Wat Chiang Man** (daily 8am–5pm), within the old city walls. Built in the 13th century under King Mengrai, it contains two important religious statues, the Crystal and Marble Buddhas – protected behind a railing, bars and glass – which were ancient long before this monastery had been conceived. Sculpted elephants surround a *chedi* at the rear of the temple.

Walk south for 15 minutes and you reach the huge, ruined **Wat Chedi Luang** (daily 8am–5pm). Built in the 15th century, it was damaged during an earthquake over 400 years ago. In the temple grounds stands a gigantic gum tree shrouded in silk which, it is said, will continue to grow for as long as the city prospers. Beneath the tree, locals leave wooden elephants and phallic objects as offerings to the guardian spirit of the city.

Continue west to find **Wat Phra Singh** (daily 8am–5pm), home to a magnificent Buddha statue. According to legend, the icon was on its way to the king when the chariot carrying it broke down in front of the temple. Believing this to be a signal that the image wished to go no further, the people installed it without question, and there it has remained ever since, along with a beautiful library and several fine carvings and sculptures.

Ho Trai (scripture library) of Wat Phra Singh

Stall at the Night Bazaar in Chiang Mai

The best time of day to visit **Wat Suan Dok** (daily 8am–5pm), which is off Suthep Road on the city outskirts, is at sunset, when the *chedi* is bathed in soft light. The ashes of the kings of Lanna are housed within the temple, which is said to hold an important relic of the Buddha.

A final temple not to miss is **Wat Jet Yot** (daily 8am–5pm), also known as the Seven Peaks because of its seven *chedis*. Local guides say it was inspired by the great Mahabodhi Temple in India in 1455, during the reign of King Tilokaraja.

For visitors who desire other forms of entertainment, drop in at the **Chiang Mai City Arts and Cultural Centre** (tel: 0 5321 7793; www.cmocity.com; Tue–Sun 8.30am–5pm) for superb exhibits and interactive displays, or the **Old Chiang Mai Cultural Centre** (tel: 0 5320 2993-5; www.oldchiangmai.com; daily 7–9.30pm), a charming old northern-style house, with traditional Lanna dance and hill tribe demonstrations. Alternatively, explore markets like **Somphet** (Moonmuang Road), or busy **Warorot** (Wich-yanon Road), where you can try exquisite local delicacies. In the evening, don't miss the **Night Bazaar**, on Chang Klan Road, which offers northern handicrafts. You'll be overwhelmed by the sheer variety, which is probably greater here than at any other market in Thailand. Animal lovers could head to **Chiang Mai Zoo and Arboretum** (www.chiangmaizoo.com; daily 8am–6pm).

Outside the city

Explore the following temples, villages and other attractions as part of either a half-day tour or a more extended itinerary. At the **Chiang Dao Elephant Training Centre** (tel: 0 5329 8553; www.chiangdaoelephantcamp.com; daily 8am–5pm, elephant training session at 10am), 56km (35 miles) north from Chiang Mai, you can watch elephants double l lifting and bathing in the river and then go elephant riding. Years ago, elephants were commonly used throughout the north for transport across inhospitable terrain and for dragging logs to the river, for floating downstream. Today, you can ride on one of the giants of the jungle, and then take a raft trip through the lush countryside.

Wooden statues, huge clay pots and coloured paper umbrellas bedeck the road to the village of **San Kamphaeng**, 13km (8 miles) east of Chiang Mai, which is known as the handicrafts centre of northern Thailand. In the factories and warehouses, you can watch the locals as they weave silk from cocoons or make lacquerware or painted umbrellas. Purchases can be shipped home, and credit cards are widely accepted.

Some 16km (10 miles) northwest of Chiang Mai is the 1,600m (5,120ft) -high peak of **Doi Suthep**. There are magnificent bird's eye views of the city and the

Silk weaving

Member of the Akha hill tribe, near Chiang Rai

surroundings from the summit and just below lies the most famous temple in North Thailand, **Wat Phra That Doi Suthep** (daily 6am–5pm). According to legend, during the 14th century a sacred white elephant sought out the site for the foundation of the temple by trumpeting three times and kneeling in homage to the Buddha. From the car park, it is a 300-step hike (or a comfortable funicular ride) to the central gold *chedi* at the top, with its royal bronze parasols at each corner. The cloister is lined with many important Buddha statues.

Continue another 4 km (2.5 miles) past the temple to reach the **Phuphing Palace** (tel: 0 5322 3065; www.bhubingpalace. org; open when the royal family is absent, mid-March–Dec daily 8.30am–4.30pm, ticket office closes at 3.30pm), where the Thai king often spends some of the winter. On weekends and holidays, if the royal family is not in residence, the grounds are opened to the public in a blaze of lavish floral displays.

Another attraction in the vicinity is the small Hmong or Meo village called **Doi Pui** ⓳. Since it is the most accessible of all Thailand's hill-tribe villages, you are unlikely to find much authenticity. Still, if you don't have time to go trekking, the village does give an idea of the hill tribes' way of life, and includes a visit to the opium museum. Children sell colourful costumes, tasselled bags and primitive handicrafts.

AMONG THE HILL TRIBES

To see the tribes in a more authentic environment, go along with an **organised trek** into the hills. You will probably have to walk considerable distances and sleep on less than luxurious floors, but with the aid of a guide, you can still locate numerous Karen tribes, who believe in the spirits of the winds and the rains, or the Lahu people, the men wearing silver buckles and black turbans and the women in calf-length tunics with yellow or white embroidery.

Known as the *chao doi*, the hill tribes are nomadic peoples who have migrated from Tibet and southern China along various routes into Burma, Thailand and Laos. In all, there are some 550,000 people, divided into six tribes: the Karen, Hmong, Akha, Mien, Lisu and Lahu, each with its own distinct dress, language and culture.

Generally, they are highland dwellers who opt to live above 1,000m (3,280ft). They earn a living from foraging, slash-and-burn agriculture and raising domestic livestock such as chickens and black pigs. All inter-tribal trade is done by barter.

Traditionally, the chao doi have also shared a common mythology. They believe that they live on top of a dragon and that they have to keep the peace to ensure that it does not move.

Travel agencies in Chiang Mai operate excursions ranging from one-day trips to more rewarding three- and four-day expeditions. Don't expect too

Trekking agencies

It is always worth dropping in to the tourist office to check which are the reliable trekking companies, as they can change from month to month. Be sure to use a guide who can speak English and, if at all possible, the tribal tongue as well, since this will greatly add to the success of the trip.

much originality, though – villagers may ask for payment for posing for photos. While some are friendly and seem to be pleased that their colourful bejewelled costumes and simple huts are a centre of attention, others have discarded just about every trace of their traditions, opting instead for jeans, T-shirts and cola.

LAMPHUN

Although legend has it that the most beautiful women in Thailand are from Lamphun, this is not the only reason for coming to this peaceful, ancient town, which can be found 30km (19 miles) south of Chiang Mai.

A large monastery in the town centre called **Wat Phra That Haripunchai** (tel: 0 5351 1104; daily 6am–6pm) is a busy educational and meditational institution. The huge, gold chedi in the middle of the monastery was begun over 1,000 years ago, and the workmen who erected it constructed their own simpler version outside the compound; it is now a ruin. Close by and built in modern style is the **Haripunchai National Museum** (tel: 0 5351 1186; Tue–Sun 9am–4pm), which has a collection of sculptures found in the Lamphun district,

Members of the Karen tribe in a village near Mae Sariang

dating from the 10th to 12th century.

You can take a pedi-cab from the centre of Lamphun to **Wat Chama Devi** (or Kukut; daily 8am–6pm), a temple that owes its existence to Queen Chama Devi, said to have founded it when she ruled the Mon kingdom of Lamphun well over 1,000 years ago. Of the original elements, most memorable is a *chedi* rising in five tiers with 60 standing Buddha images in stucco around the sides.

Look out for the *lamyai* orchards that have helped to make this region famous throughout Thailand. This delicious fruit, which is known as 'longan' in English, resembles a lychee.

River ride

The most exciting way of arriving in Chiang Rai is not by the route through the hills, nor by the 45-minute flight, but by the least comfortable option of the river-boat from the town of Tha Ton. This is a trip for the adventurous – the boats are both small and narrow, with no toilets, while the engine is as loud (though not as powerful) as that of an aeroplane. Nonetheless, it is worth the effort – the views on the 4-hour journey are spectacular.

LAMPANG

Don't be surprised if you see a horse and carriage trundling down the main road of this beautiful old town, 100km (62 miles) southeast of Chiang Mai – this is a common form of transport in **Lampang ⑳**, and the best way to explore.

There are three temples here that deserve special mention. **Wat Phra Fang** (daily 8am–5pm) has a tall, golden *chedi* with seven small shrines around the base. **Wat Phra Kaew Don Tao** (daily 8am–5pm) reveals Burmese influence and has outstanding carvings. Considered by many to be northern Thailand's most

Hill Tribe Museum, Chiang Rai

attractive temple, **Wat Phra That Lampang Luang** (daily 7.30am–5pm), situated 18km (11 miles) from Lampang near the town of **Ko Kha**, is worth a visit for its museum and fine Buddha images.

CHIANG RAI

Chiang Rai ㉑, a city located 180km (111 miles) north of Chiang Mai, is a good base for visiting nearby regional attractions. King Mengrai founded Chiang Rai in the 13th century, by chance so it is said. According to legend, his elephant ran off and took him to a spot on the Mae Kok River, where the scenery and military potential inspired him to build a town.

There are at least two temples worth a visit. At **Wat Phra Kaew** (tel: 0 5371 1385; www.watphrakaew-chiangrai.com; daily 9am–5pm), you can see a former home of the Emerald Buddha (see page 28), the country's most famous image. At the Burmese-style **Wat Doi Chom Thong** (daily 8am–5pm), you have the bonus of river views and a glimpse of the town's old quarter. Meanwhile, the **Hill Tribe Museum and Education Centre** (www.pdacr.org; Mon–Fri 8.30am–6pm, Sat–Sun 10am–6pm) sells ethnic handicrafts, with proceeds donated to hill tribe community projects.

Travel agencies in Chiang Rai operate excursions to the famous hillside temple of **Doi Tung** (daily 8am–4.30pm), perched 1,800m (6,000ft) high. On the way you pass the former Queen Mother's summer residence, an agricultural project sponsored by the Thai royal family designed to help hill tribes retain their distinctive traditions while integrating into contemporary life. The project encourages tribespeople to grow strawberries, cucumbers and cabbages, in lieu of opium. In return they receive government assistance in the form of schools and new roads.

Smaller tribal villages can still be found in the mountains north of Chiang Rai and the area around **Mae Chan**. Be warned, however: pigs, water buffalo and dogs may still wander picturesquely among the stilt houses, but modern life has not passed by unnoticed, and the children will ask for coins or, increasingly, notes. Even among the Yao villages of adobe huts with thatched roofs, many elders have learned a few English words. The women, in red-collared jackets and blue turbans, are usually more

Lisu hill tribe girls at Mae Hong Son

Mae Hong Son

interested in selling handicrafts than telling of the Yao's origins in southern China more than 200 years ago.

MAE SAI AND CHIANG SAEN

You can't go further north in Thailand than **Mae Sai**; beyond is the footbridge across the Sai River into Myanmar. This charming little backwater with a sprinkling of markets and guesthouses is a good lunchtime spot on the way to the Golden Triangle. Get there between 6am and 6pm and you'll see authorised travellers from Myanmar crossing the border into Thailand to sell products such as cheroots, packaged prunes, ivory carvings, lacquer boxes, oranges and, more discreetly, items such as gems and contraband cigarettes. In the market, take your pick from the wonderful Burmese puppets and tapestries known as *kalaga*, or pay your B10 to photograph children dressed in hill-tribe costume. It is possible to cross the bridge and visit the Burmese border town of Tachilek, although it is still not possible to travel deeper into Burma from here. Occasionally the border is closed for security reasons.

From Mae Sai, tours usually continue the 12km (7.5 miles) to the infamous Golden Triangle, which forms a three-way border between Myanmar, Laos and Thailand. This spot once saw huge quantities of opium being sent across the border, destined for heroin traders overseas. Now the trade is diminishing because of government encouragement to diversify into less sinister crops. Poppies won't be seen here, since discretion confines cultivation to the less accessible valleys, as well as to those vast areas in Myanmar that are controlled by the so-called 'opium armies'.

A short drive southeast from **Ban Sop Ruak** will bring you to the friendly market town of **Chiang Saen**, set in a marvellous location on the banks of the Mekong River. Despite its dilapidated feel, this sleepy town has a remarkably grand history. From the 10th to 13th centuries it was the seat of power for one of the earliest northern principalities – traces of this glorious past are scattered throughout.

You can easily spend an afternoon exploring a moated city wall, the Wat Phra That Chom Kitti – reputed to house part of Lord Buddha's forehead – and the ruins of several other temples. Head 10km (6 miles) north of Chiang Saen for the **Hall of Opium** (tel: 0 5378 4444-6; www.maefahluang.org; Tue–Sun 8.30am–4pm). Set up by Mae Fah Luang Foundation, it uses high-tech interactive displays to chronicle 5,000 years of the use and abuse of opiates. Visitors who have more time for leisurely travelling may also be rewarded with beautiful sunsets over the Mekong, and marvellous views of Laos, just a stone's throw away.

MAE HONG SON

December and January are the prime months to visit the town of **Mae Hong Son** ㉒, which lies between mountains 270km

(167 miles) northwest of Chiang Mai and is reached by a hair-raising, but staggeringly beautiful, eight-hour road trip – or a less bumpy 30 minute flight. At this time of year, the sky is at its bluest, the winter flowers are in full blossom and the air is cool. It doesn't really matter which month you come, however, for this town offers no shortage of year-round attractions.

Prior to 1831, when an expedition was sent here by the king of Chiang Mai in search of the rare white elephant, Mae Hong Son's history is as misty as its valleys. The expedition was so successful that a small settlement was founded, and by 1874 Mae Hong Son had become a provincial capital.

Although you're unlikely to see wild elephants, you will come across a number of Burmese-style temples around Mae Hong Son. They include **Wat Doi Kong Mu** (daily 8.30am–4.30pm), which looks down from the top of the 250m (820ft) -high Doi Kong Mu, and affords views across the green Mae Hong Son valley and towards the neighbouring Shan state. Most people like exploring the market at dawn – when hill-tribe people in traditional dress can sometimes be seen buying vegetables

⊘ SEA GYPSIES

Nearly 5,000 *Chao Lay*, or 'Sea Gypsies', have their home on the Andaman Sea. Most live in coastal shacks, between Ranong and Ko Tarutao, although the most famous, the Moken, lead a mainly nomadic life moving on boats between islands. They have no written language and their spoken languages are mainly related to Malay. The Chao Lay suffered relatively few casualties in the 2004 tsunami, and it is thought their intimacy with their environment enabled many to read the early warning signs in the sea's behaviour and flee to higher ground.

Burmese-style temple

– before going on any one of a variety of tours. Guides arrange elephant-riding and river-rafting, or will drive you to tribal villages at the Burmese border.

Around Mae Hong Son you may see the Padaung, or 'long-necked people', with their collarbones compressed by brass coils stacked up 30cm (1ft) high to make their necks appear longer than normal. Legend has it that the tribe's ancestors were a female dragon and the wind god, and it was in imitation of the image of the dragon that the women took up the unusual tradition. Inevitably, the reality now is that this appearance is primarily designed to attract tourists.

On leaving Mae Hong Son, drivers and bus passengers could return to Chiang Mai on a circular route via Mae Sariang and Hot, so that towns visited previously are not repeated. On the return journey, the relaxed crossroads town of **Pai** ㉓, a valley hamlet surrounded by mountains, is a good base for trekking. It is also a firm favourite with backpackers, so has a slew of bars with live music.

SOUTHERN THAILAND

Southern Thailand, stretching thinly down to Malaysia, gives you a choice of seas. The considerably longer eastern coast is on the Gulf of Thailand, while the west is washed by the Andaman Sea. On both sides you will find sensational beaches, while the land in between – full of rice fields, and coconut and rubber plantations – is as scenic as it is fertile.

Planes fly to Phuket, Ko Samui, and Krabi from Bangkok. Otherwise there are trains and buses, and the opportunity to explore several of the small, picturesque fishing villages along the way.

PHUKET

The island of **Phuket ㉔** (pronounced 'poo-ket') is Thailand's most expensive beach destination, with beautiful beaches and luxurious hotels, in addition to sailing, nightlife and various family attractions. Covering around 810 sq km (313 sq miles) and made up of a mountainous interior, Phuket offers national parks, inland plantations and waterfalls and is the major departure point for diving in the Andaman Sea.

The island attracts over 10 million tourists every year – over 16 times its total population – most of whom arrive by plane (55 minutes from Bangkok), although tourist coaches also make the trip in just over 14 hours, crossing the causeway from the mainland.

Although Phuket has been transformed by the invasion of tourists, and new hotels are almost as abundant as water buffalo, you are nonetheless spoiled by some of the most beautiful scenery and clearest seas in the region.

From the airport, the highway south goes through a dusty village called **Thalang Ⓐ**, the site of the island's ancient capital. Burmese invaders besieged and pillaged Thalang in 1809. In an earlier and more positive chapter of history, the city managed to withstand a siege by the Burmese that lasted longer than a month. This battle, in 1785, led to both Lady Chan and her sister Lady Muk being regarded as heroines for taking

Preparing to parasail off Phuket

command of the town's defence following the death of Lady Chan's husband, the governor. Statues of these short-haired women warriors stand on a roundabout.

The new capital, also called Phuket or **Phuket Town B**, has a host of shopping centres, cafés and seafood restaurants, along with souvenir shops that sell seashells and locally cultivated – as well as counterfeit – pearls. **Jui Tui Temple** (daily 8am–5pm) is the centre of the annual October Vegetarian Festival, when people perform acts of self-mutilation, including piercing their cheeks with skewers. It is believed that thanks to these acts Chinese gods will protect them against evil.

Phuket Orchid Garden and Thai Village (tel: 0 7628 0226; daily 9am–5.30pm) has traditional dances, elephant shows and a handicraft centre, while on Yaowaraj Road, Chillvamarket (daily 5–11pm) has a selection of eateries and shops, with frequent, free, live music events taking place, making it popular with locals.

Most visitors, however, find it hard to tear themselves away from the island's beaches. Water sports of all kinds are offered, from waterskiing to paragliding, and windsurfers, catamarans and yachts can be hired. Fresh seafood makes for memorable meals, and most will, at some stage, treat themselves to the famous Phuket lobster, which is best eaten grilled and with a dash of lime.

BEACHES AND ISLANDS

The best beaches are on the western coast of the island, where fine, white sand slopes gently into the Andaman Sea (Indian Ocean). **Patong Beach** ⓒ, 15km (9 miles) west of Phuket Town by paved road, used to be the island's most beautiful, but has become over-developed, packed with bungalows, hotels, restaurants, bars, pubs and clubs. You will also find the **Phuket Simon Cabaret** (tel: 0 7634 2011-5; www.phuket-simoncabaret.com; daily showtimes 6pm, 7.30pm and 9pm) with its *kathoey*, or 'ladyboy' shows. From Patong, visitors can take a 45-minute longtail boat ride to **Freedom Beach**, located just around the headland.

North of Patong are the lovely **Bang Thao** and **Pansea** beaches, the latter home to the Amanpuri Hotel, one of the most exclusive addresses on the island. At **Kamala** beach, the popular **Phuket Fantasea** (tel: 0 7638 5000; www.phuket-fantasea.com; theme park Fri–Wed 5.30–11.30pm, showtime 9pm) has shows combining acrobatics, pyrotechnics and performing animals.

> ### Island escapes
>
> Adventurers can escape the crowds by hiring boats to more distant, uninhabited islands – just make sure that before leaving you agree on the price and the number of islands that you will be visiting.

South of Patong, the wide beaches of **Kata** and **Karon**

have an abundance of family resorts, while further south, at **Nai Harn**, is the sophisticated cliffside hideaway of The Royal Phuket Yacht Club.

It is possible to hire a Jeep to tour the island, but some roads are steep and accidents are not uncommon. The most dramatic viewpoint is the **Laem Promthep**  promontory.

The sea views from Phuket are dotted with 30 or so uninhabited islands,

Phang Nga Bay

to which owners of long-tailed boats operate excursions for picnics and/or snorkelling. Scuba diving is first rate, either on liveaboard or day boats, with plenty of coral and brilliantly hued fish. The most favoured diving destination is the **Similan Islands** 🕒, which have National Marine Park status. Deep-sea fishing expeditions can be arranged to catch mackerel, barracuda and sailfish.

EXCURSIONS FROM PHUKET

Phuket travel agencies offer a variety of day-long excursions. Anyone who knows the James Bond film *The Man with the Golden Gun* will not want to miss visiting dramatic **Phang Nga Bay** 🕕, which contains the superb rock formations featured in the film. Long-tailed boats skim through the mangrove into a dreamscape of mad mountain tops, and at two points of the journey sail through tunnels beneath limestone islands.

The bow of a long tail by Phi Phi Don

On the way they will stop at **Ko Panyi**, where the Muslim fishing people have built a village on stilts above the sea and now enjoy the attention of thousands of tourists, who buy their woodwork and fresh fish. The real highlight, though, is **Ko Tapu** (literally 'Nail Island'), which was formed thousands of years ago as a result of an earthquake. The island rises straight up out of the water to a height of 200m (656ft).

A separate excursion is offered to **Ko Phi Phi** ㉗, which consists of two islands, Phi Phi Don and Phi Phi Leh. Boats leave from Phuket daily and the trip south lasts two hours. Day tours will take you to the Viking Cave and to beautiful Khai Nai. Tours will also, when possible, stop at the popular Maya Bay, made famous in Danny Boyle's film The Beach. However, access to tourists is being restricted to allow extensive coral reef damage to recover. Underwater enthusiasts can explore some of the richest marine life to be found in the Andaman Sea. Fish are not the only attraction either, for high up in the sea cliffs live a vast number of sea swallows. The nests that the birds build so industriously at great heights are collected at considerable risk to the islanders – it is a profitable export business, supplying Chinese restaurants with the raw material for that expensive delicacy of bird's-nest soup. Locals believe that the soup will cure skin and lung problems as well as impotence and loss of appetite. Such is the demand that some nests fetch prices as high as US$1,000 each.

KO SAMUI

Backpackers long ago thought that they could keep **Ko Samui** secret. However, this palm-fringed island, just three hours from the busy seaport town of Surat Thani, has become one of the best-known havens in the south, with idyllic accommodation and even an airport. Not that it has necessarily spoilt the laid-back feel of the place, for people are still coming here to laze on the beaches, eat excellent seafood and be pampered at one of the sumptuous spas.

Honeymooners and comfort seekers often stay on **Chaweng Beach**, which is arguably the most beautiful stretch, although packed with restaurants and discos. If you want something more chilled, head to **Bo Phut, Maenam** and **Choeng Mon** beaches. For cheaper accommodation, head for the south.

A plethora of beach sports are offered, as well as tennis, waterfall trips and even an excursion to a coconut-picking farm. For an afternoon diversion, you can hire a motor-cycle or Jeep to tour the island. The road follows the coast almost all the way round, though you should stop off at **Lamai** to see the erotic rock formations known to all as 'grandfather' and 'grandmother' rocks. Remember that the roads here are steep – and tourists with grazed knees are a fairly common sight. A safer means of transport is a *songthaew* (covered pickup truck with seats), which run almost 24 hours.

BEYOND SAMUI

Samui is the largest island in an archipelago of 80 islands that also includes the party haven of Ko Pha Ngan, the dive mecca

Divers off Ko Tao

of Ko Tao, and the stunning uninhabited ruggedness of Ang Thong National Marine Park. Ferries and speed boats shuttle visitors daily between the various shorelines, with Ko Pha Ngan being the closest.

Geared more toward backpackers than luxe travellers, **Ko Pha Ngan** is best known for its legendary **Full Moon Party** on **Hat Rin** beach. Attracting thousands of revellers each month, the party is synonymous with drug taking, despite local authorities attempting to stem the narco-consumption.

Far more tranquil is a day tour of the 40 wild islets and lagoons that comprise the beautiful **Ang Thong National Marine Park** (www.angthongmarinepark.com), which inspired the fictitious island paradise in Alex Garland's 1996 novel *The Beach*. Further north is **Ko Tao** (Turtle Island), a small, pretty island with a relaxed atmosphere. Most visitors come here for the quality dive sites, with the numerous dive shops being the island's mainstay.

NAKHON SI THAMMARAT

Thailand's most southerly provinces are plagued with Muslim separatist violence, and most governments warn against visiting Narathiwat, Yala, Pattani and Songkhla. This means fewer visitors to the area, and consequently the safe provinces are less developed and have plenty of quiet beaches and a genuine local flavour.

Nakhon Si Thammarat's **National Museum** (daily 8am–5pm) has one of Thailand's most important historical collections outside Bangkok. The town is also home to the country's most famous maker and performer of nang thalung leather shadow puppets, and **Suchart Subsin's Shadow Puppet Workshop** (tel: 0 7534 6394; daily 8.30am–4.30pm) sells puppets and stages performances for a small donation.

SATUN

While Satun Town's only real attraction is **Satun National Museum** (tel: 0 7472 3140; Wed–Sun 9am–4pm) and its Muslim lifestyle exhibitions, offshore lies **Ko Tarutao Marine National Park ㉙** (mid-Nov–mid-May). Consisting of 51 islands, it has Thailand's best coral reefs and is believed to harbour 25 percent of the world's tropical fish species. Wildlife includes whales, dolphins and dugongs, while the largest island, Ko Tarutao, offers hiking and cave exploring. The park headquarters have basic accommodation. In the 1930s and 40s Thai prisoners were exiled to Ko Tarutao, and in 2002 a series of the American reality TV show Survivor was filmed here.

Some 50km (30 miles) west, there are good dive spots at Ko Rawi, Ko Yang and Ko Hin Sorn.

Mermaid origins

Legends about seductive mermaids are believed to be based on sightings of the dugong, an inhabitant of the waters around Ko Tarutao. These strange mammals, related to the elephant, and dubbed the 'sea cow', roam the seas from Australia to East Africa, staying underwater for up to six minutes at a time. Hunters prize them for meat, oil, skin, bones and teeth, and despite them being legally protected, dugongs remain an endangered species.

Wicker baskets for sticky rice, found in the north-east

WHAT TO DO

Thailand offers an unbeatable choice of indoor and outdoor activities, even if the heat is such that sometimes all you want is a swim. If you find you are lucky enough to be in Thailand at the time of a major festival, be sure not to miss one of the country's most joyous occasions.

SHOPPING

From the moment you reach Thailand you will be astounded by the wealth of things to buy. Locally made items range from stunning silk products to finely worked wooden bowls and silver earrings, as well as clothing and fragile, colourful pots. Whatever you are looking for, you are likely to find it in **Bangkok. Pathumwan** is crammed with large, modern shopping malls and department stores where there is no shortage of either imported or local offerings.

Nor is Bangkok the only option. **Chiang Mai** is renowned for its handicrafts, while even the smaller towns in the northeast of the country offer many of their own specialities. In **Phuket**, the main Airport-Phuket highway has a good selection of handicrafts, while Chaweng at Samui is awash with typical tourist gear.

Remember that bargaining is the rule just about everywhere, apart from supermarkets and hotels – with even the large, upmarket boutiques occasionally being amenable to a little bit of negotiation. But do keep in mind that fixed-price shops may sometimes be no more expensive, and they come with the bonus of some form of guarantee. A word of caution: only buy jewellery from reputable shops.

Bangkok's Chatuchak Weekend Market

MARKETS AND BAZAARS

Air-conditioned shops might sound like the best idea in the big cities, but it is the local markets that offer the real bargains. They are definitely worth a visit, if only to see the crowds and experience the excitement. Take a camera and get there early, as the heat becomes oppressive by the middle of the day.

One of the most famous markets in Thailand is Chiang Mai's **Night Bazaar** (see page 64). Find quality silks, handicrafts, rugs and clothing for sale, among many other items. The market gets going at dusk and the vendors start packing up just before midnight.

In the capital there are several markets worth a visit. One of the biggest, most diverse and best-known markets in Bangkok is the **Chatuchak Weekend Market** (see page 39). Fruit, vegetables and spices all vie for space with food concoctions you have probably never come across before. As for take-home curios, you might like a brass temple bell, a carved buffalo horn, a hill-tribe embroidered garment, or some handmade silver jewellery. You will also find a huge selection of vintage and trendy street-style clothing, plants, rare antiques, and funky homeware and furnishings.

Smaller groups of weekday stalls can be found at Chinatown, the Thieves' Market and Pahurat, all located within easy reach of one another. **Chinatown** is worth a visit simply for the sightseeing. The **Thieves' Market** has a wide range of curios, some of them antique – but remember that you need an export certificate for genuine items. For sumptuous silks, clothing, cloth and delicate batiks, some real bargains are to be found in **Pahurat** market. Here, products from as far away as India and Malaysia are sold alongside local items.

BEST BUYS

Antiques. If you qualify as an informed collector, then you will find worthwhile objects from Thailand, Myanmar, China, Laos and Cambodia at the Thieves' Market, in smarter shops or in the provinces. Experts at the National Museum in Bangkok meet

⊘ THE ART OF BARGAINING

Want a natty wooden elephant, a lurid leather bag or even a ride in a *tuk-tuk*? Then remember to bargain for it. First ask how much the price is. Then name a figure considerably lower and somewhat less than you are prepared to pay, and eventually aim to meet up in the middle. A few helpful hints: always check the prices on several stalls to get an idea of the real cost; avoid being misled by sweet smiles and sob stories – and remember, at the end of the day, so long as you are happy with the price, it was a bargain.

the public on both Sundays and Mondays, when they vouch for the authenticity of works of art and antiquity. Export permission is required for taking genuine antiques out of the country.

Art. Paintings in several media by Thai artists, often on familiar rice paddy or temple-spire themes, are sold in galleries and shops all over the main towns. Temple stone rubbings on rice paper are another typical souvenir.

Bronze. A great Thai tradition, bronze is now used for table ware in addition to lamps, bells, candelabras and statues.

Ceramics. A particular wood is used in the kilns to fire celadon, a distinctive Asian form of pottery with a delicate green glaze. Porcelain is also made in Thailand. Ming and Ching dynasty bowls and shards turn up, salvaged from the river at Ayutthaya and Sukhothai.

Fashion. Clothes to order – allegedly in 24 hours or less – can be a bargain, but try to give the tailor several days if you want a first-rate garment. Trousers, dresses, suits, shirts and bikinis can all be made to measure. Women's ready-to-wear shops often sell good cheap copies of current European fashions. The domestic fashion industry is also coming into its own, with lots of trendy boutiques in Bangkok malls and around Siam Square.

Furniture. Rattan and hardwood furniture pieces are often bargains and can be made to order. Bangkok and Chiang Mai have the best selections. With the ongoing success of teak farming and teak recycling, teak furniture has once again become a bargain in Thailand if you find the right places. Asian rosewood is also a good buy.

Images of Buddha

Taking images of Buddha, larger than 12 centimetres (4.7 inches), or goods featuring the Thai flag out of Thailand is prohibited, and the export of antiques is strictly controlled.

Tribal crafts include miniature figures carved from wood

Gems. Precious stones such as sapphires and rubies are mined here, while others are imported at favourable prices from Myanmar, India, Sri Lanka and other countries. Bangkok claims to be the world's top gem-cutting centre. Seek out a reputable shop and avoid unrealistic bargains: fakes are common.

Handicrafts. With great skill, patience and ingenuity, the artisans of Thailand produce an apparently endless variety of hand-crafted objects. Each region has its specialities.

Homeware. Contemporary Thai design has become extremely creative in recent years, with many designers infusing traditional crafts and materials with ultra-modern twists.

Jewellery. Thai designers tend towards traditional styles, but original designs can be ordered. Choose carefully where you shop: the establishments that cater to tour buses are generally more expensive because they often pay the travel agency a 20

Lacquerware in the form of vases

percent kickback on what you spend. Thai costume jewellery can be a great bargain.

Lacquerware. Look out for pretty gold-and-black boxes in the shape of fantasy animals.

Nielloware. Black metal alloy inlaid on silver is an ancient craft now deployed on jewellery and trinkets.

Pottery. A typical Thai variety – *benjarong* ware – has a five-coloured design on a background of grey, white or black. You will also see patterned porcelain jars, plates and pots.

Thai silk and fabrics. Happy silkworms keep thousands of nimble weavers busy, hand and foot, in producing the famous, colourful Thai fabrics. Ranging from lightweight blouses to heavy bedspreads, the long-lasting fabrics live up to their worldwide reputation. Durable Thai cotton, most of which is factory-made, goes into ready-to-wear clothing, towels, some toys and tablecloths.

Umbrellas. All around Chiang Mai, locals make hand-painted parasols – to your own design, if you wish.

Wood carvings. Figurines, elephants and hippos, teak furniture, salad bowls and a variety of other knick-knacks are exquisitely carved from wood.

ENTERTAINMENT

THAI DANCE, DANCE-DRAMA AND MUSIC

The highly stylised classical *khon* drama, based on the *Ramakien* epic, was once performed solely at royal palaces for the privileged. In a *khon* performance, masks are donned for all roles except the three leads where heavy make-up and ornate costumes subdue the personality of the performers. The modern adaptations presented during dance shows are generally known as *lakhon* where no masks are worn and the movements are less stylised. The *lakhon chakri* is often performed at temple festivals and at shrines. The popular burlesque theatre, known as *likay*, is much coarser, and is interspersed with slapstick episodes. The entertaining transvestite shows always include several *likay*-type scenes. The

Wood carving

Live performance at the Saxophone Pub

shadow theatre known as *nang thalung* originated in the south of the country and is staged against a backlit white cloth screen. It is most commonly performed in South Thailand.

Classical Thai music can sound like a mishmash of contrasting tones without any pattern. To aficionados, it has a very distinct rhythm and plan. A classical *phipat* orchestra is made up of a single reed instrument, the oboe-like *phinai*, and a variety of percussion instruments.

The only places with regular traditional dance and theatre in Bangkok are **Sala Chalerm Krung** (tel: 0 2225 87578; www.sala chalermkrung.com), which hosts *khon* masked drama performances every Thursday and Friday at 7.30pm, and a few restaurants which host dinner shows. **Aksra Theatre King Power** (tel: 0 2680 9999; www.pullmanbangkokkingpower.com) has Thai and other Asian puppetry with cultural performances themed around events like cock-fighting and *MuayThai*.

NIGHTLIFE

Mention Bangkok to anybody and the chances are they will talk about the city's nightlife. Steadily, the city is welcoming a whole slew of stylish bars and clubs that are slowly helping the capital to distance itself from its salacious reputation. Lounge bars, fabulous roof-top bars and chic design-conscious clubs are all the rage now. Quality music has at last become a must with bars hosting weekly DJ-driven theme nights and also pulling in big-name international DJs.

Officially, Bangkok is divided into three nightlife zones: Thanon Silom, Thanon Ratchadaphisek and Royal City Avenue (RCA), where venues with valid dance licences open until 2am. The rest should close by 1am. In reality police bribes are common and venues might stay open later. People must be over 20 to enter clubs and almost all require you to show ID. Carry a copy of your passport, rather than the original. Good clubs include **Levels Club & Lounge** (35 Sukhumvit Soi 11; tel: 08 2308 3246; www.levelsclub.com), where – as the name suggests – there are various floors with views over the city, and **Onyx** (Thanon Phra Ram 9; tel: 08 1645 1166; www.onyxbangkok.com).

On the live music front, there are interesting local performances at **Tawandaeng German Brewhouse** (462/1 Rama 3 Rd; tel: 0 2678 11146; www.tawandang.com), while rock and blues fans head for **Saxophone Pub** (3/8 Phaya Thai Rd; tel: 0 2246 5472; www.saxophonepub.com). For rock-bottom beers visit **Cheap Charlie's** (40/2 Sukhumvit Rd), a quirky roadside bar with a somewhat eclectic-looking bar design.

Chiang Mai has few clubs. **Boy Blues Bar** (Soi 6, Changklan Rd, Kalare Night Bazaar; http://boybluesbar.com) is the venue for Thai style blues played by local talented bands with jam sessions on Monday. Down on the Ping River there is more live music at the

Advert on Soi Bangla in Patong, on the island of Phuket

Riverside Bar & Restaurant (9–11 Charoenrat Rd; tel: 0 5324 3239; www.theriver sidechiangmai.com).

Phuket is big on Irish bars like **Angus O'Toole** (516/20 Patak Rd, Hat Karon; tel: 0 7639 8262; www.otools-phuket. com) while the late night dance crowd is found at Seduction Nightclub (Thanon Bangla, Kathu District; tel: 09 2480 6234; www.seductiondisco.com).

THE GO-GO SCENE

Several thousand nightclubs and go-go bars throughout the country cater to many tastes. Although they are aimed primarily at males, women are usually welcome to come in for a drink and a look. Gay and straight bars are increasingly run in the same areas, particularly in Bangkok and Chiang Mai.

Upstairs bars are frequently a front for live sex shows. It is always wise to check the price before entering any Patpong bar. There are occasional attempts at rip-off prices; if so simply pay the bill and get in touch with the tourist police. Remember that go-go bar 'women' are not all female, and that Aids and venereal diseases are common.

Provincial nightlife is often calmer, though many towns have nightclubs with hostesses for hire, massage parlours and the like. In central Thailand, Pattaya has a comprehensive nightlife comparable with Bangkok's. Down in the far south, Phuket outdoes all other seaside tourist towns with a highly concentrated entertainment zone in Patong Beach.

SPORTS

With some of the most beautiful waters in the Far East, it is little wonder that Thailand is a beach-lover's paradise. Once you have finished sunning yourself, there is no shortage of other activities. Boats and windsurfers are available for hire at beaches, as are pedal boats and jet skis.

Fishing has only been exploited recently as a sport in Thailand, but the Andaman Sea has good options, including night fishing for shark, with boats leaving from Phuket. Good catches of sailfish, marlin and shark have also been made from Pattaya, but if all you want is a day relaxing on deck with a rod to tempt smaller snapper, mackerel or parrotfish, that can easily be arranged as well.

Scuba diving is especially good around Ko Tao and the Similan Islands, but is available at most major resorts, including Pattaya; lessons are also offered. Most dive operators have PADI Open

⊙ THAI BOXING

Thai boxing (Muay Thai) is a violent sport that combines Western boxing with Eastern martial arts. As well as using gloved fists, these agile punchers and kickers battle it out with their elbows, knees and feet. Fights are held year-round at Lumphini and Ratchadamnoen stadiums in Bangkok and at festivals and fairs around the country, where many boys begin their careers as young as seven. Tourist areas like Bangkok, Chiang Mai and Phuket have exhibition bouts and gyms where you can learn the moves yourself.

Water certification courses for beginners through to dive master, and day trips (or longer) with live-aboard facilities to the best sites. **Water-skiing, kite boarding** and **wakeboarding** fans are increasingly catered for at popular beaches. Away from the water, **golf** facilities are first rate in Bangkok, Hua Hin, Phuket and Pattaya, with several championship-standard courses available.

Trekking in the northern mountains is gaining in popularity. Week-long treks usually include three meals a day and basic camping equipment. The best town from which to begin a trekking tour is Mae Hong Son, where countless tour agencies offer trips with licensed guides.

CHILDREN'S ACTIVITIES

Although children may not take to the heat well, the upsides are that Thais love kids and there is an increasing number of facilities available for family holidays. Chiang Mai has **Chiang Mai Zoo and Arboretum** (see page 64) and the **Maesa Elephant Camp** (tel: 0 5320 6247; www.maesaelephantcamp.com; daily 8am–4pm), 30km (19 miles) from the city, where kids can learn about and ride elephants. Animal options in Bangkok are **Sea Life Ocean World** (www.sealifebangkok.com; daily 10am–9pm) and **Dusit Zoo** (www.zoothailand.org; daily 8am–6pm), while **Dream World** (www.dreamworld.co.th; Mon–Fri 10am–5pm, Sat–Sun 10am–7pm) has roller coasters. Pattaya has elephant battles and lasers at **Alangkarn Theatre** (Thu–Tue, shows at 6pm) and **Phuket Fantasea** (www.phuket-fantasea.com; theme park Fri–Wed 5.30–11.30pm, shows at 9pm) has a circus. One of the hottest attractions in recent years (and not only for kids) has been the **Art in Paradise**, an interactive 3D gallery using optical illusion so posing visitors become part of the artwork. There are branches in Bangkok, Chiang Mai and Pattaya (www.artinparadise.co.th).

CALENDAR OF EVENTS

Check precise dates before you leave as the timing of many festivals and events depends on the position of the sun or the moon.

Late January–early February Chinese New Year. Many Thais have Chinese ancestry, and this week-long Lunar New Year festival is always celebrated with much gusto.

February full moon Makha Puja. A nationwide Buddhist festival with candlelight processions around many temples.

Early February Flower carnival in Chiang Mai, with floats, parades and beauty contests.

13–15 April Songkran or Water Festival. Thai New Year is celebrated nationwide by throwing water at everybody in sight.

Early May Visaka Puja. This very important Buddhist holiday commemorates the Buddha with candlelight processions.

May The Royal Ploughing Ceremony in Bangkok. Just before the rainy season starts, the king presides over ceremonies to bring good rains to farmers.

May Bun Bang Fai (rocket) festival in the northeast. Fireworks light the sky to bring rain.

28 July The king's birthday is celebrated in Bangkok with an elaborate parade on Ratchadamnoen Klang Avenue.

July full moon Asanha Puja. Candlelight processions at every temple in Thailand to celebrate Buddha's first sermon.

12 August Mother's Day, this is a public holiday marking the King mother's birthday.

Early October Phuket Vegetarian Festival in Phuket Town. Chinese festival with male penitents piercing their bodies with knives and needles.

November full moon Thailand's most beautiful festival, Loi Krathong. Thais across the country launch small candle-laden floats on rivers and lakes (see page 58).

Late November River Kwai Historical Week in Kanchanaburi. A week-long festival to commemorate the events of World War II with memorial services and a sound-and-light show over the famous bridge.

5 December The late King Bhumibol's birthday remains a public holiday.

EATING OUT

Good food in Thailand is as ubiquitous as beaches – and often quite a lot hotter besides. If you dislike chillies, do not give up on the food. *Mai phet* (not hot), stressed at the time you order, can bring a delicious selection of cooler, more subtle flavours that may include any taste from the sweetness of coconut milk to the pungency of fresh lemon grass, garlic or nutmeg and the saltiness of fermented fish. Added to that are tropical fruits such as fresh pineapple, a little sugar, a pinch of coriander and, of course, a lashing of culinary inspiration.

Every region has its own gastronomic specialities. Up in the north, a local sausage known as *naem* is popular. The northeast is famed for its *khao niaw* (sticky or glutinous rice), normally served as an accompaniment to barbecued meat, as well as *som tam*, a tasty hot salad that combines shredded green papaya with dried shrimp or black field crabs, lemon juice, garlic, fish sauce and

⊘ STREET FARE

On the whole, the best and certainly the cheapest meals will be found at food stalls which line the streets. Housewives buy their ingredients fresh and inexpensively at the market in the early morning and prepare their best dishes. There are usually no menus as each stall offers a few specialities. Buying from food stalls poses no language difficulties, as you simply point at what you want. The food stalls may look rather dubious, but remember that unlike restaurants, everything is prepared before your very eyes. Westerners who have spent some time in Thailand have complete faith in these street-side stalls.

chillies. The south produces numerous dishes that have been influenced by the Muslim style of cooking of the Malays and, of course, all kinds of seafood dishes, including crab, squid, shark, freshly cooked lobster and mussels. Do not worry if you have a sweet tooth, you are not likely to go hungry at all. Many Thai sweets are based on rice flour, coconut milk, palm sugar and sticky rice, and just about all of them are delicious.

Kaeng mussaman curry

WHEN AND HOW TO EAT

Most Thais work all day, grab something quick for lunch and have an early dinner. But do not think that the Thai version of fast food is just a bland rice dish. A 'quick bite' often means a tasty dish (such as *pad thai*) of sautéed noodles with pork, shrimp or chicken and seasoned with tamarind juice, lime, basil, garlic and onion. Even breakfast for locals consists of dishes full of fresh herbs and spices, such as sweet curry soup with basil served with boiled rice noodles. Hotels rarely serve such traditional Thai breakfasts although they will direct you to a nearby restaurant that offers them.

Food vendors line the streets everywhere and sometimes it may seem as if everybody is eating or drinking at all hours. Some vendors operate from glass-fronted carts, others with

Try a variety of noodles at the many street stalls

just large pans on the ground. Communal tables and chairs will be nearby. Slightly more upmarket are *raan aharn* (food shops). Generally, top-end Thai restaurants have milder flavours, as they compromise for tourist palates. Bangkok boasts some of the finest restaurants in the world, including the ultra-traditional **Nahm** and the modern **Sra Bua**, conceptualised by Henrik Yde Andersen, and linked to his Michelin-starred Copenhagen restaurant Kiin Kiin. There is now a Michelin guide to the Thai capital, meaning a slew of new starred restaurants and perhaps one of the best opportunities to have a high-level culinary experience without breaking the bank.

Local markets teem with vendors selling food items such as nuts, dried meats and sweets. If you are feeling adventurous, skip the hotel breakfast and stroll through an open-air market sampling the various treats. At lunch it will be too hot to have the Thai soups so opt for a salad and noodle dish. Plan on having your main meal in the early evening, just after sunset when the temperature drops.

Soup is traditionally eaten throughout the meal. If you are a newcomer to Thai food, start off with something mild and then maybe work up to pig's intestine soup or chilli-flavoured serpents' heads. Also good to start with are curries (kaeng phet) – particularly those with a coconut-cream base, which are less piquant than Indian curries – and there is never any shortage of wonderful, fresh fish. There is no need to hold back on quantity or restrict yourself to one dish. Thais will usually order a selection and share them as a group.

When eating chillies, take a local tip and have plenty of steamed rice, which helps to soothe the stomach and will smother the fire. Nothing else is as effective, and cold drinks just make it worse.

You are unlikely to find knives on Thai tables; a spoon is often used instead. Sauces will be offered that you can use to season your dish instead of salt and pepper. One of them is *nam pla*, a salty caramel-coloured fish sauce with tiny chilli segments in it. *Nam phrik*, 'pepper water', is a much-prized concoction of pounded red chillies, shrimp paste, black pepper, garlic and onions mixed with tamarind, lemon juice, ginger and fish in an early state of fermentation.

Small bowls of roasted chillies are also served on the side for diners with a more robust constitution.

WHAT TO EAT

Appetisers. *Paw pia tawt* is a Thai spring roll enclosing sweet-and-sour bean sprouts, pork and crabmeat. *Gai hor bai toey*

Balanced diet

People order several dishes at dinner to share, with an emphasis on balance – spicy, mild, sour, salty and sweet.

consists of chicken chunks fried with sesame oil, soya sauce, oyster sauce, herbs and a drop of whisky, all in a leaf wrapper. *Krathong thong* are delicate mouth-sized patty shells filled with a delicious combination of minced chicken, sweet corn, carrots and soy sauce.

⊙ INTERNATIONAL FARE

For a change of both taste and scenery, try one of the various Asian restaurants that serve a spectrum of different cuisines, many of them at bargain prices. By far the most common is Chinese. In Bangkok you can sample the most important regional schools of Chinese cooking – Sichuanese, Cantonese, Shanghainese and Pekingese – as well as the less familiar food of the Hakka, Chiu Chow and Hunan peoples.

Restaurants specialising in food from neighbouring Cambodia, Malaysia, Burma and Laos are not easy to find, but Japanese, Korean and Vietnamese food is well-represented.

The significant population of Thais of Indian descent or Muslim religion accounts for the availability of associated foods. In Bangkok there are several Indian cafés and restaurants to choose from, selling both northern and southern dishes.

In cities, especially Bangkok, and tourist-friendly areas such as Chiang Mai, Phuket, Pattaya and Samui, there will be a good choice of international food. Italian is the most popular non-Asian food by far, but there should also be options for French, German, Mexican and Californian, as well as pub grub.

The quality of international food is steadily improving, although prices are moving accordingly, and some restaurants are very high-end, including several spectacular rooftop outfits in Bangkok.

Hot and sour shrimp soup, tom yum goong

Soup. *Tom yam* is a hot-sour soup, made with pork, shrimp, chicken or fish, which should be accompanied by steamed rice to soak up the excess chilli heat. *Kaeng jeud* is a less pungent soup made from chicken, pork and shrimp cooked with Chinese-style vegetables, glass noodles and Thai herbs and spices. *Tom kha gai* is a mildly spicy chicken soup with coconut milk and lemongrass. *Bah mee nam* is a rich broth of thin noodles, pork or chicken chunks, mixed with herbs, bean sprouts and subtle spices.

Rice and noodles. *Kao pad* is fried rice with bits of meat. *Mee grob* is crispy fried rice noodles with pork, egg, bean sprouts, shrimp, and a sweet-and-sour flavour. *Pad thai* is served many different ways, but is basically flat dried rice-flour noodles sautéed with garlic, onion, tamarind juice and a variety of spices, and served with vegetables.

Seafood. *Hor mok pla* is a fish curry with vegetables and coconut milk, served wrapped in banana leaves. *Pla preow wan* is

Mango, rice and coconut cream

fried fish covered in a thick sweet-and-sour sauce. *Gung tod* –
or crispy fried prawns – usually comes with a choice of sauces.
Pla samlee daet deow is a whole deep-fried cotton-fish traditionally served with a tangy mango salad.

Chicken and meat. *Gaeng massaman* is a beef curry – less spicy
than most – and has an overtone of peanuts. *Kao nah gai* is
sliced chicken with spring onion, bamboo shoots and steamed
rice. *Sa lad neua san* translates as roast beef salad and contains vegetables, chillies, garlic and perhaps mint. *Kaeng ped
gai naw mai* is red chicken curry with bamboo shoots, lime and
basil leaves. *Kaeng ped* is roast duck curry, sometimes served
with slices of fried aubergine.

Sweets. *Salim* is a refreshing sweet of sugared noodles with
coconut milk and crushed ice. Ice cream, pronounced 'eye-
cream', sometimes comes in original and natural flavours. A
local variation of a sundae, for instance, is coconut ice cream

sprinkled with peanuts and kernels of corn. *Khao tom mad* is sticky rice with coconut cream and bananas.

Fruit. *Somo* is a pomelo, a tropical cousin of the grapefruit, and is served divided into sections. *Sap-pa-rot*, or pineapple, is a familiar fruit but twice as tasty on its home ground. More exotic local fruits are rarely on restaurant menus, but can be discovered at markets and street stalls. Just point if you do not know the name. *Ngor* (rambutan) looks like a hairy and overdeveloped strawberry; the fruit is inside. *Lamut*, a light-brown fruit that has to be peeled, is syrupy sweet, with a taste reminiscent of fresh figs. *Durian*, that green monster with spiky thorns, contains bits of custard-like fruit around egg-shaped piths. Its smell is often compared to that of a rubbish tip, although its creamy interior is deliciously sweet and luscious. Try local oranges, bananas, mangoes, papayas, practically every fruit imaginable, except apples and pears, which do not grow here and are expensive.

WHAT TO DRINK

Iced water is frequently served at the start of a meal. It is almost bound to be safe to drink in any decent restaurant, but if in doubt ask for a bottle of water and skip the ice (see page 122). Thais usually drink water or cold tea *(cha jin yen)* throughout their meal, along with beer or whisky with dinner.

Because of high import duty, wines are very expensive in Thailand, including the few locally produced labels. Even in a modest restaurant, an undistinguished wine could cost more than the whole dinner. Thailand also produces beer, such as Singha, Kloster and Chang. All are stronger than you might expect.

Thai whisky, on the other hand, is weaker and cheaper than you would think, and usually ordered by the small bottle in a 'set' with soda and ice. Mekhong is the best-known brand.

TO HELP YOU ORDER

Could we have a table? **Kor toh dai mai?**

I'd like a/an/some... **Chan yak dai ...**

beef **neua**

beer **beer**

bread **khanom-pang**

chicken **kai**

coffee **kafae**

curry **kaeng**

egg **khai**

fish **pla**

meat **neua**

menu **maynu/raigarn arharn**

milk **nom**

noodles **kwaytio**

pork **moo**

rice **kao**

salt **kloua**

shrimp **kung**

soup **soop**

sugar **nam tan**

tea **cha**

water **nam**

wine **low wai**

Street food for sale in northern Thailand

PLACES TO EAT

We have used the following symbols to give an idea of the price for a three-course meal for one, including wine, cover and service:

$$$$ over US$50
$$$ US$30–50
$$ US$15–30
$ less than US$15

BANGKOK

Biscotti $$$ *Four Seasons Hotel, 155 Ratchadamri Road, tel: 0 2126 8866 ext. 1229-30,* www.biscottibangkok.com. Open daily for lunch and dinner. One of the most popular Italian restaurants in Bangkok is casual but elegant with a contemporary flair and an open kitchen. There is a wood-fired oven for the inventive pizzas (such as the lobster tail pizza with forest mushrooms) and the fragrant *focaccia* bread with herbs. Risottos, pastas and a few meat dishes round out the menu.

Celadon $$$$ *The Sukhothai, 13/3 South Sathorn Road, tel: 0 2344 8888,* www.sukhothai.com. Open daily for lunch and dinner. Wonderfully located in the Zen-like Sukhothai hotel, overlooking a lotus pond. Here you can sample Royal Thai cuisine served by very knowledgeable staff who can help you combine dishes to create a most memorable meal. Banana blossom salad, spicy kingfish soup and sweet-and-sour tofu are just a few of the specialities. Desserts are outstanding.

Chim by Siam Wisdom $$$$ *66 Soi Sukhumvit 31 Yak 4, tel: 0 2260 7811,* www.catbox.fr. Open daily for dinner. With a Michelin star you might have to double take when looking at the prices of the set menus. Sure, they are quite some way above the street food rate cards, but you might not get the chance to try Michelin-rated food at such a low price again. Thaninthorn "Noom" Chantrawan is the chef

behind the culinary wisdom, which he garnered over the course of 14 years at some of the finest restaurants in London.

China House $$$$ *The Mandarin Oriental hotel, 48 Oriental Avenue, tel: 0 2659 9000 ext. 739*, www.mandarinoriental.com. Open daily for lunch and dinner. The beautiful 1930s Shanghainese art deco interior features red lanterns, carved wood and ebony pillars. Miniature black-and-white photos and Chinese calligraphy cover the walls; a brass samovar steams in the central tearoom. It is a wonderful setting for top quality dishes like hot-and-sour soup filled with fresh herbs and sweet lobster meat.

The Deck by Arun Residence $$$ *Arun Residence, 36–38 Soi Pratoo Nok Yoong, tel: 0 2221 9158*, www.arunresidence.com. Open daily for lunch and dinner. Just two minutes' walk from Wat Pho, this cute place has outdoor seating, river views of Wat Arun and a bar, Amorosa, on the third floor. A mixed Thai and Euro fusion menu features plates such as carpaccio of tea-smoked duck. Book ahead (if you can) for a riverside table.

Harmonique $$ *22 Charoenkrung Soi 34, tel: 0 2237 8175*. Open Mon–Sat for lunch and dinner. Occupying several old Chinese shophouses with leafy courtyards, and filled with antiques, this is a charming restaurant near the French Embassy. Because there is usually a large contingent of Western diners, the spices are subdued, but the food is generally of a very high standard.

Long Table $$$ *Floor 25, The Column Residence, Sukhumvit Soi 16, tel: 0 2302 2557/9*, www.longtablebangkok.com. Open daily for dinner. A classy modern Thai restaurant designed with panache. Fantastic city views and a very long communal table are the focal points as you dine, while films on overhead monitors roll to a funky soundtrack. Yellow curry with crab and foie gras with dried shrimp and tamarind are both standouts.

Mango Tree Surawong $$ *37 Soi Tantawan, Surawongse Road, tel: 0 2236 2820*. Open daily for lunch and dinner. This lovely Thai restaurant is housed within a charming old house offering indoor/outdoor dining just steps from the busy Patpong neighbourhood. Specialities include fresh and spicy mango salad, chicken baked in pandanus leaf and a variety of green curries. There is Thai dancing on weekend evenings.

Nahm $$$$ *Metropolitan Hotel, 27 South Sathorn Road, tel: 0 2625 3388,* www.comohotels.com . Open daily for lunch and dinner. Run by Australian chef David Thompson, this Thai restaurant has a traditional menu, which includes intriguing flavours that are becoming harder to find in modern Thai cooking. Regional dishes like relishes of snail, shrimp, peanuts and Thai basil and grilled prawn with citrus and sour fruits relish are just two of the unique spins on Thai food.

New York Steakhouse $$$$ *JW Marriott Hotel, 4 Sukhumvit Soi 2, tel: 0 2656 7700,* www.marriott.com. Open daily for dinner. This steakhouse is a pleasant and very contemporary restaurant serving the best steaks in the city. Aged to perfection, grain-fed Angus beef is flown in from the US along with excellent (and more affordable) Australian steaks. There is also a large selection of seafood including fresh lobster, swordfish and salmon.

Seafood Market and Restaurant $$$ *89 Sukhumvit Soi 24, Klongtoey, tel: 0 2261 2071.* In this seafood market-cum-restaurant you can select your dinner while it is still alive and have it cooked the way you like. Alternatively, those who do not dare to look their food in the eye may select dishes from the set menu. Stir-fried crab with curry powder and spicy soup with shrimp are recommended.

Sirocco $$$$ *63/F, Lebua at State Tower, 1055/111 Silom Road, tel: 0 2624 9555,* www.lebua.com/sirocco. Open daily for dinner. This spectacular 200 metre (656ft) -high rooftop restaurant has magnificent views of the river. Greco-Roman architecture and a jazz band add to the sense of occasion. While the food can be inconsistent, it is often excellent. In the same complex there is the classy Distil Bar, the Sky Bar for cocktails, the Italian eatery Mezzaluna, and the alfresco pan-Asian seafood restaurant Breeze.

Sra Bua $$$$ *Siam Kempinski Hotel, 991/9 Rama I Road, tel: 0 2162 9000,* www.kempinskibangkok.com. Open daily for lunch and dinner. This branch of Copenhagen's Michelin-starred Kiin Kiin has a playful approach to Thai food. Dishes are artfully presented – a green curry mousse in a flower pot, soups served as tiny jellies and red curry ice-cream. It is centrally-located, behind Siam Paragon shopping mall.

Tables Grill $$$$ *Grand Hyatt Erawan Hotel, 494 Ratchadamri Road, tel: 0 2254 1234*, www.tablesgrill.com. Open daily for lunch and dinner. Oxidised mirrors and waiters in white aprons aid the smart Parisian interior in this restaurant designed by Tony Chi. Billed as classic European, it is full of old stalwarts like Sunday roast, lobster bisque and champagne risotto. Chefs cook some dishes in the open at copper-topped tables.

Theo Mio $$$ *InterContinental Bangkok, 973 Ploenchit Road, tel: 0 2656 0444*, bangkok.intercontinental.com. Open daily for lunch and dinner. This Italian restaurant comes courtesy of British chef (and Italian cuisine specialist) Theo Randall. There is a floor of large black and white checks, marble counter displays of wines, bread and cold cuts. The menu eschews obvious Italian exports for dishes like creamy Burrata slow cooked with red peppers, and Randall's award winning Cappaletti di Vitello with porcini mushroom sauce.

CHIANG MAI

The Gallery $$ *25–29 Charoenrat Road, tel: 0 5324 8601*, www.thegallery-restaurant.com. Open 24 hours daily. This lovely restaurant is located on the banks of the River Ping in an old teakwood house that doubles as an art gallery. There is a wide variety of northern Thai dishes as well as a good selection of vegetarian specialities, plus a small wine list.

Huen Phen $ *112 Rachamankha, tel: 08 1882 1544*. Open daily for lunch and dinner. This old wooden house located just inside the old city walls is decorated with local antiques and is reputed to serve some of the best northern Thai dishes in Chiang Mai. Good picks are *laap khua* (spicy minced-pork salad) and *kaeng hang-leh* (savoury, Burmese-influenced curry).

PHUKET

Baan Rim Pa $$$$ *223 Prabaramee Road, Patong, tel: 0 7634 0789*, www. baanrimpa.com. Open daily for lunch and dinner. Exquisitely prepared

Thai food is presented in this restaurant on a cliff overlooking the ocean. It includes such specialities as steamed fish in pickled-plum sauce and hot-and-sour soup with fish and vegetables. There is also a good selection of vegetarian dishes.

Boathouse Wine & Grill $$$ *182 Koktanode Road, Kata Beach, tel: 0 7633 0015*, www.boathousephuket.com. Open daily 11am–11pm. Offering fine views of the Andaman Gour, this beach front restaurant offers refined Thai and European dining as well as seafood specialties. There is a large wine selection and indoor and outdoor seating is available.

Tamarind Spa Restaurant $$ *Banyan Tree Phuket, 33, 33/27 Moo 4, Srisoonthorn Road, Cherngtalay, Amphur Talang, tel: 0 7637 2400*, www.banyantree.com. Open daily for lunch and dinner. This cool, airy and shaded restaurant is located alongside the serene and Zen-like lap pool at a luxurious resort hotel. The unusual (but very affordable) menu features low-calorie specialities such as soba-noodle salad with fresh greens, vegetable juice cocktails and delicious sandwiches. Only the freshest market ingredients are used, along with local herbs and spices, to add a subtle fusion of Thai flavours to every dish.

KO SAMUI

The Beach Club $$$ *BuriRasa Village Resort & Spa, 11/2 Moo 2 Chaweng Beach, tel: 0 7723 0222*, www.burirasa.com. Open daily for lunch and dinner. This smart, wooden beachside restaurant, with some tables on the sand, plates modern Californian/Pacific Rim dishes. Specialities include scallops, duck with black rice and soba noodles with seared ahi tuna. Desserts like chocolate air cake with tonka bean ice cream are exquisite.

La Boudoir $$$ *Soi 1 Mae Nam, tel: 8 5783 1031*. Owned by an expatriate couple from France, this small cosy restaurant, with flamboyant décor, serves enjoyable French fare and great cocktails. It has a romantic setting for alfresco dining. Slightly off the beaten track, but well worth a visit.

Poppies Restaurant $$$ *Poppies Samui resort, Chaweng Beach, tel: 0 7742 2419*, www.poppiessamui.com. Open daily for lunch and dinner.

One of the most romantic restaurants on the island, it is right on the beach and serves Thai cuisine infused with a Western twist, such as the popular prawn cakes with plum sauce and charcoal-roasted duck. There is also an excellent selection of fusion dishes such as the chicken filled with crabmeat and baked in a seafood sauce.

CHIANG RAI

Salung Kham $$ *384/3 Paholyothin Road, tel: 0 5371 7192*, www.salung khamhotel. Open daily for lunch and dinner. The Northern Thai menu includes Chiang Rai sausage, curries, and steamed herbal chicken with bamboo shoots. The indoor section is decorated with Thai handicrafts and there is also a pleasant garden.

MAE HONG SON

Fern Restaurant $ *87 Khunlumpraphat Road, tel: 0 5361 1374*. This rustic restaurant near Jong Kum Lake is one of the town's best. The house speciality is tasty and crunchy fern shoots, served either stir-fried or as a spicy warm salad. The typically spicy dishes are cooked with a deft touch and are not too overpowering.

HUA HIN

Brasserie de Paris $$$ *3 Naresdamri Road, tel: 0 3253 0637*, www. brasseriedeparis.net. Open daily for lunch and dinner. Sit upstairs at this wooden pier restaurant for views of fishing boats bobbing on the waves. It has delicious, freshly caught seafood served French-style, such as rock lobster *au beurre blanc*.

Chao Lay $$$ *15 Naresdamri Road, tel: 0 3251 3436*. Open daily for lunch and dinner. One of the most popular of several Thai restaurants on stilts over the sea, the menu features all kinds of seafood, grilled, deep-fried and steamed, either freshly caught or live from tanks downstairs.

A-Z TRAVEL TIPS

A SUMMARY OF PRACTICAL INFORMATION

A

ACCOMMODATION

Thailand's accommodation rates vary widely in each category, so shop around for bargains. In high season, from November to March, it is best to book well ahead. Prices are high and many hotels have a compulsory gala dinner at Christmas and New Year. In low season discounts in excess of 50 percent are common, although hotels in less visited places may close for part of the time.

Top-end hotels are generally excellent and even mid-range and budget lodgings will often have a pool. The term 'resort' in Thailand may merely translate as a countryside or beachside location, and may not imply all the features you'd expect. High-end and mid-range places charge 10 percent service and seven percent VAT.

Serviced apartments, available in major destinations, can save money while having many facilities you'd find in a hotel. Most hotel booking sites will list serviced apartments.

New design-conscious properties have widened the choice of accommodation, and many places have villas in both beach and jungle settings. Guesthouses often provide clean and decent rooms, while the Deep South islands have some beach huts with perhaps only a fan and cold shower, but the natural scenery amply compensates. Rangers huts in national parks can also be very cheap.

Youth hostels are found in Bangkok and Chiang Mai, and to a lesser extent in Ayutthaya, Kanchanaburi and Phuket. The International Youth Hostel Federation has a Thailand page (www.tyha.org) with hostel listings. Thailand is also expanding its range in home-stays and eco-tourism, where visitors interact more with the local community. These are largely village initiatives, such as Ban Mae Kampong near Chiang Mai and Ayutthaya's Ban Rang Jorakae (tel: 0 3530 5441).

Do you have a (double) room? **Mee hong (kuu) mai?**

AIRPORTS

Air service to Bangkok is excellent with non-stop flights arriving daily from London, Sydney, the US, many European, and most Asian cities. **Suvarnabhumi Airport** (pronounced 'su-wan-na-poom'; BKK; call centre tel: 0 2132 1888; www.suvarnabhumiairport.com) is approximately 30km (19 miles) east of the city. It handles all international flights to and from Bangkok as well as many domestic connections.

Air-conditioned taxis are available from the counter outside the arrival hall. Tell the desk clerk your destination and this will be written in Thai on a slip and handed to the driver. Make sure the driver turns on the meter. There will be an airport surcharge of B50 payable to the driver on arrival. If you have agreed to use the expressway for a quicker journey, there will be extra toll fees (B70). The trip from the airport to Bangkok's hotels takes about 40 minutes. Expect to pay B350–450 to reach the city centre.

The Suvarnabhumi Airport Rail Link (SARL) opened in 2010. There are three services: the City Line, calling at eight stations en route to Phaya Thai; and the Express Line direct to Bangkok City Air Terminal, at Makkasan, where passengers can check in and drop luggage, and another Express Line to Phaya Thai. Tickets are B15–45 (City Line) and B150 (Express Line; round trip) with journey times of 30 minutes, 15 and 17 minutes respectively. The trains run from 6am until midnight.

BMTA Buses run from 5am until 10pm along five routes: to Happy Land, Samuthprakarn, Rangsit (2 lines), Samae Dam Garage. Tickets are B32–35. The S1 shuttle service operates between the airport and Khaosan. Tickets cost B60. The transfer bus service to Don Muaeng Airport (old Bangkok International Airport; http://donmueangairportthai. com) operates between 5am and midnight and is free of charge.

Chiang Mai International Airport (CNX; tel: 0 5327 0222; http://chiang maiairportthai.com) is 6km (4 miles) west of the city. To get to the city centre, order a taxi (B140–160, rides are not metered in Chiang Mai). The airport shuttle bus connects to some of the bigger hotels and costs B60 or hail a 'red car' (rot daeng or song thae; usually B30–40), which is a van like vehicle with two parallel bench seats inside.

Phuket International Airport (HKT; tel: 0 7632 7230; http://phuketairport thai.com) is 28km (18 miles) north of Phuket Town. Metered red-and-yellow taxis take 30 minutes to Phuket Town for around B500, or the beaches for around B650–700. Buses run from 9am until 8pm to Phuket Town only. Tickets are B100 and the journey takes around one hour (www.airportbus phuket.com). **Hat Yai International Airport** (HDY; tel: 0 7425 1007 12; http:// hatyaiairportthai.com) is a major airport in southern Thailand. **Ko Samui Airport** (USM; tel: 0 7742 5012; www.samuiairportonline.com), privately owned, 13.3km (3 miles) north of Chaweng Beach.

B

BICYCLE AND MOPED HIRE

Although cycling is difficult in Bangkok traffic, bikes can be rented at several hotels and guesthouses. In Ayutthaya, Pattaya, Ko Samui, Phuket and Chiang Mai, bikes and mopeds are more readily available at roadside outlets. Spice Roads (tel: 0 2381 7490; www.spiceroads.com) has bicycles for hire and organises wide-ranging trips of up to 14 days around the country.

BUDGETING FOR YOUR TRIP

Bangkok is inexpensive when compared to most major cities. There are approximately B44 to one pound and B31 to one US dollar.

Transport. Taxi: B40–200.

Metro, Skytrain B15–42 per trip.

Domestic one-way flight example: Bangkok to Phuket B2,200.

Domestic rail ticket example: Bangkok to Surat Thani B1,579 (first class sleeper), B297 (third class).

Domestic bus ticket example (air-conditioned bus): Bangkok to Chiang Mai B534.

A short *tuk-tuk* fare: B40–50.

Meals. You can save lots of money by eating street food, and in many cases it is tastier, too. A meal will cost between B30–100, half the price of a budget diner. Main courses in moderate international restaurants are B350–750, and in expensive restaurants B1,000–2,500. The cheapest bottle of wine in a restaurant is around B900, while beer in a pub is B50–200.

Other money-saving tips are to use multi-trip passes on the Bangkok Skytrain and Metro, and check bars and restaurant websites for cheap deals, even in hotels, as entertainment competition is fierce.

CAR HIRE (see also Driving)

Although driving can be stressful in Thailand many roads are excellent, making car hire a realistic idea, particularly in the countryside.

Several international hire companies operate in Thailand, including **Avis** (2/12-13 Wireless Road, Bangkok, tel: 0 2251 1131, www.avisthai land.com), **Budget** (201/2 Mahidol Road, Chiang Mai, tel: 0 5320 2871, www.budget.co.th) and **Hertz** (72/8-9 North Sathorn Road, Bangkok, tel: 0 2266 4666, www.hertzthailand.com), with rates starting around B850 a day. Local firms, such as **Phuket Car Rent** (23/3 Moo 1 Sakoo, Thalang, Phuket, tel: 08 9724 2823, www.phuketcarrent.com) and **Sathorn Car Rent** (6/8-9 Sathorn Nua Rd, Silom Bangrak, Bangkok, tel: 0 2633 8888, www.sathorncarrent.com) start from B800 a day, but check insurance is included (opt for the full package, including Collision Damage Waiver).

It is possible to hire a vehicle with driver, from an extra B300–500 per day, plus a surcharge for overnight stays.

CLIMATE

Thailand has three seasons: hot from March to May, rainy from June to October, and cool from November to February. For tourists from more temperate regions, it is just plain hot, amplified by humidity levels above 70 percent. The countryside is generally milder, with Chiang Mai having cool season temperatures of 13–28°C (55–82°F). The height of the rainy season is September, with over 300mm (11.8 inches) of rainfall in Bangkok and over 400mm (15.7 inches) in the south. The Gulf, around Ko Samui, receives only light rain from June to October and has a second high season in June and July.

	J	F	M	A	M	J	J	A	S	O	N	D
av. max. (°F)	89	91	93	95	93	91	90	90	89	88	87	87
av. max. (°C)	32	33	34	35	34	33	32	32	32	31	31	31
av. min. (°F)						76	76	76	76	75	72	68
av. min. (°C)	20	22	24	25	25	25	24	24	24	24	22	20
rainy days	2	2	4	5	14	16	19	21	23	17	7	1

CLOTHING

Light and loose clothes are best for Thailand, preferably of natural fibres, which breathe better. A hat will protect from the sun, and it is best to carry a light mac or umbrella during the rainy season. Convenience stores sell them if you get caught out.

CRIME AND SAFETY (See also Emergencies)

Thailand is generally very safe, although a few precautions are wise. Beware of pickpockets in crowded marketplaces, carry bags away from the roadside to thwart motorbike bag-snatchers, and avoid being flash with your cash, particularly around red-light areas. It is advisable to avoid the southern provinces of Narathiwat, Yala, Pattani and Songkhla, where there is a high risk of Muslim separatist violence. You should also better refrain from trips to Preah Vihear and Ta Krabey temples, which are subject to the Cambodian–Thai border dispute.

Thais tend to be non-confrontational, so casual harassment and sexual crimes against women are uncommon. That said, like anywhere, it is not a great idea to walk alone on quiet streets or beaches late at night. Thailand has tough drug laws; indulge at your peril. In times of trouble it is best to contact the Tourist Police hotline: 1155.

D

DISABLED TRAVELLERS

Thailand is a major challenge for disabled travellers, and a companion is highly advisable. Pavements are often uneven and crowded with obstructions, and there are few wheelchair ramps in buildings. There are no facilities to speak of in any of the transport networks. Wheelchair Tours to Thailand (tel: 0 2720 5395; www.wheelchairtours.com) specialises in package tours for the disabled.

DRIVING

Road conditions. Driving in Thailand is on the left; overtake and give way to the right. Highway tolls apply to some expressway sections, especially in Bangkok. Roads are generally in good condition but main routes are very busy. There is only a rudimentary driving test, however, so drivers largely learn by intuition. Road courtesy is low, with right-of-way determined by size. Tailgating and dangerous overtaking are also common. That said, once you are acclimatised, driving in Thailand is not too uncomfortable.

Rules and regulations. Visitors need an International Driver's Licence. The official speed limit is 60kph (37mph) in towns, 80kph (50mph) on main main roads, and 120kph (75mph) on motorways. Seat belts are compulsory. Drink driving is against the law, with an alcohol limit of 50mg per 100 millilitres. The law requires that if you have an accident, you don't move the vehicle to the side of the road, but leave everything as it is, so police can make an assessment.

Fuel. Readily available in both regular and super.

Parking. If stuck for somewhere to park on the street, try a temple, as they often have public parking spaces for a small fee.

If you need help. Telephone the agency from which you rented the car to come and rescue you. In an emergency dial the Tourist Police hotline: 1155 or the Highway Police Patrol Centre, tel: 1193.

Road signs. Most road signs are in English.

accident **u-bat-fi-het**
collision **rot chon**
flat tyre **yang baen**
Help! **chuey duey!**
Police! **tam ruat!**

ELECTRICITY

The standard current in Thailand is 220-volt, 50-cycle AC. Most hotel rooms have an electrical outlet for shavers; some have 110-volt sockets, too. Plugs are two-pin and you'll need adaptors (and transformers depending on where you are coming from).

EMBASSIES AND CONSULATES

Australia: 181 Wireless Road, Bangkok; tel: 0 2344 6300; www.thailand. embassy.gov.au

Canada: 990 Rama IV Road, Abdulrahim Place, 15th Floor, Bangkok; tel: 0 2646 4300; www.canadainternational.gc.ca

Ireland: 208 Wireless Road, 12th Floor, Bangkok; tel: 0 2016 1360; www. dfa.ie

New Zealand: M Thai Tower, 87 Wireless Road, All Seasons Place, 14th Floor, Bangkok; tel: 0 2254 2530; www.nzembassy.com

South Africa: M Thai Tower, 87 Wireless Road, All Seasons Place, 12th Floor, Bangkok; tel: 0 2092 2900; www.dirco.gov.za/bangkok

UK: 14 Wireless Road, Bangkok; tel: 0 2305 8333; www.ukinthailand. fco.gov.uk

US: 95 Wireless Road, Bangkok; tel: 0 2205 4000; https://th.usembassy.gov

EMERGENCIES

In case of an emergency dial **191**. For less dire emergencies, contact the Tourist Police on **1155**.

ETIQUETTE

Thais are remarkably tolerant and forgiving of foreigners' eccentricities, but there are a few things that are liable to upset them.

Thais have great reverence for the monarchy and disapprove of disrespect towards the Institution. Standing for the National Anthem in cinemas is expected.

Disrespect towards Buddha images, temples or monks is not taken lightly. Women should take care to avoid any accidental contact with monks; monks observe a vow of chastity that prohibits being touched by (or touching) women.

Thai Buddhism regards the head as a wellspring of wisdom and the feet as unclean. For this reason, it is insulting to touch another person on the head, point one's feet at anything, or step over another person.

At temples, the scruffy and the underclad are frequently turned away, so dress appropriately.

G

GETTING THERE

Air travel. Suvarnabhumi Airport (see Airports) is the main gateway to Thailand. From the UK, the main airlines flying direct are British Airways (www.britishairways.com) and Thai Airways International (THAI) (www.thaiairways.com), all from London Heathrow, with a flight time of around 11 hours.

From Australia, Qantas flies from Sydney (9hrs) and Thai Airways flies from Brisbane (9hrs), Melbourne (9hrs), Perth (7hrs) and Sydney (9hrs).

International airports. Phuket, Chiang Mai and Samui handle international flights from Asian cities like Hong Kong and Singapore.

Rail travel. Comfortable trains run from Singapore to Bangkok, including the luxury service run by the Venice-Simplon Orient Express, known as the Eastern and Oriental Express.

H

HEALTH AND MEDICAL CARE

No vaccinations are required to enter Thailand. Malaria and dengue persist in rural areas but less so in Bangkok. When in the countryside, especially in the monsoon season, apply mosquito repellent on exposed skin at all times – dengue mosquitoes are most active in the day.

Never drink the tap water anywhere in the country. Bottled water is readily available everywhere. Responsible restaurants serve bottled water and pure ice, but be cautious about the ice in drinks at roadside stands.

Many Westerners suffer some kind of intestinal discomfort from the spicy food, the excessive heat and the unusual ingredients. Spare your digestive system by experimenting gradually until you're more accustomed to the Thai cuisine. Avoiding fresh vegetables and unpeeled fruit is a good idea except at the top hotels and restaurants, and avoid uncooked foods at market stalls.

Ensure you buy health insurance before travelling. Most major hospitals in Thailand accept credit cards and are of a high standard in Bangkok and other cities. Prices for medical services are significantly below equivalent charges in Europe and the US. There is always a pharmacy open 24 hours. Pharmacies nationwide are well-equipped and can dispense many medications over the counter that requires a prescription in Western countries.

---

a bottle of drinking water **nam yen neung khuad**
I need a doctor **pom/chan tong karn maw**
I need a dentist **pom/chan tong karn maw fan**

L

LANGUAGE

Although English is widely used in hotels and shops and is the best-known Western language in Thailand, try to use some simple phrases in Thai. The Thai language spoken in Bangkok is understood everywhere in the country, though there are many dialects and sub-dialects. Like Chinese, Thai uses intonation to distinguish between otherwise identical words, which makes it a difficult language for foreigners. Each syllable can have up to five different meanings depending on how it is pronounced; there are 44 consonants plus dozens of vowels, compounds and tone marks. If all this doesn't discourage you, consider Rachasap, a special language used only when speaking to or about Thai royalty.

Listen to Thai people to learn how to intone useful words. You will find a brief list of useful expressions below.

one **neung**
two **sorng**
three **sarm**
four **see**
five **har**
six **hok**
seven **jet**
eight **(b)paet**
nine **gao**
ten **sip**
eleven **sip-eht**
twelve **sip-sorng**
thirteen **sip-sarm**
fourteen **sip-see**
fifteen **sip-har**
sixteen **sip-hok**

seventeen **sip-jet**
eighteen **sip-(b)paet**
nineteen **sip-gao**
twenty **yee-sip**
thirty **sarm-sip**
forty **see-sip**
fifty **har-sip**
sixty **hok-sip**
seventy **jet-sip**
eighty **(b)paet-sip**
ninety **gao-sip**
one hundred **roy**
Monday **wan jan**
Tuesday **wan ang karn**
Wednesday **wan put**
Thursday **wan pa ru hat**
Friday **wan suk**
Saturday **wan sow**
Sunday **wan ar tit**
thank you **korp khun kap (if you are a man) ka (if you are a woman)**
hello/goodbye **sawatdee kap (if you are a man) ka (if you are a woman)**
today **wan nee**
tomorrow **prung nee**
good/bad **dee/lehw**
big/small **yai/lek**
cheap/expensive **took/phaeng**
hot/cold **rorn/yen**
When does ... open/close? ... **pert/pit meua rai?**
What's the fare to ...? **(b)pai ... kit thao rai?**
stop here **jop teenee**

turn right **lieo khwa**
turn left **lieo sai**
Could you speak more slowly? **Poot char long dai mai?**
I don't understand **mai kao chai**
I'm sorry/excuse me **kor thort**

LGBTQ TRAVELLERS

Thai people's general tolerance towards others extends to sexual orientation and gay lifestyles, particularly in Bangkok. There are many gay clubs and bars, and a lively party scene amid the terrace drinkers of Silom Soi 4. Chiang Mai and Phuket also have several gay-friendly venues. *Katoeys* (ladyboys) are similarly high profile. The lesbian scene is more discreet, but there are a few women-only places in Bangkok. There are on-off Gay Pride Festivals in Bangkok, Phuket and Pattaya. Useful resources are www.utopia-asia.com, www.bangkoklesbian.com and the specialist gay travel company Purple Dragon (www.purpledrag.com).

M

MEDIA

The *Bangkok Post* and *The Nation* are Thailand's leading English-language newspapers. They are available at most hotels and airports and are updated daily online at www.bangkokpost.com and www.nation multimedia.com. Useful listings magazines include *BK* (www.bk.asia-city.com) for Bangkok, *Citylife* (www.chiangmainews.com) in Chiang Mai, and *Pattaya Mail* (www.pattayamail.com) in Pattaya.

There are six terrestrial Bangkok TV channels, and many programmes are foreign shows, which are dubbed into Thai. There is also a cable television network with international channels, including BBC News, HBO, ESPN and MTV Thailand, that is available in most leading hotels. Radio stations include Eazy FM (105.5FM), with middle-of-the road music, and

Virgin HITZ/FMX (95.5 FM) playing contemporary dance and pop.

MONEY

Currency. The unit of currency in Thailand is the baht (abbreviated THB, Bt or B), divided into 100 satang. Banknotes come in denominations of B20, 50, 100, 500 and 1,000. Coins are 25 and 50 satang, and B1, 2, 5 and 10.

Banks and exchange facilities. Normally the exchange rate at banks is the most favourable. After the banks are closed you can change money at your hotel, at exchange booths or at shops displaying a sign in English saying 'money changer'.

Banks and money-changers in tourist towns will accept virtually any major currency.

Credit cards. Major hotels, restaurants and shops are accustomed to the well-known international charge cards. Small eateries and small shops tend to accept cash only.

ATMs. Facilities for using your debit or credit card to withdraw money automatically are widely available in Thailand, especially in Bangkok.

O

OPENING HOURS

Business hours are 8.30am–noon and 1–4.30pm, Monday–Friday for government offices. Banks are open 8.30am–3.30pm. Department stores are usually open 10am–10pm seven days a week. Hours are extended just before Christmas, New Year and Chinese New Year. In seaside tourist areas, many shops are open from early in the morning until 11pm or even midnight during the high season. Note that many state-run museums are closed on Monday and Tuesday.

P

POLICE

A special force of Thai Tourist Police operates in crucial areas of Bangkok and throughout the country, such as near tourist attractions and major hotels. The officers, all of whom speak passable English, stand ready to protect or advise foreigners. They wear the beige military-style uniform of ordinary Thai police, but with 'Tourist Police' shoulder patches. Dial 1155 from any phone in the country to reach the Tourist Police. The Royal Thai Police Headquarters is at Rama 1 Road, Pathum-wan Bangkok, tel: 0 2252 2344.

POST OFFICES

Bangkok's main post office is open 8am–8pm Monday–Friday, and 8am–1pm Saturday–Sunday. Branch offices, found at airports and throughout the country, are usually open Mon–Fri 8am–4.30pm and Sat 9am–noon. You can send letters and postcards airmail, which should arrive within five days to a week in Europe or North America. Many newspaper shops sell stamps and there are red post boxes on the streets.

PUBLIC HOLIDAYS

Since many Thai holidays and festivals are fixed to the lunar calendar, the dates vary from year to year. Banks are closed on these days, but daily life is not necessarily disrupted. The only notable exception is Chinese New Year, a time when most businesses are closed.

1 January **New Year's Day**
6 April **Chakri Day, honouring Rama I**
13–15 April **Songkran (Water Festival)**
1 May **Labour Day**
28 July **HM the King's Birthday**
12 August **Mother's Day**
23 October **Chulalongkorn Day, honouring Rama V**
5 December **Father's Day and National Day**
10 December **Constitution Day**
31 December **New Year's Eve**
Variable dates
Chinese New Year (1st month of the lunar calendar, usually Jan/Feb).

Maka Puja (full moon in February). Commemoration of meeting at which the Buddha preached the doctrines of Buddhism.

Visakha Puja (full moon in May). Celebrates the birth, enlightenment and death of the Buddha. Most holy Buddhist ceremonial day.

Royal Ploughing Day (Variable May date based on astrological observations). Before the rainy season starts the king presides over ceremonies to bring good rains to farmers.

Asanha Puja (full moon in July). Celebrates Buddha's first sermon.

T

TELEPHONES

Thailand's country code is 66. To make an overseas phone call from Thailand, first dial 001 followed by the country code (without the preceding 0) and area code. If you need international call assistance, dial 100. To avoid hotel surcharges on phone calls, call from one of the public telephones located on streets and in post offices. Rates (usually per minute with a 3-minute minimum) are posted in English. Prepaid international phone cards can also be used. These can be bought at post offices, 7 Eleven stores, shops displaying the ThaiCard sign and the office of the Communications Authority of Thailand (tel: 1322; www.cattelecom.com). For local directory assistance, dial 1133.

Mobile phones. Mobiles with international roaming facility can connet to the local Thai network. Check with your service provider if you are unsure. An alternative is to buy a local SIM card with a pre-paid value. Local mobile network operators include: AIS (www.ais.co.th), DTAC (www.dtac.co.th) and True (www3.truecorp.co.th).

TIME ZONE

Thailand time is GMT plus 7 hours throughout the year. When it is noon in Bangkok in winter, it is 9pm the day before in Vancouver and Los Angeles, midnight in Toronto and New York, 5am in Dublin and London, 7am in Johannesburg, 4pm in Sydney and 6pm in Auckland.

TIPPING

Tipping is not generally a custom in Thailand, although it is more prevalent in Bangkok, Phuket and Pattaya. Restaurants and hotels will add a service charge of 10 percent to your bill. People leave loose change left over from their bill both in cafés and taxis. Otherwise, tip massage therapists and hairdressers 10 percent and maids and porters B20.

TOILETS

Try to find a hotel or restaurant. In luxury establishments the toilets are spotless. Away from the main centres, you will encounter hole-in-the-floor toilets. Some public toilets are free.

Where are the toilets? **Hong nam yu tee nai?**

TOURIST INFORMATION

The **Tourism Authority of Thailand (TAT)** runs information stands in the arrivals hall of Suvarnabhumi, Chiang Mai and Phuket airports.

You can also obtain leaflets, maps and advice at the organisation's head office: 1600 New Phetburi Road, Makkasan, Ratchathewi, Bangkok 10400; tel: 0 2250 5500 or 1672; www.tourismthailand.org; daily 8.30am–4.30pm. Other Bangkok branches are located in the building of the Ministry of Tourism and Sports (4 Ratchadamnoen Nok Road, Wat Somanat, Pom Prap Sattru Phai; daily 8.30am –4.30pm), Suvarnabhumi Airport Gate 3 and Gate 10 (both open 24 hours).

Branch offices of TAT are also located in Chiang Mai, Kanchanaburi, Nakhon Ratchasima (Korat), Pattaya, Ko Samui and Phuket. In Chiang Mai the address is: 105/1 Chiang Mai, Lamphun Road, tel: 0 5324 8604, and in Phuket, 191 Thalang Road, Phuket Town; tel: 0 7621 1036.

Overseas representatives of TAT can be found in the following countries: **Australia:** Level 20, 56 Pitt Street, Sydney 2000; tel: +61-2-9247 7549; www.thailand.net.au.

UK: 1st Floor, 17–19 Cockspur Street, Trafalgar Square, London SW1Y 5BL; tel: +44-207-925 2511; www.tourismthailand.co.uk.

US: 611 North Larchmont Boulevard, Los Angeles, CA 90004; tel: 1-323-461 9814; 61 Broadway, Suite 2810, New York, NY 10006; tel: 1-212-432 0433.

TRANSPORT

Domestic flights. The main domestic airline is Thai Airways (tel: 0 2356 1111, 0 2288 7000; www.thaiairways.com), followed by Bangkok Airways (tel: 0 2270 6699 or 1771, www.bangkokair.com). Budget airlines are Nok Air (tel: 1318 or 0 2900 9955; www.nokair.com), Air Asia (tel: 0 2515 9999; www.airasia.com) and Orient Thai (tel: 0 2229 4260 or 1126; http://flyorientthai.com).

Ferries. The main ferries are from the mainland to the Gulf islands of Ko Samui, Ko Phangan and Ko Chang. Seatran Ferry (tel: 0 7725 1555, 0 2240 2582; www.seatranferry.com) from Donsak to Ko Samui runs 14 boats a day, 6am–7pm, with tickets at B130 for passengers, and B420 for a car with a driver. Koh Chang Ferry (tel: 0 3952 8288) runs from Laem Ngop to Ko Chang 6.30am–5pm. Passenger return tickets are B120, cars B150.

Trains. Thailand's state railway (tel: 0 2222 0175, hotline: 1690; www.railway.co.th) is an efficient means of seeing the country, although for many routes, buses are quicker. Travel agents, hotel desks and the information office at the main (Hualamphong) railway station can advise you on timetables and fares. Bangkok's main stations are: Hualamphong on Rama IV Road, for the north, east and northeast and for express trains to the south, and Thonburi on Bangkok Noi on Rod Fai Road, for the west and slower trains to the south.

Popular routes are Bangkok to Chiang Mai (8.30am–10pm, first class fare B593) and Bangkok to Ayutthaya (4.20am–10.25pm, first class fare B66).

Intercity coaches. Government buses are operated by the Transport Company Ltd (tel: 1490; www.transport.co.th). They are known locally as Bor Kor Sor (BKS), and have terminals at every town. Buy tickets (VIP, 1st and 2nd classes) at any BKS station or online from www.thaiticketmajor.com.

Popular routes include Bangkok to Phuket (14 hours) and Bangkok to Chiang Mai (11 hours).

Skytrain (BTS). The Bangkok Transit System (Tourist Information Centre: tel: 0 2617 7341, hotline: 0 2617 6000; www.bts.co.th) is an elevated train service, better known as Skytrain. Trains operate from 6am–midnight. Single-trip fares vary according to distance, starting at B15 and rising to B42. Self-service ticket machines are found at all station concourses. Tourists may find it useful to buy the unlimited ride 1-Day Pass (B130) or the 30-Day Adult Pass (which comes in four types: B405 for 15 rides, B625 for 25, B920 for 40 and B1,100 for 50). The 30-day pass should be added to a Rabbit Card, which you will need to purchase (B150). All are available at station counters.

Metro (MRT or subway). Bangkok's metro line (Customer Relations: tel: 0 2624 5200) operates from 6am to midnight. Fares start at B16, increasing B2–3 every station, with a maximum fare of B42. You can buy passes with unlimited rides: the 1-Day Pass (B120), 3-Day Pass (B230), 30-Day Pass (B1,400) and the stored-value Adult Card (B230, includes a B50 deposit).

Taxis. Taxis in Bangkok are metered, air-conditioned and inexpensive. The flag fall is B35 for the first km, then B5.5–8 per kilometre, depending on distance travelled. If stuck in traffic, a small per-minute (usually B2) surcharge kicks in. It is best to hail them on the streets, as those parked outside hotels often hustle for a no-meter fare. Fares, however, are negotiated for longer distances outside Bangkok: for instance, to Pattaya (B1,500), Koh Samet (B2,500) or Hua Hin (3,000). The following taxi companies will take bookings for a B20 surcharge: Siam Taxi (hotline: 1661), Nakhornthai Transportation (tel: 0 2878 9000).

Tuk-tuks. Tuk-tuks are brightly coloured three-wheeled taxis. Negotiate the fare before you set off. In Bangkok, expect to pay B40–50 for short journeys of around 10 minutes or less, and B50–200 for longer journeys.

Songthaew. *Songthaew* are pick-up trucks with two benches in the back and operate like buses, usually with a loose route, but occasionally able to make detours. Hail one on the street and state your destination.

Fares start around B8–12. Bargain for a price before you get in.

Motorcycle taxis. Motorcycle taxi stands are noticeable by their drivers; a gathering of men in fluorescent, numbered vests found at the mouth of many sois. Short journeys, such as the length of a street, will cost B10–30. Longer rides (B80–200 should get you a half-hour trip) are more expensive during rush hour (8–10am and 4–6pm).

Buses. In Bangkok buses come in air conditioned or non-air conditioned varieties. Municipal and private operators all come under the charge of the Bangkok Mass Transit Authority (tel: 1348 or 0 2248 0339; www.bmta.co.th). Chiang Mai also has several bus routes, but most towns rely on tuk-tuks and songthaew.

Boats. Bangkok's most common waterborne transport is the Chao Phraya Express Boat Company (tel: 0 2445 8888; www.chaophrayaexpressboat.com), which runs services between Nonthaburi pier in the north to Ratburana in the south. Boats run every 10–20 minutes 6am–8pm, and stop at different piers according to the coloured flag on top of the boat. Yellow and green flags are fastest, but stop at only 12 piers, while orange flags are slowest but stop at every pier. On Saturday and Sunday only orange-flagged boats are in operation. There is also no flag route from Nonthaburi to Wat Rajsinkorn. Tickets cost B10–32 and are purchased from the conductor on board or at some pier counters. The Chao Phraya Tourist Boat (tel: 0 2866 3163-4) operates daily 9.30am–5.30pm and a one day river pass costs B180. The ticket is valid for an unlimited number of rides within the day; you can also use it on the regular express boats. This hop-on-and-hop-off service begins at the Sathorn pier and travels upriver to the Phra Athit pier, stopping at eight major piers along the way. Boats leave every 30 minutes.

Cross-river ferries. Bangkok's ferries are used for getting from one side of the river to the other. They cost from B2.5 per journey, and operate from 5am to 10pm or later.

Longtail boat taxis. Bangkok water taxis ply the inner canals, from the centre of town to outlying districts. Tell the conductor your destination when you get on, as boats do not stop otherwise. Tickets cost B5–10; services are roughly every 10 minutes from 6am–7pm.

V

VISAS AND ENTRY REQUIREMENTS

For a visit not exceeding 30 days, visitors from many countries, including the UK, Ireland, Canada, Australia, New Zealand, South Africa and the US, do not need a visa to enter Thailand, just a passport valid for at least 6 months, and a return or onward ticket. Visas can usually be extended by up to 30 days at immigration offices throughout the country. If you plan to stay more than a month, obtain a 60-day visa at a Thai consulate or embassy in your country before leaving home. Check www.thaivisa.com or the websites of Thailand's immigration (www.immigration.go.th) and the Ministry of Foreign Affairs (www.mfa.go.th) for details.

W

WEBSITES

www.tourismthailand.org The official site of the Tourism Authority of Thailand with information on all aspects of travel within the country.

www.bangkokpost.com The internet version of the daily English-language newspaper.

www.phuketgazette.net The website of Phuket's English-language newspaper has news and events related to the island.

www.bangkoktourist.com Information on Bangkok from the Bangkok Tourist Bureau.

www.khaosanroad.com Backpackers' resource with accommodation, work advice, upcountry travel and forums.

WEIGHTS AND MEASURES

Thailand uses the metric system, except for their traditional system of land measurement (1 rai = 1,600 sq metres) and their weight of gold (1 baht = 15.2 grammes).

RECOMMENDED HOTELS

Luxury hotels in Bangkok are among the world's least expensive and most travellers take advantage of the many promotional rates offered at the city's world-class establishments. It is imperative to make advance reservations for the high season, from December to March, especially for the resort destinations of Phuket and Ko Samui. During the low season, from April to October, there are almost always rooms to be had. The Tourist Authority of Thailand (TAT) has airport and city-centre offices in all major destinations; many are open seven days a week. All hotels are air-conditioned. A seven percent Value Added Tax (VAT) and 10 percent service charge is added to hotel bills. Unless noted below, all hotels accept major credit cards. Published, or 'rack' rates, may be high at the hotels listed below, but always ask for promotional rates which offer up to 60 percent savings. Reservations made through tour operators or through the TAT will also normally ensure a lower price than the hotel's rack rates. Always check the hotel's website (where available) as many hotels offer 'internet-only' rates, allowing you to make substantial savings.

The following price categories are for accommodation for two people per night, including tax.

$$$$	over US$280
$$$	US$140–280
$$	US$70–140
$	less than US$70

BANGKOK

Arun Residence $$$ *38 Soi Pratoo Nok Yoong, Thanon Maharat, Rattanakosin, tel: 0 2221 9158-9,* www.arunresidence.com. A small riverbank hotel with views of Wat Arun; it is located just a short walk away from Wat Pho and 100 year-old Chinese shophouses. Rooms have Wi-Fi access and iPod docks. There is a French-Thai restaurant, The Deck, and a rooftop bar that makes an atmospheric spot for cocktails. Six rooms.

Intercontinental Bangkok $$$ *973 Ploenchit Road, tel: 0 2656 0444,* www.ihg.com. In the heart of the shopping district, steps from Chit Lom Skytrain station, this hotel is an excellent choice. The deluxe rooms are spacious with large sound-proofed windows overlooking the bustling city. There are five restaurants, a pool, health club, spa and a beauty salon. There is a very cute Italian restaurant and wine bar, called Theo Mio, on site. 381 rooms.

The Mandarin Oriental $$$$ *48 Oriental Avenue, tel: 0 2659 9000,* www. mandarin-oriental.com/bangkok. More than 140 years old, the world-renowned Oriental Hotel is Bangkok's longest-established luxury hotel. All the rooms are plush, with special touches such as hard-wood floors in the bathrooms. As well as the Oriental Spa, there is a Thai cooking school, seven of the city's best restaurants, two swimming pools and a health club. Afternoon tea is served in the Authors' Lounge, named in honour of the many famous writers who have stayed at the hotel. 395 rooms.

Marvel Hotel $ *30 Sukhumvit Soi 22, Bangkok 10110, tel: 0 2262 0000,* www.marvelhotelbangkok.com. The shopping district of Sukhumvit, including the Emporium shopping complex, is just a few minutes' walk from this well-priced, full-service hotel. Located near Phrom Phong Skytrain station, the rooms come with telephones, satellite television and bathrooms with hairdryers. There is an outdoor swimming pool, a gym, a 24-hour bar and an Italian restaurant. 221 rooms.

Le Méridien $$$$ *40/5 Surawong Road, tel: 0 2232 8888,* www.lemeri dien.com/bangkoksurawong. This sleek, modernist hotel, just 50 metres from Patpong district, is a fully wired techno vision of brushed concrete, glass and funky nightclub lighting effects. Rooms have full-wall windows, flat screen TVs and 'rainforest' showers. The signature restaurant, Bamboo Chic, fuses Thai, Japanese and Chinese cuisines to a techno soundtrack, and has sake and *shouchu* lists alongside the wine. 282 rooms.

The Peninsula $$$$ *333 Charoen Nakhon Road, Khlong San, tel: 0 2861 2888,* www.peninsula.com. This 39-storey luxury hotel has great river views and decor that is international and contemporary but with neat Asian undertones. The marble bathrooms have steam-free TVs, there is an outdoor pool, a health club, and six excellent bars and restaurants, including Mei Jiang, one of the best Chinese in the city. Free shuttle boats to Tha Sathorn pier. 370 rooms.

Shanghai Mansion $$ *479–481 Yaowarat Road, tel: 0 2221 2121*, www.shanghaimansion.com. A classy boutique hotel in a part of town that is often written off as lacking in decent lodgings. The artful decor results in accommodation with lovely over-the-top chinoiserie, four-poster beds and vibrant saturated hues, many reflecting those you see in the nearby market alleyways. It also has free internet access, a spa, and free a tuk-tuk shuttle to major attractions. 76 rooms.

Le Siam $$ *3 Convent Road, Silom, Bangkok 10500, tel: 0 2233 5345*, www.swisslodge.com. Formerly known as The Swiss Lodge, this is a small boutique hotel located near the nightlife and shopping districts, and the Saladaeng Skytrain station. It is Swiss-managed with friendly, knowledgeable staff and elegant rooms with teak furniture and marble bathrooms. There is 24-hour room service, a small pool with sundeck and a Swiss café. 55 rooms.

The Siam Hotel $$$$ *Khao Road, Khwaeng Wachira Phayaban, tel: 0 2206 6999*, www.thesiamhotel.com. The art deco marvel that is The Siam takes its lead from the Jazz Age, with megaphones and vintage posters setting the tone amid a serene inner-city oasis of leafy interiors and lofty ceilings. This is decadence on the Chao Phraya. There is a Muay Thai ring, pool and spa and even a cooking school here. 39 rooms.

Take a Nap $ *920–926 Rama 4 Road, Suriyawongse, tel: 0 2637 0015*, www.takeanaphotel.com. Basic but cutely attired rooms, each with an artistic theme, such as Japanese waves, Pop Art, and the child-like Happy Forest, painted on the wall. They also have air-conditioning and a few TV stations, but no fridge or wardrobe. Close to the Patpong night market and a five-minute walk to the Skytrain and subway stations. 30 rooms.

CHIANG MAI

Chiang Mai Plaza Hotel $ *92 Sridonchai Road, Chang Khlan, tel: 0 5382 0920.* Within walking distance of the Night Bazaar and the Ping River, this large tourist hotel offers great value. Its spacious public areas are tastefully decorated with Thai art and maintain a relaxed ambience. In the evenings a small Northern Thai music ensemble performs in the main lobby. Facilities include a fitness centre, large outdoor pool and two restaurants serving Thai and international cuisine. Free Wi-Fi internet access available. 467 rooms and eight suites.

Dhara Dhevi $$$$ *51/4 Chiang Mai-San Kamphaeng Road, tel: 0 5388 8888,* www.dharadhevi.com. A stunning complex in extensive grounds with villas modelled on local Lanna architecture. In communal areas there are replicas of famous buildings such as the ancient Palace of Mandalay in Burma. Top class restaurants include the French Farang Ses and the Chinese Fujian. 123 suites and villas.

The Four Seasons Resort Chiang Mai $$$$ *502 Moo 1, Mae Rim-Samoeng Old Road, tel: 0 5329 8181,* www.fourseasons.com/chiangmai. Thirty minutes from the airport, this world-renowned, lushly landscaped resort hotel overlooks tranquil rice paddies. Accommodation is in two-storey teak pavilions, luxuriously furnished with every amenity, including internet access and huge bathrooms with deep tubs. These also come with private *sala* (a traditional-style covered verandah) with an oversized day bed and colourful Thai pillows. There is an infinity pool, tennis courts, a spa, a fitness centre and several outstanding restaurants and bars. A shuttle service to the Night Bazaar is provided daily. 98 lodgings, including pavilions, villas and private residencies.

Karinthip Village $$$ *50/2 Chang Moi Kao Road, Changmoi Tb. Muang Ap., tel: 0 5323 54 14-8,* www.karinthipvillage.com. Located just outside the old city, Karinthip Village occupies a quiet landscaped corner opposite Wat Chomphu. The three guest wings contain rooms decorated in different themes: Chinese, Thai or colonial. Facilities include a Thai-Western restaurant, large pool and a spa. 67 rooms.

CHIANG RAI

Dusit Island Resort $$$ *1129 Kraisorasit Road, Vieng District, tel: 0 5360 7999*, www.dusit.com. A great hotel located on an island in the Kok river, across from the city centre. Rooms have large picture windows overlooking the city and mountains. There is a large outdoor pool, tennis courts, fitness centre, a steak house, a Chinese restaurant and a Thai café. 271 rooms.

CHIANG SAEN/THE GOLDEN TRIANGLE

Anantara Resort and Spa Golden Triangle $$$$ *229 Moo 1, Chiang Saen tel: 0 5378 4084*, http://goldentriangle.anantara.com. A most unusual low-rise hotel (two-storey buildings) set amid 81 hectares (200 acres) of manicured gardens. The spacious and comfortable rooms, with sunken bathrooms, all come with a large terrace overlooking the Mekong River, Myanmar and Laos. An elephant camp offers local elephant treks and elephant training lessons. One free activity for every night of stay. 77 rooms and suites.

MAE HONG SON

The Dai Resort $ *158 Toongkongmoo Village, tel: 0 5361 3964*. Owned by a Shan family, The Dai is a lovely property with several Shan-style houses spread across landscaped grounds. The spacious rooms have air conditioning and are warmly decorated with bamboo-thatched walls and wood trim. There is also space in the grounds for camping. 11 rooms.

PHUKET

Amanpuri $$$$ *Pansea Beach, tel: 0 7632 4333,* www.amanpuri.com. The premier property of the exclusive Aman resorts chain has a private beach where every imaginable water sport is available. Pavilions with wood floors and ocean views are scattered on the hillside amid coconut and palm trees. There is a beautiful pool and the hotel has its own fleet of yachts for anything from day trips to overnight cruises. It has 40 pavilions as well as 30 private villas.

Banyan Tree $$$$ *33 Moo 4 Srisoonthorn Road, Amphoe Talang, 83110, tel: 0 7632 4374*, www.banyantree.com. The epitome of luxury in the midst of a manicured development at Bang Tao Bay. All the villas have wood floors, plush furniture and private outdoor Jacuzzis; some come with private pools, although few overlook the sea. There are free-form and lap pools, tennis courts, water sports, a spa and fitness centre, a golf school and course, cooking classes, and several outstanding restaurants. 108 villas.

Cape Sienna Hotel & Villas $$$$ *18/40 Moo 6, Nakalay Road, Kamala, Kathu, tel: 0 7633 7300*, www.capesienna.com. Modern accommodation with good views over Kamala Beach. All rooms have sea views, private balconies, flat screen TVs and wireless broadband. There are good sea views, too, from its restaurants, bars and spa. This is an adult-friendly resort so only allows children under 12 in family villas, all of which overlook the sea. 146 rooms and nine villas.

Marina Phuket Resort $$$$ *47 Karon Road, Karon Beach, tel: 0 7633 0625*, www.marinaphuket.com. Small, simply furnished bungalows are scattered on a hillside a few minutes' walk from the sandy beach at Karon. The jungle-like foliage means some rooms remain quite dark throughout the day; the sea view units offer breathtaking scenery to look at. There are two restaurants and a small pool. 104 rooms.

The Nai Harn $$$$ *23/3 Vises Road, Nai Harn Beach, tel: 0 7638 0200*, www.thenaiharn.com. A lovely hideaway on a cliff above a white-sand beach. The Nai Harn offers understated luxury in well-equipped rooms that feature oversized terraces with magnificent ocean views. The spa has outdoor treatment rooms overlooking the Andaman Sea and there is a pool, two restaurants and a spa. 110 rooms.

Thavorn Beach Village and Spa $$$ *6/2 Moo 6, Nakalay Bay, Patong, tel: 0 7629 0334*, www.thavornbeachvillage.com. Close to the bustle of Patong, yet tranquil enough with its own private beach. A cable car transports guests from the open-air main lobby to the comfortable rooms built high on a hill. The grounds are lush and service is of a high standard. There is a large lagoon swimming pool, a spa and an excellent Thai restaurant. 194 rooms.

KO SAMUI

Ampha Place Hotel $ *67/59 Moo 1, Thanbol Maenam, tel: 0 7733 2129,* www.samui-ampha-hotel.com. This simple, but well-run place has smart ensuite rooms, each with international TV channels, a balcony and free Wi-Fi access. There is a small café and bar beside the outdoor pool. The location is secluded and quiet, about 150 metres (165 yards) to the beach and a ten minute walk into the village of Maenam.

Bo Phut Resort & Spa $$$$ *12/12 Tambol Bo Phut, Surat Thani, tel: 0 7724 5777,* www.bophutresort.com. This 9-hectare (23-acre) luxury resort prides itself on its quiet, restful atmosphere. There is a lovely stretch of private sandy beach with every water sport imaginable. Accommodation is in villas scattered across the grounds, all meticulously decorated with an authentic flair. There is a spa, a glorious pool and three restaurants. 32 Thai-style villas and 29 suites.

Centara Grand Beach Resort $$$$ *38/2 Moo 3, Borpud, Chaweng Beach, tel: 0 7723 0500,* www.centralhotelsresorts.com. This is a large resort hotel in the midst of bustling Chaweng Beach. Rooms are comfortable with their own little private balconies, all with ocean views. There is a fitness centre, spa and three excellent restaurants. 208 rooms.

The Imperial Boat House Beach Resort $$ *83 Moo 5, Choeng Mon Beach, tel: 0 7742 5041,* www.melia.com. This splendid property features comfortable hotel rooms, including 34 rice barge suites with wood floors, luxury bathrooms and amenities. Public areas feature a pool, a beachside restaurant and a bar. 210 rooms.

Poppies Samui $$$ *Chaweng Beach, tel: 0 7742 2419,* www.poppies samui.com. Excellent location at the quieter end of Chaweng Beach, this is a small property with understated luxury in each of its private cottages which are decorated with fine Thai silk and gleaming teak floors and furniture. The bathrooms feature a sunken bath opening onto a private garden. There is a pool surrounded with natural rock, an outstanding restaurant on the beach and a spa. 24 cottages.

The Tongsai Bay $$$$ *84 Moo 5, Bo Phut, Tongsai Bay, tel: 0 7724 5480,* www.tongsaibay.co.th. On a quiet bay with a private beach, this hideaway is one of the most luxuriously unpretentious retreats in Thailand. The cottages, scattered on a hillside, all have teak floors, open-air terraces and secluded outdoor tubs. The villas have indoor and outdoor bedrooms (mosquito nets are provided), which is an unusual feature for a tropical vacation. It has a mix of 44 cottages, 24 beachfront suites and 15 villas.

HUA HIN

Evason Hua Hin Resort and Spa $$$ *9 Moo 5 Parknampran Beach, Pranburi, Prachuab Khiri Khan, tel: 0 3263 2111,* www.sixsenses.com. Modern elegance situated along an isolated beach with the option of villas that come with their own private pools. The Six Senses Spa offers a range of treatments, including Thai and Himalayan Singing Bowl massage. 240 rooms and suites as well as 40 pool villas.

KO PHI PHI

Holiday Inn Resort Phi Phi Island $$ *Laemtong Beach, Phi Phi Island, Krabi, tel: 0 7562 7300,* www.phiphi.holidayinn.com. These bungalows in a smart resort at the remote northerly end of the island have garden or sea views. The resort also has a spa and holds Thai cooking classes in one of its restaurants. Its isolation means tranquillity, though sightseeing is best accomplished by boat. 77 bungalows, split between beachfront and garden locations.

DICTIONARY

ENGLISH–THAI DICTIONARY

adj adjective   **adv** adverb   **BE** British English   **n** noun   **v** verb   **prep** preposition

A

abroad ต่างประเทศ
dtaang•bpra•tet

accept ยอมรับ
yorm•ráhp

access เข้าถึง
kôu•tŭeng

accident อุบัติเหตุ
uh•bàht•dtih•hèt

accommodation ที่พัก
têe•páhk

accompany มาด้วย
mar dôary

acetaminophen พารา
เซตตามอล *par•rar•
sèht•dtar•môhn*

across ตรงข้าม
dtrong•kârm

acupuncture ฝังเข็ม
făhng•kěhm

adapter ปลั๊กแปลง
ไฟฟ้า *bpláhk bplaeng
fi•fár*

additional เพิ่มเติม
pêrm•dterm

address ที่อยู่
têe•yòo

admission charge ค่า
เข้า *kâr•kôu*

adult ผู้ใหญ่ *pôo•yi*

after หลังจาก
lăhng•jàrk

afternoon ตอนบ่าย
dtorn bie

agree เห็นด้วย
hěhn•dôary

air (tire) ลม *lom*;
อากาศ *ar•gàrt*

air conditioning
แอร์ *ae*

air mattress ที่นอน
อัดลม *têe•norn
âht lom*

airline สายการบิน
sǐe•garn•bihn

airmail ไปรษณีย์
อากาศ *bpri•sah•nee
ar•gàrt*

airport สนามบิน
sah•nǎrm•bihn

airsickness เมาเครื่อง
บิน *mou krûeang•bihn*

alarm clock นาฬิกา
ปลุก *nar•lí•gar bplùhk*

allergy ภูมิแพ้
poom•páe

allow อนุญาต
ah•núh•yârt

allowance ค่าใช้จ่าย
kâr chi•jie

almost เกือบจะ
gùeap•jàh

alone คนเดียว
kon•deaw

already แล้ว *láew*

alter (a garment)
แก้ *gâe*

alternate สลับ
sah•làhp

aluminum foil
กระดาษฟอยล์
grah•dàrt fory

ambassador
เอกอัครราชทูต
*èk•àhk•kah•rârt•
chah•tôot*

ambulance รถ
พยาบาล *rót
pah•yar•barn*

American อเมริกัน
ah•me•rih•gahn

amount จำนวน
jahm•noarn

amusement park สวน
สนุก *sŏarn sah•nùhk*

and และ *lá*

anemia โรคโลหิตจาง
rôek loe•hìht jarng

anesthetic ยาชา
yar•char

animal สัตว์ *sàht*

antacid ยาลดกรด *yar
lót gròt*

antibiotics ยา
ปฏิชีวนะ *yar bpah•
dtìh•chee•wah•náh*

antique ของเก่า
kŏrng gòu

antiseptic cream ครีม
แก้อักเสบ *kreem gâe
àhk•sèp*

any ใด *di*

anyone ใคร *kri*

anything อะไร *a•ri*

apartment
อพาร์ตเมนต์
ah•pàrt•méhn

apologize ขอโทษ
kŏr•tôet

appointment นัด *náht*

approve ยอมรับ
yorm•ráhp

approximately
ประมาณ *bprah•marn*

area code รหัสพื้นที่
rah•hàht púeen•tée

arm แขน *kǎen*

aromatherapy อโรมา
เทอราปี *ah•roe•mâr
te•rar•pêe*

around รอบ ๆ
rôrp•rôrp

arrivals ขาเข้า
kǎr•kôu

arrive มาถึง *mar•tŭeng*

art gallery หอศิลป์
hǒr•sǐhn

arthritis โรคไขข้อ
เสื่อม *rôek kǐ•kôr
sùeam*

ashtray ที่เขี่ยบุหรี่ *tée
kèar buh•rèe*

ask ถาม *tǎrm*

aspirin แอสไพริน
áet•sah•pi•rihn

assistance ความ
ช่วยเหลือ *kwarm
chôary•lŭea*

asthma โรคหอบหืด
rôek hòrp•hùeet

ATM เอทีเอ็ม
e•tee•ehm

attack *v* ทำร้าย
tahm•ríe; *n* การทำร้าย
garn tahm•ríe

attractive มีเสน่ห์ *mee
sah•nè*

audio guide เทปนำ
เที่ยว *tép nahm•tîeaw*

authentic แท้ *táe*

available ว่าง *wârng*

away ห่าง *hàrng*

B

baby เด็กอ่อน *dèhk òrn*

baby bottle ขวดนมเด็ก *kòart•nom dèhk*

baby food อาหารเด็ก *ar•hărn dèhk*

babysitter พี่เลี้ยงเด็ก *pêe•léang dèhk*

back หลัง *lăhng*

backache ปวดหลัง *bpùat•lăhng*

backpack เป้สะพาย หลัง *bpê sah•pie lăhng*

bad เลว *lew*

bag กระเป๋า *grah•bpŏu*

baggage [BE] กระเป๋า *grah•bpŏu*

baggage claim ที่ รับกระเป๋า *têe ráhp grah•bpŏu*

bakery ร้านเบเกอรี่ *rárn be•ger•rêe*

balcony ระเบียง *rah•beang*

ball ลูกบอล *lôok•bohn*

ballet บัลเลต์ *bahn•lê*

bandage ผ้าพันแผล *pár pahn plăe*

bank ธนาคาร *tah•nar•karn*

bar บาร์ *bar*

barber ร้านตัดผม *ผู้ชาย rárn dtàht•pŏm pôo•chie*

bargain ตอราคา *tòr rar•kar*

basement ชั้นใต้ดิน *cháhn tí•dihn*

basket ตะกร้า *dtah•grâr*

basketball บาสเก็ต ตบอล *bárt•sah•gèht bohn*

bath อางน้ำ *àrp•nárm*

bathroom ห้องน้ำ *hôhng•nárm*

battery แบตเตอรี่ *bàt•dter•rêe*

be เป็น *bpehn*

beach ชายหาด *chie•hàrt*

beautiful สวย *sŏary*

because เพราะว่า *práh•wâr*

bed เตียง *dteang*

bedding เครื่องนอน *krûeang•norn*

bedroom ห้องนอน *hôhng•norn*

before ก่อน *gòrn*

begin เริ่ม *rêrm*

behind หลัง *lăhng*

belong เป็นของ *bpehn kŏhng*

belt เข็มขัด *kĕhm•kàht*

bet พนัน *pah•nahn*

between ระหว่าง *rah•wârng*

beware ระวัง *rah•wahng*

bicycle จักรยาน *jàhk•grah•yarn*

big ใหญ่ *yì*

bike path ทางจักรยาน *tarng jàhk•grah•yarn*

bikini บิกินี่ *bih•gih•nêe*

bill บิล *bihn*

binoculars กล้องส่อง ทางไกล *glôhng sòhng tarng gli*

bird นก *nók*

birthday วันเกิด *wahn•gèrt*

bite กัด *gàht*

blanket ผ้าห่ม *pâr•hòm*

bleed เลือดออก *lûeat•òrk*

blister แผลพุพอง *plăe púh•porng*

blood เลือด *lûeat*

blood pressure ความ ดันเลือด *kwarm•dahn lûeat*

blouse เสื้อผู้หญิง *sûea pôo•yĭhng*

board กระดาน *grah•darn*

boarding card ตั๋ว ขึ้นเครื่อง *dtŏar kûen krûeang*

boat trip ทัวร์ทางเรือ *toar tarng ruea*

bone กระดูก *grah•dòok*

book หนังสือ *năhng•sŭee*

bookstore ร้านหนังสือ *rárn năhng•sŭee*

boots รองเท้าบูท *rorng•tôw bóot*

born เกิด *gèrt*

borrow ยืม *yueem*

botanical garden สวน พฤกษศาสตร์ *sŏarn prúek•sah•sàrt*

bother รบกวน *róp•goarn*

bottle ขวด *kòart*

bottle opener ที่เปิด ขวด *têe bpèrt kòart*

bowl ชาม *charm*

box กล่อง *glòhng*

boxing ชกมวย *chók•moary*

boy เด็กผู้ชาย *dèhk•pôo•chie*

bra ยกทรง *yók•song*

bracelet สร้อยข้อมือ *sôry kôr•muee*

brake v หยุด *yùht*; n เบรก *brèk*

break แตก *dtàek*

breakfast อาหารเช้า *ar•hărn chów*

breast หน้าอก *nâr•òk*

breastfeed ให้นม *hî•nom*

breathe หายใจ *hĭe•ji*

bridge สะพาน *sah•parn*

bring เอามา *ou•mar*

British (person) คน อังกฤษ *kon ahng•grìht*

brochure แผ่นพับ *pàen•páhp*

broken เสีย *sĕa*

broom ไม้กวาด *mie•gwàrt*

browse เปิดดู *bpèrt•doo*

bruise รอยฟกช้ำ *rory fók•cháhm*

bucket ถัง *tăhng*

Buddha image พระพุทธรูป *práh•púht•tah•rôop*

bug แมลง *mah•laeng*

build สร้าง *sârng*

building ตึก *dtùek*; อาคาร *ar•karn*

burn ไหม้ *mî*

bus รถเมล์ *rót•me*

bus station สถานีขนส่ง *sah•tăr•nee kŏn•sòng*

bus stop ป้ายรถเมล์ *bpîe rót•me*

bus ticket ตั๋วรถเมล์ *dtŏar rót•me*

business ธุรกิจ *túh•ráh•gìht*

business card นามบัตร *narm•bàht*

business center ศูนย์ บริการทางธุรกิจ *sŏon bor•rih•garn tarng túh•ráh•gìht*

business class ชั้น ธุรกิจ *túh•ráh•gìht*

business district ย่านธุรกิจ *yârn túh•ráh•gìht*

busy ยุ่ง *yûhng*

but แต่ *dtàe*

button (clothing) กระดุม *grah•duhm*; **(device)** ปุ่ม *bpùhm*

buy ซื้อ *súee*

by โดย *doey*

bye สวัสดี *sah•wàht•dee*

C

cafe ร้านกาแฟ *rárn gar•fae*

calendar ปฏิทิน *bpah•dtih•tihn*

call (phone) โทรศัพท์ *toe•rah•sáhp;* **(summon)** เรียก *rêak*

camera กล้องถ่ายรูป *glôhng tìe•rôop*

camp ตั้งแคมป์ *dtâhng•kaem*

campsite ทัดแคมป์ *tée dtâhng•káem*

can กระป๋อง *grah•bpŏhng*

can opener ที่เปิด กระป๋อง *tée bpèrt grah•bpŏhng*

canal คลอง *klorng*

cancel ยกเลิก *yók•lêrk*

cancer มะเร็ง *mah•rehng*

candle เทียน *tean*

candy store ร้านขาย ขนม *rárn kĭe kah•nŏm*

canoe เรือแคนู *ruea kae•noo*

car รถยนต์ *rót•yon*

car hire [BE] รถเช่า *rót•chôu*

car park [BE] ที่จอดรถ *tée jòrt rót*

car rental รถเช่า *rót•chôu*

car seat ที่นั่งในรถ สำหรับเด็ก *tée•nâhng ni rót sâhm•ráhp dèhk*

carafe เหยือก *yùeak*

card บัตร *bàht*

careful ระวัง *rah•wahng*

carpet พรม *prom*

carry-on luggage กระเป๋าถือขึ้นเครื่อง *grah•bpŏu tŭee kûen krûeang*

cart รถเข็น *rót•kĕhn*

carton (of cigarettes) กล่อง *glòhng*

cash v ขึ้นเงิน *kûen•ngern;* n เงินสด *ngern•sòt*

cash register เครื่องคิด เงิน *krûeang kít•ngern*

cashier แคชเชียร์ *káet•chea*

casino คาสิโน *kar•sih•noe*

catch จับ *jàhp*

cathedral โบสถ์ฝรั่ง *bòet fah•ràhng*

caution ระมัดระวัง *rah•máht rah•wahng*

cave ถ้ำ *tâhm*

CD ซีดี *see•dee*

CD player เครื่องเล่นซีดี *krûeang lêhn see•dee*

cell phone โทรศัพท์ มือถือ *toe•rah•sáhp muee•tŭee*

cemetery สุสาน *sùh•sărn*

ceramics เซรามิก *se•rar•mihk*

certificate ใบรับรอง bi *ráhp•rorng*

change v เปลี่ยน *bplèan;* **(money)** v แลกเงิน *lâek ngern;* n เงินทอน *ngern•torn*

charcoal ถ่าน *tàrn*

charge v คิดเงิน *kìht•ngern;* n ค่า *kâr*

cheap ถูก *tòok*

check n **(bank)** เช็ค *chéhk;* v ตรวจ *dtròart;* v **(luggage)** ฝาก กระเป๋า *fàrk grah•bpŏu*

check in เช็คอิน *chéhk•ihn*

check out เช็คเอาท์ *chéhk•òu*

check-in desk โต๊ะเช็ค อิน *dtó chéhk•ihn*

checking account บัญชีกระแสรายวัน *bahn•chee grah•săe rie•wahn*

chemical toilet ส้วม เคมี *sôarm ke•mee*

chemist [BE] ร้านขาย ยา *rárn kĭe yar*

cheque [BE] เช็ค *chéhk*

chest หน้าอก *nâr•òk*

child เด็ก *dèhk*

child seat ที่นั่งเด็ก *tée•nâhng dèhk*

children's menu เมนู สำหรับเด็ก *me•noo sâhm•ráhp dèhk*

children's portion ขนาดสำหรับเด็ก *kah•nàrt sâhm•ráhp dèhk*

choose เลือก *lûeak*

church โบสถ์ *bòet*

cigar ซิการ์ *síh•gâr*

cigarette บุหรี่ *bùh•rèe*

cinema [BE] โรงหนัง *roeng•năng*

clean adj สะอาด *sah•àrt;* v ทำความ สะอาด *tahm kwarm sah•àrt*

clearance (sale) ลด ราคา *lót rar•kar*

cliff หน้าผา *nâr•păr*

cling film [BE] ฟิล์ม ถนอมอาหาร *feem tah•nŏrm ar•hărn*

clinic คลีนิค *klee•nihk*

clock นาฬิกา *nar•líh•gar*

close (shut) ปิด *bpìht;* **(near)** ใกล้ *glî*

clothes shop [BE] ร้าน ขายเสื้อผ้า *rárn kĭe sûea•pâr*

clothing store ร้าน ขายเสื้อผ้า *rárn kĭe sûea•pâr*

club คลับ *kláhp*

coast ชายฝั่ง *chie•fàhng*

coat เสื้อโค้ท *sûea•kóet*

coat check ที่รับฝาก เสื้อโค้ท *tée ráhp fàrk sûea•kóet*

code รหัส *rah•hàht*

coin เหรียญ *rĕan*

cold (weather) adj หนาว *nŏw;* n หวัด *wàht*

collapse ล้ม *lóm*

colleague เพื่อน ร่วมงาน *pûean•rôarm•ngarn*

collect (call) โทรเก็บ เงินปลายทาง *toe gèhp ngern bplie tarng*

color สี *sĕe*

comb หวี *wĕe*

come มา *mar*

commission ค่าบริการ *kâr bor•rih•garn*

company บริษัท *bor•rih•sàht*

compartment ที่ใส่ของ *tée sì körng*

computer คอมพิวเตอร์ *kohm•pihw•dtêr*

concert คอนเสิร์ต *kohn•sèrt*

conditioner (hair) ครีมนวดผม *kreem nôart pŏm*

condom ถุงยางอนามัย *tŭhng•yarng ah•nar•mi*

conductor (bus) รถ กระเป๋า *rót grah•bpŏu rót*

conference การ ประชุมสัมมนา *garn bprah•chuhm săhm•mah•nar*

confirm ยืนยัน *yueen•yahn*

congratulations ขอ แสดงความยินดี *kŏr sah•daeng kwarm yihn•dee*

connect เชื่อมต่อ chûeam•dtòr

connection การเชื่อม ต่อ garn chûeam•dtòr

conscious รู้สึกตัว róo•sùek dtoar

conservation area เขต อนุรักษ์ kèt ah•nú•ráhk

constant คงที่ kong•têe

constipation ท้องผูก ah•gahn tórng•pòok

consulate กงสุล gong•sùhn

consult ปรึกษา bprùek•săr

contact v ติดต่อ dtìht•dtòr; n การติดต่อ garn dtìht•dtòr

contact lens คอนแท็ค เลนส์ korn•tàk•lehn

contact lens solution น้ำยาคอนแท็ค เลนส์ náhm•yar kohn•tàk•lehn

contraceptive คุมกำเนิด kuhm•gahm•nèrt

control ควบคุม kôarp•kuhm

convention การประชุม garn bprah•chuhm

convention hall ห้อง คอนเวนชั่น hôhng kohn•wen•chăhn

cook v ทำอาหาร tahm ar•hărn; n คนครัว kon•kroar

cool เย็น yehn

copy ทำสำเนา tahm săhm•nou

corkscrew ที่เปิด จุกก๊อก têe bpèrt jùhk•gòhk

corner มุม muhm

correct ถูกต้อง tòok•dtôhng

cosmetic เครื่องสำอาง krûeang săhm•arng

cost n ค่าใช้จ่าย kâr chí•jìe; v ราคา rar•kar

cot เตียงพับ dteang•páhp

cottage กระท่อม grah•tôhm

cotton ผ้าฝ้าย pâr fîe

cough ไอ

counter เคาน์เตอร์ kóu•dtêr

country ประเทศ bprah•têt

country code รหัส ประเทศ rah•hàht bprah•têt

course วิชา wíh•char

cover charge ค่าบริการ ต่อหัว kâr bor•rih•garn dtòr hŭa

craft shop ร้านขาย งานฝีมือ rárn kăi ngarn•fĕe•muee

cramp (sports) ตะคริว dtah•krihw; ปวดประจำเดือน bpòart bprah•jahm•duean

credit card บัตรเครดิต bàht kre•dìht

crib เปลเด็ก bple dèhk

crowd ฝูงคน fŏong•kon

cruise ล่องเรือ lôhng•ruea

crutch ไม้เท้า mí•tów

crystal คริสตัล kríhts•dtàhn

cup ถ้วย tôary

currency เงิน ngern

currency exchange office ที่รับแลกเงิน têe ráhp lâek ngern

curtain ผ้าม่าน pâr•mârn

customer service บริการลูกค้า bor•rih•garn lôok•kár

customs ศุลกากร sŭhn•lah•gar•gorn

cut v (knife) บาด bàrt; n บาดแผล bàrt•plăe

cute น่ารัก nâr•ráhk

D

daily รายวัน rie•wahn

damage เสียหาย sĭe•hăi

damp ชื้น chúeen

dance เต้นรำ dtêhn•rahm

dance club คลับเต้นรำ kláhp dtêhn•rahm

dangerous อันตราย ahn•dtah•rie

dark มืด mûeet

day วัน wahn

day trip ทัวร์วันเดียว toar wahn deaw

dead ตาย dtie

deaf หูหนวก hŏo•nòark

deck chair เก้าอี้ผ้าใบ gôu•êe pâr•bi

declare แสดงรายการ สิ่งของ sah•daeng rie•garn sìhng•kŏrng

decorative ตกแต่ง dtok•dtàeng

deep ลึก lúek

degree องศา ong•săr

delay ช้า chár

delete ลบ lóp

delicious อร่อย ah•ròhy

deliver ส่ง sòng

delivery การส่ง garn•sòng

dental floss ไหมขัดฟัน mĭ kàht fahn

dentist หมอฟัน mŏr fahn

denture ฟันปลอม fahn bplorm

deodorant ยาระงับ กลิ่นตัว yar rah•ngáhp glìhn•dtoar

depart จาก jàrk

department store ห้าง สรรพสินค้า hârng sàhp•pah•sĭhn•kár

departure gate ประตู ทางออกขึ้นเครื่อง bprah•dtoo tarng•òrk kûen krûeang

departures ขาออก kăi•òrk

deposit v ฝากเงิน fàrk ngern; n เงินมัดจำ ngern máht•jahm

describe อธิบาย ah•tíh•bie

destination ปลายทาง bplie•tarng

detail รายละเอียด rie•lah•èat

detergent ผงซักฟอก pŏng•sáhk•fôrk

detour ทางเบี่ยง tarng•bèang

develop พัฒนา páht•tah•nar

diabetes โรคเบาหวาน rôek bou•wărn

diabetic adj เบาหวาน bou•wărn; n คนเป็น โรคเบาหวาน kon bpehn rôek bou•wărn

dial (phone) กด gòt

diaper ผ้าอ้อม pâr•ôrm

diarrhea ท้องร่วง tórng•rôarng

dice v หั่น hàhn; n ลูกเต๋า lôok•dtŏu

dictionary พจนานุกรม pót•jah•nar•núh•grom

diesel ดีเซล dee•sen

diet การควบคุมอาหาร kôarp•kuhm ar•hărn

difficult ยาก yârk

digital ดิจิตอล dih•jih•dtohn

dine กินอาหาร gihn ar•hărn

dining car รถเสบียง rót sah•beang

dining room ห้องอาหาร hôhng ar•hǎrn

dinner อาหารเย็น ar•hǎrn yehn

direct adj ตรง dtrong; v กำกับ gahm•gàhp

direction ทิศ tíht

director (com-pany) ผู้อำนวยการ pôo•ahm•nuoary•garn

directory (phone) สมุด โทรศัพท์ sàh•mùht toe•rah•sàhp

dirty สกปรก sòk•gra•bpròk

disabled adj พิการ pih•garn; n คนพิการ kon pih•garn

disconnect ตัดการ เชื่อมต่อ dtàht garn chûeam•dtòr

discount ส่วนลด sòarn•lót

dish จาน jarn

dishwasher เครื่องล้าง จาน krûeang lárng jarn

dishwashing liquid น้ำยาล้างจาน náhm•yar lárng jarn

display case ตู้โชว์ tôo•choe

disposable ใช้แล้วทิ้ง chí láew tíhng

dissolve ละลาย lah•lai

distance ระยะทาง ráh•yáh•tarng

disturb รบกวน róp•guarn

dive ดำน้ำ dahm•nárm

diving equipment อุปกรณ์ดำน้ำ ùhp•bpah•gorn dahm•nárm

divorce หย่า yàr

dizzy เวียนศีรษะ wean sěe•sàh

do ทำ tahm

dock อู่เรือ òo•ruea

doctor หมอ mǒr

dog สุนัข sùh•náhk

doll ตุ๊กตา dtúhk•gah•dtar

dollar ดอลลาร์ dohn•lâr

domestic ในประเทศ ni bprah•têt

donation เงินบริจาค ngern bor•rih•jàrk

door ประตู bprah•dtoo

dosage (medi-cine) ขนาดรับ ประทาน kah•nàrt ráhp•bprah•tarn

double คู่ kôo

double room ห้องคู่ hôhng kôo

downstairs ชั้นล่าง cháhn lárng

downtown ย่านใจกลาง เมือง yârn ji•glarng mueang

dress ชุดกระโปรง chúht grah•bproeng

drink v ดื่ม dùeem; n เครื่องดื่ม krûeang•dùeem

drip หยด yòt

drive ขับ kàhp

driver คนขับ kon kàhp

driver's license ใบขับขี่ bi•kàhp•kèe

drown จมน้ำ jom nárm

drowsy ง่วง ngûarng

drugstore ร้านขายยา rárn kǐe yar

dry adj แห้ง hâeng

dry clean ซักแห้ง sàhk•hâeng

dry cleaner ร้านซักแห้ง rárn sàhk•hâeng

dummy [BE] จุกนม jùhk•nom

during ระหว่าง rah•wàrng

duty (tax) ภาษี par•sěe

duty-free ร้านค้าปลอด ภาษี rárn•kár bplòrt par•sěe

E

ear หู hǒo

earache ปวดหู bpòart hǒo

earrings ตุ้มหู dtûhm•hǒo

east ทิศตะวันออก tíht dtah•wahn•òrk

easy ง่าย ngîe

eat กิน gihn

economy class ชั้น ประหยัด cháhn bprah•yàht

electrical outlet ปลั๊ก ไฟ bpláhk•fi

electronic ไฟฟ้า fi•fár

elevator ลิฟต์ lihp

e-mail อีเมล์ ee•mew

e-mail address อีเมล์ แอดเดรส ee•mew àht•drét

embassy สถานทูต sah•tǎrn•tôot

emergency ฉุกเฉิน chùhk•chěrn

emergency brake เบรคฉุกเฉิน brèk chùhk•chěrn

emergency exit ทางออกฉุกเฉิน tarng•òrk chùhk•chěrn

emergency service บริการฉุกเฉิน bor•rih•garn chùhk•chěrn

empty ว่าง wârng

end v จบ jòp; n ปลาย bplie

engaged หมั้น mâhn

England (ประเทศ) อังกฤษ (bprah•têt) ahng•grìht

English (language) ภาษาอังกฤษ par•sǎr ahng•grìht; **(person)** คนอังกฤษ kon ahng•grìht

engrave สลัก sah•làhk

enjoy สนุก sàh•nùhk

enlarge ขยาย kah•yǐe

enough พอ por

entrance ทางเข้า tarng•kôu

entry visa วีซ่าเข้า ประเทศ wee•sâr kôu bprah•têt

envelope ซองจดหมาย sorng•jòt•mǐe

equipment เครื่องมือ krûeang•muee

error ข้อผิดพลาด kôr•pìht•plârt

escalator บันไดเลื่อน bahn•di•lûean

essential จำเป็น jahm•bpehn

e-ticket ตั๋ว อิเล็กทรอนิกส์ dtǔar ee•léhk•tror•nihk

Eurocheque ยูโรเช็ค yoo•roe chéhk

evening ตอนเย็น dtorn•yehn

event เหตุการณ์ hèt•garn

every ทุก túhk

exact แน่นอน nâe•norn

examination การสอบ garn•sòrp

example ตัวอย่าง dtoar•yàrng

except ยกเว้น yók•wéhn

excess luggage กระเป๋าเกิน grah•bpǒu gern

exchange แลกเปลี่ยน lâek•bplèan

exchange rate อัตรา แลกเปลี่ยน *àht•dtrar lâek•bplèan*

excursion ทัวร์ระยะสั้น *toar rah•yáh sân*

exhausted หมดแรง *mòt raeng*

exit v ออก *òrk*; n ทางออก *tarng•òrk*

expensive แพง *paeng*

express mail ไปรษณีย์ ด่วน *bpri•sah•nee dòarn*

extension (phone) เบอร์ต่อ *ber dtòr*

extra เพิ่ม *pêrm*

eye ตา *dtar*

eyebrow คิ้ว *kíhw*

F

fabric เนื้อผ้า *núea•pâr*

face หน้า *nâr*

facility สถานที่ *sah•tărn•têe*

faint เป็นลม *bpehn•lom*

family ครอบครัว *krôrp•kroar*

famous มีชื่อเสียง *mee chûee•sĕang*

fan พัดลม *páht•lom*

far ไกล *gli*

farm ฟาร์ม *farm*

fast เร็ว *rehw*

fast food อาหารจาน ด่วน *ar•hărn jarn dòarn*

faucet ก๊อกน้ำ *góhk•nárm*

faulty บกพร่อง *bòk•prôhng*

favorite ที่ชอบ *têe chôrp*

fax แฟกซ์ *fák*

fax machine เครื่อง แฟกซ์ *krûeang fák*

fax number เบอร์แฟกซ์ *ber fák*

feature รูปแบบ *rôop•baep*

feed ป้อน *bpôrn*

feeding bottle [BE] ขวดนม *kòart•nom*

feel รู้สึก *róo•sùek*

female เพศหญิง *pêt•yĭhng*

ferry เรือข้ามฟาก *ruea kârm•fârk*

fever ไข้ *kî*

field ทุ่ง *tûhng*

fight ต่อสู้ *dtòr•sôo*

fill เติม *dterm*

fill out กรอก *gròrk*

fill up เติมให้เต็ม *dterm hî dtehm*

filling (dental) ที่อุดฟัน *têe•ùht•fahn*

film หนัง *năhng*

find หา *hăr*

fine (health) สบายดี *sah•bie dee*

finger นิ้ว *níhw*

fire ไฟ *fi*

fire alarm สัญญาณไฟ ไหม้ *săhn•yarn fi•mî*

fire escape ทางหนีไฟ *tarng nĕe fi*

fire exit ทางหนีไฟ *tarng nĕe fi*

fire extinguisher ถัง ดับเพลิง *tăhng dàhp•plerng*

first ที่หนึ่ง *têe nùeng*

first class ชั้นหนึ่ง *cháhn nùeng*

fishing ตกปลา *dtòk•bplar*

fitting room ห้องลอง เสื้อผ้า *hôhng lorng sûea•pâr*

fix (repair) ซ่อม *sôhm*

flash (camera) แฟลช *flát*

flashlight ไฟฉาย *fi•chĭe*

flat [BE] (apartment) แฟลต *flát*

flavor รสชาติ *rót•chârt*

flea market ตลาดนัด *dtah•làrt náht*

flight เที่ยวบิน *têaw•bihn*

flight attendant พนักงานต้อนรับ *pah•náhk•ngarn dtôhn•ráhp*

flight number เที่ยวบิน ที่ *têaw•bihn têe*

floor (level) ชั้น *cháhn*

flower ดอกไม้ *dòrk•mée*

flu ไข้หวัดใหญ่ *kî•wàht•yì*

flush (toilet) กด ชักโครก *gòt cháhk•krôek*

fly บิน *bihn*

fog หมอก *mòrk*

follow ตาม *dtarm*

food อาหาร *ar•hărn*

food poisoning อาหาร เป็นพิษ *ar•hărn bpehn•píht*

foot เท้า *tów*

football [BE] ฟุตบอล *fúht•bohn*

footpath [BE] ทางเท้า *tarng•tów*

for เพื่อ *pêua*

for sale สำหรับขาย *săhm•ràhp kĭe*

foreign ต่างชาติ *dtàrng•chârt*

forest ป่า *bpàr*

forget ลืม *lueem*

fork ส้อม *sôhm*

form แบบฟอร์ม *bàep•form*

formal dress ชุดเป็น ทางการ *chúht bpehn tarng•garn*

formula (baby) นมผง เด็ก *nom•pŏng•dèhk*

fountain น้ำพุ *nárm•púh*

fracture ร้าว *rárw*

free ว่าง *wârng*

freezer ตู้แช่แข็ง *dtôo•châe•kăeng*

frequent บ่อย *bòhy*

fresh สด *sòt*

friend เพื่อน *pûean*

from จาก *jàrk*

front ด้านหน้า *dârng•nâr*

frying pan กระทะ *grah•táh*

fuel น้ำมัน *náhm•mahn*

full เต็ม *dtehm*

fun สนุก *sah•núhk*

funny ตลก *dtah•lòk*

furniture เฟอร์นิเจอร์ *fer•nih•jêr*

G

gallery หอศิลป์ *hŏr•sĭn*

game เกม *gem*

garage โรงรถ *roeng•rót*

garbage bag ถุงใส่ขยะ *tŭhng sì kah•yàh*

garden สวน *sŏarn*

gas เบนซิน *ben•sihn*

gas station ปั๊มน้ำมัน *bpáhm•náhm•mahn*

gate ประตู *bprah•dtoo*

gauze ผ้าก๊อซ *pâr•górt*

gear เกียร์ *gear*

genuine แท้ *táe*

get off (bus, train, etc.) ลง *long*

gift ของฝาก *kŏrng•fàrk*

gift store ร้านกิฟต์ช็อป *rárn gíp•chôhp*

girl เด็กหญิง *dèhk•yĭhng*

give ให้ *hî*

glass แก้ว *gâew*

glasses (optical) แว่นตา *wâen•dtar*

gloves ถุงมือ *tŭhng•muee*

go ไป *bpi*

gold ทอง *torng*

golf กอล์ฟ *górp*

golf club ไม้กอล์ฟ *mí•górp*

golf course สนาม กอล์ฟ *sah•nǎrm górp*

good ดี *dee*

goodbye สวัสดี *sah•wàht•dee*

gram กรัม *grahm*

grass หญ้า *yâr*

Great Britain สหราชอาณาจักร *sah•hàh•rât•chah•ar•nar•jàhk*

grocery store ร้าน ขายของชำ *rárn kǐe kǒrng•chahm*

group กลุ่ม *glùhm*

guarantee รับประกัน *ráhp bprah•gahn*

guesthouse เกสต์เฮาส์ *gét•hóus*

guide (person) ไกด์ *gí*

guide book หนังสือ นำเที่ยว *nǎhng•sǔee nahm•têaw*

guide dog สุนัขนำทาง *sùh•nàhk nahm tarng*

guided tour ทัวร์นำเที่ยว *toar nahm•têaw*

guided walk ทัวร์เดิน นำเที่ยว *toar dern nahm•têaw*

guitar กีตาร์ *gee•dtâr*

gym โรงยิม *roeng•yihm*

gynecologist สูติ นรีแพทย์ *sǒo•dtìh•nah•ree•pâet*

H

hair ผม *pǒm*

hairbrush แปรง แปรงผม *bpraeng bpraeng•pǒm*

hairdresser ช่างทำผม *chârng tahm•pǒm*

halal ฮาลาล *har•larn*

half ครึ่ง *krǔeng*

hammer ฆ้อน *kórn*

hand มือ *muee*

hand luggage กระเป๋า ถือ *grah•bpǒu tǔee*

handbag [BE] กระเป๋า ถือ *grah•bpǒu tǔee*

handicapped adj พิการ *píh•garn*; n (person) คนพิการ *kon píh•garn*

handicrafts หัตถกรรม *hàht•tah•gahm*

hanger ไม้แขวนเสื้อ *mi•kwǎen•sûea*

happy มีความสุข *mee kwarm•sùhk*

harbor ท่าเรือ *târ•ruea*

hard แข็ง *kǎng*

hardware store ร้าน ขายเครื่องมืออุปกรณ์ *rárn kie krûeang•muee úhp•bprah•gorn*

hat หมวก *mòark*

have มี *mee*

hay fever โรคแพ้อากาศ *rôek páe•ar•gàrt*

head หัว *hǒar*

headache ปวดหัว *bpòart•hǒar*

health สุขภาพ *sùhk•kah•pârp*

health food store ร้าน ขายอาหารสุขภาพ *rárn kie ar•hǎrn sùhk•kah•pârp*

health insurance ประกัน สุขภาพ *bprah•gahn sùhk•kah•pârp*

hear ได้ยิน *dî•yin*

hearing aid เครื่อง ช่วยฟัง *krûeang•chôary•fahng*

hearing impaired พิการทางหู *píh•garn tarng•hǒo*

heart หัวใจ *hǒa•ji*

heart attack หัวใจวาย *hǒa•ji wary*

heart condition โรค หัวใจ *rôek hǒa•ji*

heat ความร้อน *kwarm•rárn*

heavy หนัก *nàhk*

heel ส้น *sôn*

height (person) ความ สูง *kwarm•sǒong*

hello สวัสดี *sah•wàht•dee*; (phone) ฮัลโหล *hahn•lǒe*

helmet หมวกนิรภัย *mòark níh•ráh•pi*

help n ความช่วยเหลือ *kwarm chôary•lǔea*; v ช่วย *chôary*; (request) ช่วยด้วย *chôary•dôary*

here ที่นี่ *têe•nêe*

high สูง *sǒong*

highchair เก้าอี้เด็ก *gôu•êe dèhk*

highway ทางหลวง *tarng•lǒarng*

hike เดินป่า *dern•bpàr*

hill เนินเขา *nern•kǒu*

hire เช่า *chôu*

hold ถือ *tǔee*

hole รู *roo*

holiday [BE] วันหยุด *wan yùht*

home บ้าน *bârn*

homemade ทำเอง *tahm•eng*

honeymoon ฮันนีมูน *hahn•nee•moon*

horn (car) แตร *dtrae*

horse ม้า *már*

horse racing แข่งม้า *kàeng•már*

horseback riding ขี่ม้า *kèe•már*

horsetrack ลู่แข่งวิ่ง *lôo*

már *wíhng*

hospital โรงพยาบาล *roeng pah•yar•barn*

hot adj ร้อน *rórn*; (spicy) เผ็ด *pèht*

hotel โรงแรม *roeng•raem*

hour ชั่วโมง *chôar•moeng*

house บ้าน *bârn*

how ยังไง *yahng•ngi*

how many *tôu•ri*

how much เท่าไหร่ *tôu•ri*

hug กอด *gòrt*

hungry หิว *hǐhw*

hunt ล่า *lâr*

hurry รีบ *rêep*

hurt เจ็บ *jèhp*

I

ibuprofen อีบูโปรเฟน *ee•boo•bproe•fen*

identification บัตร ประจำตัว *bàtr bprah•jahm•dtoar*

ill [BE] ไม่สบาย *mî sah•bare*

illegal ผิดกฎหมาย *piht gòt•mǐe*

imitation (fake) ของ เลียนแบบ *kǒrng lean•bàep*

important สำคัญ *sǎhm•kahn*

improve ปรับปรุง *bpràhp•bpruhng*

in ใน *ni*

include รวม *roarm*

indigestion อาหารไม่ ย่อย *ar•hǎrn mî yôhy*

indoor pool สระว่ายน้ำ ในร่ม *sàh wîe•nárm ni•rôhm*

inexpensive ไม่แพง *mî paeng*

infection การติดเชื้อ
garn dtiht•chúea

inflammation อาการ
อักเสบ ar•garn
àhk•sèp

informal ไม่เป็นทางการ
mî bpehn tarng•garn

information ข้อมูล
kôr•moon

information desk
ประชาสัมพันธ์
bprah•char•
sǎhm•pahn

injection ฉีดยา
chèet yar

injure บาดเจ็บ bàrt•jèhp

innocent บริสุทธิ์
bor•rih•sùht

insect แมลง mah•laeng

insect bite แมลงกัด
ต่อย mah•laeng gàht
dtóhy

insect repellent ยา
กันแมลง yar gahn
mah•laeng

insert แทรก sâek

inside ข้างใน kârng•ni

insist ยืนกราน
yueen•grarn

insomnia นอนไม่หลับ
norn•mî•làhp

instant messenger
โปรแกรมส่งข้อความ
bproe•graem sòng
kôr•kwarm

instead แทนที่ taen•têe

instructions คำสั่ง
kahm•sàhng

instructor ผู้สอน
pôo•sǒrn

insulin อินซูลิน
ihn•soo•lihn

insurance ประกันภัย
bprah•gahn•pi

interest (hobby) ความ
สนใจ kwarm sǒn•ji

international ระหว่าง

ประเทศ rah•wàrng
bprah•têt

**International
Student Card** บัตร
นักศึกษาสากล bàht
náhk•sùek•sǎr sǎr•gon

internet อินเตอร์เน็ต
ihn•dter•nèht

internet cafe
อินเตอร์เน็ต
คาเฟ่ ihn•dter•nèht
kar•fâe

internet service
บริการอินเตอร์เน็ต
bor•rih•garn
ihn•dter•nèht

interpreter ล่าม lârm

intersection สี่แยก
sèe•yâek

introduce แนะนำ
ná•nahm

invite เชิญ chern

iron n เตารีด dtou•rêet;
v รีด rêet

itch คัน kahn

itemized แยกตาม
รายการ yâek dtarm
rie•garn

J

jacket เสื้อแจ็กเก็ต
sûea ják•gèht

jar ขวด kòart

jaw ขากรรไกร kâr
gahn•gri

jazz แจส jáet

jeans ยีนส์ yeen

jet lag เจ็ทแล็ก jéht•làk

jet-ski เจ็ทสกี jéht
sah•gee

jeweler ร้านขายเครื่อง
ประดับ rárn kǐe krûeang
bprah•dàhp

jewelry เครื่องประดับ
krûeang bprah•dàhp

job งาน ngarn

join ต่อ dtòr

joke เรื่องตลก rûeang

dtah•lòk

journey การเดินทาง
garn dern•tarng

K

keep เก็บ gèhp

keep out ห้ามเข้า
hârm kôu

key กุญแจ guhn•jae

key cord สี่กุญแจ ...

key ring พวงกุญแจ
poarng guhn•jae

kiddie pool สระเด็ก
sàh dèhk

kidney ไต dti

kilogram กิโลกรัม
gih•loe grahm

kilometer กิโลเมตร
gih•loe mét

kind adj ใจดี ji•dee;
(type) ประเภท
bprah•pêt

kiss จูบ jòop

kitchen ห้องครัว
hôhng•kroar

kitchen foil [BE]
กระดาษฟอยล์
gràh•dàrt fory

knee เข่า kòu

knife มีด mêet

knock เคาะ kóh

know รู้จัก róo•jàhk

kosher โคเชอร์
koe•chêr

L

label ป้าย bpîe

lace ผ้าลูกไม้ pâr
lôok•mie

lactose intolerant กิน
นมไม่ได้ gihn nohm
mî dîe

ladder บันได bahn•di

lake ทะเลสาบ
tah•le•sàrp

lamp โคมไฟ koem•fi

land ที่ดิน têe•dihn

lane เลน len

large ใหญ่ yi

last (previous) ที่
แล้ว têe•láew; **(final)**
สุดท้าย sùht•tíe

late สาย sǐe

launderette [BE] ร้าน
ซักรีด rárn sáhk•rêet

laundromat ร้านซักรีด
ร้าน ... ...

laundry service บริการ
ซักรีด bor•rih•garn
sáhk•rêet

lawyer หมายความ
tah•nie•kwarm

laxative ยาระบาย yar
rah•bie

lead นำ nahm

leader (group) ผู้นำ
pôo•nahm

learn เรียน rean

leather หนัง nǎhng

leave v ออกจาก
òrk•jàrk; **(deposit)**
ฝากไว้ fàrk•wí

left ซ้าย síe

**left-luggage office
[BE]** แผนก
สัมภาระ pàh•nàek
sǎhm•par•ráh

leg ขา kǎr

legal ถูกกฎหมาย tòok
gòt•mie

lend ให้ยืม hî•yueem

length ความยาว
kwarm•yarw

lens เลนส์ lehn

less น้อยกว่า nóry gwàr

lesson บทเรียน
bòt•rean

let ปล่อย bplòhy

letter จดหมาย jòt•mǐe

level ระดับ rah•dàhp

library ห้องสมุด hôhng
sah•mùht

life ชีวิต chee•wíht

life boat เรือชูชีพ *ruea choo•cheep*

lifeguard ยามไลฟ์การ์ด *yarm li•gàrt*

lifejacket เสื้อชูชีพ *sûea choo•cheep*

lift [BE] ลิฟต์ *lihp*

light adj **(weight)** เบา *bou;* **(color)** อ่อน *òrn; v* จุดไฟ *jùht fi; n* ไฟ *fi*

lightbulb หลอดไฟ *lòrt•fi*

lighter ไฟแช็ก *h•chàhk*

lighthouse ประภาคาร *bprah•par•karn*

like v (same) เหมือนกับ *mǔean•gàhp;* **(want)** อยากได้ *yàrk•dâi;* **(please)** ชอบ *chôrp*

line เส้น *sêhn*

linen ลินิน *lih•nihn*

lip ริมฝีปาก *rihm•fěe•bpàrk*

lipstick ลิปสติก *lihp•sah•dtihk*

liquor store ร้านขายเหล้า *rárn kǐe lôu*

liter ลิตร *liht*

little น้อย *nóry*

live v อยู่ *yòo;* **(performance)** adj สด *sòht*

lobby (theater, hotel) ล็อบบี้ *lóhp•bêe*

local ท้องถิ่น *tórng•tihn*

lock ล็อก *lóhk*

log off ออกจากระบบ *òrk•jàrk rah•bòp*

log on เข้าระบบ *kôu rah•bòp*

long ยาว *yow*

long-distance bus รถ บัสทางไกล *rót bâht tarng gli*

look ดู *doo*

loose หลวม *lǒarm*

lorry [BE] รถบรรทุก *rót bahn•túhk*

lose หาย *hǐe*

lost หลงทาง *lǒng•tarng*

lost and found office แผนกของหาย *pah•nàek kǒrng•hǐe*

lost-property office [BE] แผนกของหาย *pah•nàek kǒrng•hǐe*

lottery ล็อตเตอรี่ *lóht•dter•rêe*

loud ดัง *dahng*

love รัก *ráhk*

low ต่ำ *dtàhm*

luggage กระเป๋า *grah•bpǒu*

luggage cart รถเข็น กระเป๋า *rót kěhn grah•bpǒu*

luggage trolley [BE] รถเข็นกระเป๋า *rót kěhn grah•bpǒu*

lunch อาหารกลางวัน *ar•hǎrn glarng•wahn*

lung ปอด *bpòrt*

M

magazine นิตยสาร *niht•tah•yah•sǎrn*

mail v จดหมาย *jòt•mǐe; v* ส่งจดหมาย *sòng jòt•mǐe*

mailbox ตู้จดหมาย *dtôo jòt•mǐe*

main สำคัญ *sǎhm•kahn*

make-up v แต่งหน้า *dtàeng•nâr*

male เพศชาย *pêt•chie*

mall ศูนย์การค้า *sǒon garn•kár*

man ผู้ชาย *pôo•chie*

manager ผู้จัดการ *pôo•jàht•garn*

mandatory บังคับ *bahng•káhp*

manicure ทำเล็บมือ *tahm léhp•muee*

many หลาย *lǐe*

map แผนที่ *pǎen•têe*

market ตลาด *dtah•làrt*

marry แต่งงาน *dtàeng•ngarn*

mask หน้ากาก *nâr•gàrk*

mass (church) มิสซา *míht•sar*

massage นวด *nôart*

matches ไม้ขีด *mí•kèet*

matinée รอบกลางวัน *rôrp glarng•wahn*

mattress ที่นอน *têe•norn*

maybe อาจจะ *àrt•jah*

meal อาหาร *ar•hǎrn*

measure วัดขนาด *wáht kah•nàrt*

measurement การวัด *garn wáht*

mechanic ช่าง *chârng*

medication การใช้ยา *garn chi ya*

medicine ยา *yar*

medium ขนาดกลาง *kah•nàrt glarng*

meet พบ *póp*

meeting การประชุม *garn bprah•chuhm*

meeting room ห้อง ประชุม *hôhng bprah•chuhm*

member สมาชิก *sah•mar•chihk*

memorial อนุสาวรีย์ *ah•núh•sǎ•wah•ree*

memory card เมมโมรี่ การ์ด *mem•moe•rêe gárt*

mend (clothes) ชุน *chuhn*

menstrual cramps ปวดประจำเดือน *bpòart bprah•jahm•duean*

menu เมนู *may•noo*

merge รวม *roarm*

message ข้อความ *kôr•kwarm*

metal โลหะ *loe•hàh*

microwave (oven) (เตา)ไมโครเวฟ *[dtou] mi•kroe•wép*

midday [BE] เที่ยง *têang*

midnight เที่ยงคืน *têang•kueen*

migraine ไมเกรน *mi•gren*

mini-bar มินิบาร์ *míh•níh•bar*

minute นาที *nar•tee*

mirror กระจกเงา *grah•jòk ngou*

missing หาย *hǐe*

mistake ผิดพลาด *piht•plârt*

mobile phone [BE] โทรศัพท์มือ ถือ *toe•rah•sàhp muee•tǔee*

money เงิน *ngern*

money order ธนาณัติ *tah•nar•náht*

monsoon มรสุม *mor•rah•sǔhm*

month เดือน *duean*

mop ไม้ถูพื้น *mie tǒo•púeen*

moped จักรยาน มอเตอร์ไซค์ *jàhk•grah•yarn mor•dter•sì*

more มากกว่า *mârk•gwàr*

morning ตอนเช้า *dtorn•chóu*

mosque สุเหร่า *sùh•ròu*

mosquito bite ยุงกัด *yuhng•gàht*

motion sickness เมา รถ *mou rót*

motor เครื่องยนต์ *krûeang•yon*

motorboat เรือยนต์ *ruea yon*

motorcycle มอเตอร์ไซค์
mor•dter•si

motorway [BE] ทางด่วน *tarng•dòarn*

mountain ภูเขา
poo•kŏu

mouth ปาก *bpàrk*

move ขยับ *kah•yàhp*

movie หนัง *năhng*

movie theater โรงหนัง
roeng•năhng

Mr. นาย *nie*

Mrs. นาง *narng*

much มาก *mârk*

mugging จี้ *jée*

muscle กล้ามเนื้อ
glârm•néua

museum พิพิธภัณฑ์
pih•piht•tah•pahn

music ดนตรี *don•dtree*

must ต้อง *dtôhng*

N

nail เล็บ *léhp*

nail file ตะไบขัดเล็บ
dtah•bi kàht léhp

nail salon ร้านทำเล็บ
rárn tahm•léhp

name ชื่อ *chûee*

napkin กระดาษเช็ดปาก
grah•dàrt chéht bpàrk

nappy [BE] ผ้าอ้อม
pâr•ôrm

nationality สัญชาติ
săn•chârt

native พื้นเมือง
púeen•mueang

nature ธรรมชาติ
tahm•mah•chârt

nature trail ทางเดินชม
ธรรมชาติ *tarng•dern
chom tahm•mah•chârt*

nausea คลื่นไส้ *klúecn sî*

near ใกล้ *glî*

nearby ใกล้ๆ *glî•glî*

necessary จำเป็น

neck คอ *kor*

necklace สร้อยคอ
sôry•kor

need ต้องการ
dtôhng•garn

network เครือข่าย
kruea•kìe

never ไม่เคย *mî•kery*

new ใหม่ *mì*

news ข่าว *kìw*

newspaper
หนังสือพิมพ์
năhng•sŭee•pihm

newsstand แผงขาย
หนังสือพิมพ์ *păeng kĭe
năhng•sŭee•pihm*

next ถัดไป *tàht•bpi*

next to ติดกับ
dtiht•gàhp

nice ดี *dee*

night กลางคืน
glarng•kueen

night club ไนท์คลับ
ní•kláhp

no ไม่ *mî*

noisy เสียงดัง
sĕang•dang

non-smoking ห้าม
สูบบุหรี่ *hârm
sòop•buh•rèe*

non-stop (flight) เที่ยว
บินตรง *tîaw•bihn
trong*

noon เที่ยง *têang*

normal ธรรมดา
tahm•mah•dar

north เหนือ *nŭea*

nose จมูก *jah•mòok*

not ไม่ *mî*

nothing ไม่มีอะไร *mî
mee ah•ri*

notify แจ้ง *jâeng*

now ตอนนี้ *dtorn•née*

number เบอร์ *ber*

nurse พยาบาล
pah•yar•barn

O

office ที่ทำงาน *têe
tahm•ngarn*

off-peak (ticket) ช่วง
ออฟพีค *chôarng
órp•péek*

often บ่อย *bòhy*

OK โอเค *oe•ke*

old เก่า *gòu*

on บน *bon*

one-way ticket เที่ยว
เดียว *tîaw•deaw*

only เท่านั้น *tôu•náhn*

open เปิด *bpèrt*

opening hours เวลา
ทำการ *we•lar
tahm•garn*

opera โอเปร่า
oo•bpe•râr

operation ผ่าตัด
pàr•dtàht

opposite ตรงข้าม
dtrong•kârm

optician ช่างตัดแว่น
chârng dtàht•wäen

or หรือ *rŭee*

orchestra วงออเคสตร้า
wong or•kés•trâr

order สั่ง *sàhng*

organize จัดระบบ *jàht
rah•bòp*

original ตั้งเดิม
dâhng•derm

out ออก *òrk*

outdoor กลางแจ้ง
glarng•jâeng

outdoor pool สระกลาง
แจ้ง *sàh glarng•jâeng*

outside ข้างนอก
kârng•nôrk

oven เตาอบ *dtou•òp*

over (more than)
มากกว่า *mârk•gwàr*

overcharge คิดเงินเกิน
kiht•ngern gern

overlook จุดชมวิว *jùht
chom wihw*

overnight ข้ามคืน
kârm•kueen

owe เป็นหนี้ *bpehn nêe*

own เป็นเจ้าของ *bpehn
jôu•kŏrng*

owner เจ้าของ
jôu•kŏrng

oxygen ออกซิเจน
ôhk•sih•jêhn

P

pacifier จุกนม
jùhk•nom

pack ห่อ *hòr*

package พัสดุ
páht•sah•dùh

paddling pool [BE] สระ
เด็ก *sàh dèhk*

padlock กุญแจคล้อง
guhn•jae klórng

pail ถัง *tăhng*

pain เจ็บ *jèhp;* (muscle) ปวด *bpòart*

painting (picture) ภาพ
วาด *pârp•wârt*

pair คู่ *kôo*

pajamas ชุดนอน
chúht•norn

palace วัง *wahng*

panorama ภาพ
พาโนรามา *pârp
par•noe•rar•mâr*

pants กางเกงขายาว
garng•geng kăr•yow

panty hose ถุงน่อง
tŭhng•nôhng

paper towel กระดาษ
เช็ดมือ *grah•dàrt
chéht•muee*

paracetamol [BE]
พาราเซตตามอล
*par•rar•séht•
dtar•môhn*

parcel [BE] พัสดุ
páht•sah•dùh

park ก สวนสาธารณะ
sŏarn săr•tar•rah•náh;
v จอดรถ *jòrt•rót*

parking garage อาคาร จอดรถ ar•karn jòrt•rót

parking lot ที่จอดรถ têe jòrt•rót

partner หุ้นส่วน hûhn•sòarn

party งานปาร์ตี้ ngarn bpar•dtêe

passport หนังสือเดินทาง nǎhng•sǔee dern•tarng

password รหัส rah•hàht

passport หนังสือ เดินทาง

pavement [BE] ทางเท้า tarng•tów

pay จ่าย jìe

pay phone โทรศัพท์ สาธารณะ toe•rah•sàhp sǎr•tar•rah•náh

payment การจ่ายเงิน garn jìe•ngern

pedestrian คนเดินถนน kon dern tah•nǒn

pediatrician หมอเด็ก mǒr•dèhk

pedicure ทำเล็บเท้า tahm lée•tów

pen ปากกา bpàrk•gar

penicillin เพนิซิลลิน pe•níh•sih•lihn

per ต่อ dtòr

performance การแสดง garn sah•daeng

perhaps บางที้ barng•tee

period (menstrua-tion) ประจำเดือน bprah•jahm•duean

person คน kon

petrol [BE] เบนซิน ben•sihn

petrol station [BE] ปั๊มน้ำมัน bpáhm náhm•mahn

pharmacy ร้านขายยา rárn kǐe yar

phone โทรศัพท์ toe•rah•sàhp

phone call โทรศัพท์ toe•rah•sàhp

phone card บัตร โทรศัพท์ bàht toe•rah•sàhp

phone directory สมุด โทรศัพท์ sah•mùht toe•rah•sàhp

phone number เบอร์ โทรศัพท์ ber lee rah sàhp

photocopy ถ่ายเอกสาร tìe èk•gah•sǎrn

photograph รูป rôop

phrase วลี wáh•lee

pick up รับ ráhp

picnic ปิคนิค bpíhk•níhk

picnic area ที่ปิคนิค têe bpíhk•níhk

piece ชิ้น chíhn

pill ยา yar

pillow หมอน mǒrn

PIN รหัสพิน rah•hàht pihn

place สถานที่ sah•tǎrn•têe

plan แผน pǎen

plane เครื่องบิน krûeang•bihn

plaster [BE] เฝือก fúeak

plastic พลาสติก plárt•sah•dtihk

plastic wrap ฟิล์ม ถนอมอาหาร feem tah•nǒrm•ar•hǎrn

plate จาน jarn

platform ชานชาลา charn•char•lar

play v เล่น lêhn; **(theater)** ละคร lah•korn

playground สนาม เด็กเล่น sah•nǎrm

dèhk lêhn

playpen คอกเด็กเล่น kòrk dèhk lêhn

please กรุณา gah•rúh•nar

plug ปลั๊กไฟ bpláhk•fi

plunger ที่ดูดส้วม tée dòot sôarm

pneumonia ปอดบวม bpòrt•boarm

poison ยาพิษ yar•píht

police ตำรวจ dtahm•ròat

police report ใบแจ้ง ความ bi•jǎeng•kwarm

police station สถานี ตำรวจ sah•tǎr•nee dtahm•ròat

pond บ่อน้ำ bòr•nárm

pool สระว่ายน้ำ sàh wìe•nárm

popular เป็นที่นิยม bpehn•têe níh•yom

port ท่าเรือ târ•ruea

porter คนยกกระเป๋า kon yók grah•bpǒu

portion ขนาด kah•nàrt

post [BE] v ส่งจดหมาย sòng jòt•mǐe; n จดหมาย jòt•mǐe

post office ที่ทำการ ไปรษณีย์ têe tahm•garn bpri•sah•nee

postage ค่าแสตมป์ kâr sah•dtaem

postbox [BE] ตู้จดหมาย dtôo jòt•mǐe

postcard โปสการ์ด bpòet•sah•gàrt

pot หม้อ môr

pottery เครื่องปั้นดินเผา krûeang•bpâhn dihn•pǒu

pound (weight) ปอนด์ bporn

pound sterling เงิน

dèhk lêhn

ปอนด์ ngern•bporn

practice ฝึก fùek

pregnant ท้อง tórng

prepaid phone card บัตรโทรศัพท์ แบบเติม เงิน bàht toe•rah•sàhp bàep dterm•ngern

prescription ใบสั่งยา bi sàhng•yar

present (time) ปัจจุบัน bpàht•jùh•bahn; n ของ ขวัญ kǒrng•kwǎhn

price ราคา rar•kar

print ปริ้นท์ prihn

prison คุก kúhk

private ส่วนตัว sòarn•dtoar

problem ปัญหา bpahn•hǎr

produce store ร้านขาย ผักผลไม้ rárn kǐe pàhk pǒn•lah•mí

profession อาชีพ ar•chêep

program โปรแกรม bproe•graem

prohibited ห้าม hârm

pronounce ออกเสียง òrk•sěang

public สาธารณะ sǎr•tar•rah•náh

pull ดึง dueng

pump ปั๊ม bpáhm

pure แท้ táe

purpose วัตถุประสงค์ wáht•tùh•bprah•sǒng

purse กระเป๋าสตางค์ grah•bpǒu sah•tarng

push ผลัก plàhk

push-chair [BE] รถเข็น เด็ก rót•kěhn dèhk

put ใส่ sì

Q

quality คุณภาพ kuhn•nah•pârp

queue [BE] v เข้าคิว
kôw•kihw; n คิว kihw

quick เร็ว rehw

quiet เงียบ ngêap

R

racetrack ลู่แข่ง
lôo•kàeng

racket (tennis) ไม้
chúea•tûee die
แบดมินตัน mí tennghit

railway station
[BE] สถานีรถไฟ
sah•tăr•nee rót•fi

rain ฝนตก fŏn dtòk

raincoat เสื้อกันฝน
sûea gahn fŏn

rape ข่มขืน kòm•kũeen

rapids แก่ง gàeng

rash เป็นผื่น bpehn
pùeen

razor มีดโกน mêet•goen

razor blade ใบมีดโกน
bi mêet•goen

reach เอื้อม ûeam

reaction ปฏิกิริยา
bpah•dtih•gih•rih•yar

read อ่าน àrn

ready พร้อม prórm

real (genuine) แท้ táe

receipt ใบเสร็จ bi•sèht

receive ได้รับ dî•ráhp

reception (desk) แผนก
ต้อนรับ pah•năek
dtôrn•ráhp

receptionist
พนักงานต้อนรับ
pah•náhk•ngarn
dtôrn•ráhp

recommend แนะนำ
ná•nahm

reduce ลด lót

reduction ส่วนลด
sùan•lót

refrigerator ตู้เย็น
dtôo•yehn

refund v คืนเงิน
kueen•ngern; n เงินคืน

ngern•kueen

region เขต kèt

regular ธรรมดา
tahm•mah•dar

relationship ความ
สัมพันธ์ kwarm
săhm•pahn

reliable เชื่อถือได้
chûea•tŭee die

religion ศาสนา
sàrt•sà•năr

remember จำได้
jahm•dîe

remove เอาออก ou•òrk

renovation ปรับปรุง
ใหม่ bpràhp•bpruhng mi

rent เช่า chôu

rental car รถเช่า
rót•chôu

repair ซ่อม sôhm

repeat ซ้ำอีกที sáhm
êek•tee

replace แทนที่ taen•têe

report แจ้งความ
jàeng•kwarm

reservation การจอง
garn•jorng

reservation desk
แผนกรับจอง pah•năek
ráhp•jorng

reserve จอง jorng

reservoir อ่างเก็บน้ำ
àrng•gèhp nárm

responsibility ความ
รับผิดชอบ kwarm
ráhp•piht•chôhp

rest v พัก páhk

rest area ที่พักริมทาง
têe•páhk rihm tarng

restaurant ร้านอาหาร
rárn ar•hărn

restroom ห้องน้ำ
hôhng•nárm

retired เกษียณ
gah•sĕan

return (come back)
กลับ gláhp; (give

back) คืน kueen

return ticket [BE] ตั๋ว
ขากลับ dtŏar kăr•gláhp

right (correct) ถูก
tòok; (direction)
ขวา kwăr

ring v กดกระดิ่ง gòt
grah•dihng; (jewelry)
n แหวน wăen

river แม่น้ำ mâe•nárm

road ถนน tà•nŏn

robbery การปล้น karn
bplôn

romantic โรแมนติก
roe•maen•dtihk

roof หลังคา lăhng•kar

room ห้อง hôhng

room service รูม
เซอร์วิส room•ser•wiht

rope เชือก chûeak

round adj กลม glom; n
(golf) รอบ rôrp

round-trip ticket ตั๋วไป
กลับ dtŏar bpi•gláhp

route เส้นทาง sên•tarng

row v พาย pie; n แถว
tăew

rowboat เรือพาย
ruca•pie

rubbish [BE] n ขยะ
kah•yàh

rude หยาบคาย yàrp•kie

rush เร่ง rêng

S

safe n ตู้เซฟ dtôo•sèf;
adj ปลอดภัย bplòrt•pi

safety ความปลอดภัย
kwarm bplòrt•pi

safety pin เข็มกลัด
kĕhm•gláht

sale [BE] ลดราคา lót
rar•kar

sales tax ภาษีมูลค่า
เพิ่ม par•sĕe moon•kâr
pêrm

same แบบเดียวกัน

bàep•deaw•gahn

sand ทราย sie

sandals รองเท้าแตะ
rorng•tów dtà

sanitary napkin ผ้า
อนามัย pâr ah•nar•mai

sanitary pad [BE] ผ้า
อนามัย pâr ah•nar•mai

sauna ซาวน่า soww•nâr

save เก็บรักษา gèhp
ráhk•săi

savings account บัญชี
ออมทรัพย์ bahn•chee
orm•sáhp

say พูด pôot

scale ตาชั่ง dtar•châhng

scarf ผ้าพันคอ pâr
pahn kor

schedule ตาราง
dtar•rarng

scissors กรรไกร
gahn•gri

screwdriver ไขควง
kĭ•koarng

sea ทะเล tah•le

seafront ติดทะเล dtiht
tah•le

seasickness เมาเรือ
mou ruea

seat (on train, etc.) ที่
นั่ง têe nâhng

seat belt เข็มขัดนิรภัย
kĕhm•kàht nih•ráh•pi

sedative ยาระงับ
ประสาท yar rah•ngáhp
bprah•sàrt

see เห็น hĕhn

self-service บริการ
ตนเอง bor•rih•garn
dton•eng

sell ขาย kĭe

seminar สัมมนา
săhm•mah•nar

send ส่ง sòng

senior citizen ผู้สูงอายุ
pôo sŏong ar•yúh

separate แยก yâek

separated แยกกันอยู่
yâek gahn yòo
serious จริงจัง
jihng•jahng
serve เสิร์ฟ sèịp
service (work) บริการ
bor•rih•garn;
(church) สวดมนต์
sòart•mon
service charge ค่า
บริการ kâr
bor•rih•garn
service included รวม
ค่าบริการ roarm kâr
bor•rih•garn
set menu อาหารชุด
ar•hǎrn chúht
sew เย็บ yéhp
sex (gender) เพศ pêt;
(activity) เซ็กซ์ séhk
shadow เงา ngou
shallow ตื้น dtûeen
shampoo แชมพู
chaem•poo
shape รูปร่าง rôop•rârng
sharp คม kom
shave โกนหนวด
goen•nòart
shaving cream ครีม
โกนหนวด kreem
goen•nòart
sheet (bed) ผ้าปูที่นอน
pâr bpoo têe•norn
ship เรือ ruea
shock ช็อก chóhk
shoe รองเท้า rorng•tów
shoe repair ซ่อม
รองเทา sôhm
rorng•tów
shoe store ร้านขาย
รองเท้า rárn kǐe
rorng•tów
shop assistant
พนักงานขาย
pah•nákk•ngarn kǐe
shopping ช็อปปิ้ง
chóhp•bpîhng

shopping area ย่าน
ช็อปปิ้ง yârn
chóhp•bpîhng
shopping basket
ตะกร้าช็อป
ปิ้ง dtah•grár
chóhp•bpîhng
shopping cart รถเข็น
rót•kěhn
**shopping centre
[BE]** ศูนย์การค้า
sǒon•garn•kár
shopping mall
ศูนย์การค้า
sǒon•garn•kár
shopping trolley [BE]
รถเข็น rót•kěhn
short สั้น sâhn
shorts กางเกงขาสั้น
garng•geng kǎr•sân
shoulder ไหล่ li
show n การแสดง garn
sah•daeng; v แสดง
sah•daeng
shower v อาบน้ำ
àrp•nárm; n ห้องอาบ
น้ำ hôhng àrp•nárm
shut ปิด bpiht
sick ไม่สบาย mî sah•bie
side effect ผลข้างเคียง
pǒn kârng•keang
sidewalk ทางเท้า
tarng•tów
**sight (attrac-
tion)** สถานที่ท่อง
เที่ยว sàh•tǎrn•têe
tôhng•têaw
sightseeing tour ทัวร์
ชมเมือง toar chom
mueang
sign n ป้าย bpîe; v ชื่อ
ชื่อ sehn•chûee
single (marital status)
เป็นโสด bpehn•sòet
single room ห้องเดี่ยว
hôhng•dèaw
sink อ่าง àrng

sit นั่ง nâhng
site สถานที่
sàh•tǎrn•têe
size ขนาด kah•nàrt
skin ผิวหนัง pǐhw•nǎhng
skirt กระโปรง
grah•bproeng
sleep นอน norn
sleeping bag ถุงนอน
tǔhng•norn
sleeping car ตู้นอน
dtôo•norn
sleeping pill ยานอน
หลับ yar norn•làhp
sleeve แขนเสื้อ kǎen
sûea
slice v ฝาน fǎrn; n
ชิ้น chíhn
slippers รองเท้าแตะ
rorng•tów dtà
slow ช้า chár
small เล็ก léhk
smell n กลิ่น glìhn; v
ได้กลิ่น dî•glìhn
smoke สูบบุหรี่
sòop•bùh•rèe
smoking area บริเวณ
สูบบุหรี่ bor•rih•wen
sòop•bùh•rèe
snack อาหารว่าง
ar•hǎrn wârng
snack bar สแน็คบาร์
sah•nák bar
sneakers รองเท้าผ้าใบ
rorng•tów pâr•bi
snorkel สนอกเกิล
sah•nórk•gêrn
snow หิมะ hìh•máh
soap สบู่ sah•bòo
soccer ฟุตบอล
fúht•bohn
sock ถุงเท้า tǔhng•tów
sold out ขายหมด
kǐe mòt
some บาง barng
someone บางคน
barng kon

something บางอย่าง
barng yàrng
sometimes บางครั้ง
barng kráhng
somewhere บางที่
barng têe
soon ในไม่ช้า
ni•mî•chár
soother [BE] จุกนม
jùhk•nom
sore ปวด bpòart
sore throat เจ็บคอ
jehp•kor
sorry ขอโทษ kǒr•tôet
sour เปรี้ยว bprêaw
south ทิศใต้ tíht dtîe
souvenir ของที่ระลึก
kǒrng•têe•rah•lúek
souvenir store ร้าน
ขายของที่ระลึก rárn kǐe
kǒrng•têe•rah•lúehk
spa สปา sàh•bpar
space ที่ว่าง têe•wârng
spare สำรอง
sǎhm•rorng
spatula ตะหลิว
dtah•lǐhw
speak พูด pôot
special พิเศษ pih•sèt
specialist (doctor)
หมอเฉพาะทาง mǒr
chah•póh•tarng
spell สะกด sah•gòt
spend (money) ใช้จ่าย
chí•jie
sponge ฟองน้ำ
forng•nárm
spoon ช้อน chórn
sport กีฬา gee•lar
**sporting goods
store** ร้านขาย
เครื่อง กีฬา rárn kǐe
krûeang•gee•lar
sports club สปอร์ตคลับ
sah•bpòrt kláhp
spot (place, site)
จุด jùht

spouse คู่สมรส *kôo sŏm•rót*

sprain แพลง *plaeng*

stadium สนามกีฬา *sah•nàrm gee•lar*

staff พนักงาน *pah•nák•ngarn*

stair บันได *bahn•di*

stamp แสตมป์ *sà•dtaem*

stand ยืน *yuuen*

standard มาตรฐาน *mârt•dtah•tărn*

standby ticket ตั๋วสำรอง *dtŏar sǎhm•rorng*

start เริ่ม *rêrm*

statue รูปปั้น *rôop•bpân*

stay อยู่ *yòo*

steal ขโมย *kah•moey*

steep ชัน *chahn*

stiff (muscle) เมื่อย *mûeay*

stolen ถูกขโมย *tòok kah•moey*

stomach ท้อง *tórng*

stomachache ปวดท้อง *bpòart•tórng*

stop v จอด *jòrt*; (bus) n ป้ายรถเมล์ *bpîe rót•me*

store ร้านค้า *rárn•kár*

store directory [BE] รายการสินค้า *rie•garn rárn•kár*

store guide รายการสินค้า *rie•garn rárn•kár*

stove เตา *dtou*

straight (ahead) ตรง ไป *dtrong bpi*

stream ลำธาร *lahm•tarn*

street ถนน *tah•nŏn*

stroller รถเข็นเด็ก *rót•kĕhn dèhk*

strong แข็งแรง *kǎeng•raeng*

student นักศึกษา *náhk sùek•săr*

study ศึกษา *sùek•săr*

style สไตล์ *sah•tie*

subtitled มีซับไตเติล *mee sáhp•dti•dtern*

subway รถไฟใต้ดิน *rót•fi tí•dihn*

subway map แผนที่ รถไฟใต้ดิน *păn•tîe rót•fi tái•dihn*

subway station สถานีรถไฟใต้ดิน *sah•tăr•nee rót•fi tie•dihn*

suggest แนะนำ *ná•nahm*

suit ชุดสูท *chúht•sòot*

suitable เหมาะสม *mòh•sŏm*

suitcase กระเป๋า เดินทาง *grah•bpŏu dern•tarng*

sun (light) แดด *dàet*

sunbathe อาบแดด *àrp•dàet*

sunblock ครีมกันแดด *kreem gahn•dàet*

sunburn แดดเผา *dàet pŏu*

sunglasses แว่น กันแดด *wâen•gahn•dàet*

sunscreen ครีมกันแดด *kreem gahn•dàet*

sunstroke ลมแดด *lom•dàet*

suntan lotion โลชั่น อาบแดด *loe•châhn àrp•dàet*

superb เยี่ยมมาก *yêam•mârk*

supermarket ซุปเปอร์มาร์เก็ต *súhp•bpêr•mar•gèht*

supervision การดูแล *garn doo•lae*

supplement v เสริม *sěrm*

suppository ยาเหน็บ *yar nèhp*

sure แน่นอน *nâe•norn*

surfboard กระดานโต้คลื่น *grah•darn dtôe•klùuen*

swallow กลืน *glueen*

swamp ที่ลุ่มน้ำ *tîe lôom nárm*

sweatshirt เสื้อ สเวตเชิร์ต *sûea sah•wéht•chèrt*

sweep กวาด *gwàrt*

sweet adj หวาน *wǎrn*

swelling บวม *boarm*

swim ว่ายน้ำ *wîe•nárm*

swimming pool สระ ว่ายน้ำ *sàh wîe•nárm*

swimming trunks กาง เกงว่ายน้ำ *garng•geng wîe•nárm*

swimsuit ชุดว่ายน้ำ *chúht wîe•nárm*

swollen บวม *boarm*

symbol สัญลักษณ์ *sǎhn•yah•láhk*

symptom อาการ *ar•garn*

synagogue โบสถ์ยิว *bòet•yihw*

T

table โต๊ะ *dtóh*

take เอา *ou*

talk พูด *pôot*

tall สูง *sŏong*

tampon ผ้าอนามัยแบบ สอด *pâa•ah•nar•mi bàep•sòrt*

taste v ชิม *chihm*; n รสชาติ *rót•chârt*

taxi แท็กซี่ *táek•sêe*

taxi rank [BE] ที่จอดรถ รถแท็กซี่ *tîe jòrt•rót táek•sêe*

taxi stand ที่จอดรถ แท็กซี่ *tîe jòrt•rót táek•sêe*

team ทีม *teem*

telephone n โทรศัพท์ *toe•rah•sàhp*

telephone booth ตู้ โทรศัพท์ *dtôo toe•rah•sàhp*

telephone call โทรศัพท์ *toe•rah•sàhp*

telephone number เบอร์โทรศัพท์ *ber toe•rah•sàhp*

tell บอก *bòrk*

temperature อุณหภูมิ *uhn•hah•poom*

tennis เทนนิส *tehn•níht*

tennis court สนาม เทนนิส *sah•nărm tehn•nít*

tent เต็นท์ *dtéhn*

terminal เทอร์มินอล *ter•mih•nôrn*

text (SMS) v ส่งข้อความ *sòng kôr•kwarm*

Thai (language) ภาษา ไทย *par•sǎr ti*; (person) คนไทย *kon ti*

Thailand ประเทศไทย *bprah•têt ti*

thank ขอบคุณ *kòrp•kuhn*

that นั่น *nân*

theater (movie) โรง หนัง *roeng•nǎhng*; (play) โรงละคร *roeng•lah•korn*

theft ขโมย *kah•moey*

then (afterwards) แล้ว ก็ *láew•gôr*

there ที่นั่น *tîe•nâhn*

thermometer ปรอท *bprah•ròrt*

thick หนา *nǎr*

thief ขโมย *kah•moey*

thigh ต้นขา *dtôn•kǎr*

thin บาง *barng*

thing สิ่งของ *sihng•kŏrng*

think คิดควา *kiht•wâr*

thirsty หิวน้ำ *hĭhw•nárm*

this นี่ *nêe*

throat คอ *kor*

through ผ่าน *pàrn*

ticket ตั๋ว *dtŏar*

ticket inspector คน ตรวจตั๋ว *kon dtròart ...*

ticket office แผนก จำหน่ายตั๋ว *pah•nàek jahm•nìe dtŏar*

tie เนคไท *néhk•tie*

tight คับ *káhp*

tile กระเบื้อง *grah•bûeang*

time เวลา *we•lar*

timetable [BE] ตาราง *dtar•rarng*

tin opener [BE] ที่ เปิดกระป๋อง *têe bpèrt gra•bpŏhng*

tip (service) v ทิป *tihp*

tire (vehicle) ยาง *yarng*

tired เหนื่อย *nùeay*

tissue กระดาษทิชชู่ *grah•dàrt tiht•chôo*

to (place) ถึง *thŭeng*

tobacco ยาสูบ *yar•sòop*

today วันนี้ *wahn•née*

toe นิ้วเท้า *níhw•tóu*

toilet [BE] ห้องน้ำ *hôhng•nárm*

toilet paper กระดาษ ชำระ *grah•dàrt chahm•ráh*

tomorrow พรุ่งนี้ *prûhng•née*

tongue ลิ้น *líhn*

tonight คืนนี้ *kueen•née*

too เกินไป *gern•bpi*; (also) เหมือนกัน *mŭean•gahn*

tooth ฟัน *fahn*

toothache ปวดฟัน *bpòart fahn*

toothbrush แปรงสีฟัน *bpraeng sĕe•fahn*

toothpaste ยาสีฟัน *yar sĕe•fahn*

torn ฉีก *chèek*

tough เหนียว *nĕaw*

tour ทัวร์ *toar*

tour guide ไกด์ทัวร์ *gi toar*

tour information *náhk•tôhng•têaw*

tourist office สำ นักงานท่องเที่ยว *săhm•náhk•ngarn tôhng•têaw*

tow truck รถลาก *rót•lârk*

towel ผ้าเช็ดตัว *pâr•chéht•dtoar*

tower หอคอย *hŏr•kory*

town เมือง *mueang*

toy ของเล่น *kŏrng lên*

toy store ร้านขายของ เล่น *rárn kĭe kŏrng•lên*

traditional ดั้งเดิม *dâhng•derm*

traffic การจราจร *garn jah•rar•jorn*

trail เส้นทางเดินป่า *sên tarng dern•bpàr*

trailer รถพวง *rót•pôarng*

train รถไฟ *rót•fi*

train station สถานี รถไฟ *sah•tăr•nee rót•fi*

tram รถราง *rót•rarng*

transfer (finance) โอน เงิน *oen•ngern*

translate แปล *bplae*

translation คำแปล *kahm•bplae*

translator ผู้แปล *poo•bplae*

transport v ขนส่ง *kŏn•sòng*

trash ขยะ *kah•yáh*

trash can ถังขยะ *tăhng kah•yáh*

travel ท่องเที่ยว *tôhng•têaw*

travel agency บริษัท ทัวร์ *bor•rih•sàht toar*

travel sickness (by car) เมารถ *mou rót*; (by boat) เมาเรือ *mou ruea*

traveler's check เช็ค เดินทาง *chéhk dern•tarng*

traveller's cheque [BE] เช็คเดินทาง *chéhk dern•tarng*

treatment การรักษา *garn ráhk•săr*

tree ต้นไม้ *dtôn•mí*

trim เล็ม *lehm*

trip การเดินทาง *garn dern•tarng*

trolley รถเข็น *rót•kĕhn*

trousers [BE] กางเกง ขายาว *garng•geng kăr•yow*

truck รถบรรทุก *rót bahn•túhk*

true จริง *jihng*

T-shirt เสื้อยืด *sûea•yûeet*

tumor เนื้องอก *núea•ngôrk*

tunnel อุโมงค์ *uh•moeng*

turn เลี้ยว *léaw*

turn off ปิด *bpiht*

turn on เปิด *bpèrt*

TV ทีวี *tee•wee*

tweezers แหนบ *nàep*

twist บิด *biht*

type ชนิด *chah•níht*

typical ธรรมดา *tahm•mah•dar*

ugly น่าเกลียด *nâr•glèat*

umbrella ร่ม *rôm*

unconscious หมดสติ *mòt sah•dtih*

under ใต้ *dtíe*

underground station [BE] สถานีรถไฟ ใต้ดิน *sah•tăr•nee rót•fi tíe•dihn*

understand เข้าใจ *kôu•ji*

unit หน่วย *nòary*

United Kingdom สห ราชอาณาจักร *sah•hàh ràrt•chah ar•nar•jàhk*

United States สหรัฐอเมริกา *sah•hàh•ráht ah•me•rih•gar*

until กระทั่ง *grah•tâhng*

upstairs ชั้นบน *cháhn•bon*

urgent ด่วน *dòarn*

use ใช้ *chí*

username ชื่อผู้ใช้ *chûee pôo•chí*

vacant ว่าง *wârng*

vacation วันหยุด *wahn•yùht*

vacuum cleaner เครื่องดูดฝุ่น *krûeang dòot•fùhn*

valet service บริการรับจอดรถ *bor•rih•garn•ráhp jòrt•rót*

valid ใช้ได้ *chí•dîe*

validate รับรอง *ráp rorng*

valuable มีค่า *mee kâr*

value มูลค่า *moon•kâr*

VAT [BE] ภาษีมูลค่า เพิ่ม *par•sĕe moon•kâr pêrm*

vehicle รถ *rót*
very มาก *mârk*
view วิว *wihw*
viewpoint จุดชมวิว *jùht chom wihw*
village หมู่บ้าน *mòo•bârn*
vineyard ไร่องุ่น *rî âh•ngùhn*
visa วีซ่า *wee•sâh*
visit เยี่ยม *yêam*
visiting hours เวลา เยี่ยม *we•lar yêam*
visually impaired พิการทางสายตา *pih•garn tarng sǎry•dtar*
volleyball วอลเล่ย์บอล *wohn•lê•bohn*
vomit อาเจียน *ar•jean*

W

wait รอ *ror*
waiter พนักงานบริการ ชาย *pah•náhk•ngarn• bor•garn chie*
waiting room ห้องพัก ผู้โดยสาร *hôhng•páhk pôo•doey•sǎrn*
waitress พนักงาน บริการหญิง *pah•náhk• ngarn•bor•garn•yǐng*
wake ปลุก *bplúhk*
wake-up call บริการ โทรปลุก *bor•rih• garn•toe bplùhk*
walk เดิน *dern*
wall กำแพง *gahm•paeng*
wallet กระเป๋าเงิน *grah•bpǒu ngern*
ward (hospital) วอร์ด คนไข้ *wôrt kon•kî*
warm อุ่น *ùhn*
warning คำเตือน *kahm•dtuean*
washing machine เครื่องซักผ้า *krûeang• sáhk•pâr*
watch นาฬิกาข้อมือ *nar•lih•gar kôr•muee*
water น้ำ *nárm*
water ski สกีน้ำ *sah•gee nárm*
waterfall น้ำตก *náhm•dtòk*
waterproof กันน้ำ *gahn•nárm*
wave คลื่น *klúeen*
way ทาง *tarng*
wear ใส่ *sì*
weather อากาศ *ar•gàrt*
weather forecast พยากรณ์อากาศ *pah•yar•gorn ar•gàrt*
wedding งานแต่งงาน *ngarn dtàeng•ngarn*
week สัปดาห์ *sàhp•dar*
weekday วันธรรมดา *wahn tahm•mah•dar*
weekend วันเสาร์-อาทิตย์ *wahn sǒu ar•tíht*
weigh ชั่ง *châhng*
weight น้ำหนัก

welcome ยินดีต้อนรับ *yihn•dee dtôrn•ráhp*
west ทิศตะวันตก *tiht dtah•wahn•dtòk*
wetsuit เว็ทสูท *wéht•sòot*
what อะไร *ah•rì*
wheelchair รถเข็นคน พิการ *rót kěhn kon pih•garn*
wheelchair ramp ทาง ขึ้นสำหรับรถ เข็น คนพิการ *tarng kûen sǎhm•ràhp rót kêhn kon pih•garn*
when เมื่อไหร่ *mûea•rì*
where ที่ไหน *têe•nǐ*
who ใคร *kri*
why ทำไม *tahm•mi*
wide กว้าง *gwârng*
wildlife สัตว์ป่า *sàht bpàr*
wind ลม *lom*
windbreaker เสื้อกันลม *sûea gahn lom*
window หน้าต่าง *nâr•dtàrng*
window seat ที่นั่งริม หน้าต่าง *têe•nâhng rihm nâr•dtàrng*
windsurfing เล่นวินด์ เซิร์ฟ *lêhn wihn•sérp*
windy ลมแรง *lom raeng*
wipe เช็ด *chéht*
wireless ไร้สาย *rí•sǐe*
wish (bless) v อวยพร *oary•porn*

with กับ *gàhp*
withdraw (bank) ถอน เงิน *tǒrn•ngern*
withdrawal ถอน *tǒrn*
without ไม่ใส่ *mì•sì*
witness พยาน *pah•yarn*
wood (material) ไม้ *mie*
wool ผ้าขนสัตว์
work ทำงาน *tahm•ngarn*
wrap หอ *hòr*
write เขียน *kěan*
wrong ผิด *piht*

X

x-ray เอ็กซเรย์ *éhk•sah•re*

Y

yacht เรือยอชท์ *ruea yórt*
year ปี *bpee*
yes ครับ? *kráhp?*; คะ/ค่ะ
yesterday เมื่อวาน *mûea•warn*
young เด็ก *dèhk*
youth เด็ก *dèhk*
youth hostel ที่พัก เยาวชน *têe páhk you•wah•chon*

Z

zipper ซิป *síhp*
zoo สวนสัตว์ *sǒarn•sàht*

THAI-ENGLISH DICTIONARY

ก

กงสุล **gong•sŭln** consulate

กด **gòt** press; dial (phone)

กดกระดิ่ง **gòt grah•dìhng** v ring

กดชักโครก **gòt chákh•krôek** flush (toilet)

กรรไกร **gahn•gri** scissors

กรอก **gròrk** fill out (form)

กรอบแว่น **gròrp wâen** frame (glasses)

กระจกเงา **gràh•jòk ngou** mirror

กระดาน **grah•darn** board

กระดานโต้คลื่น **grah•darn dtôe•klûuen** surfboard

กระดาษชำระ **grah•dàrt chahm•ráh** toilet paper

กระดาษเช็ดปาก **grah•dàrt chéht bpàrk** napkin

กระดาษเช็ดมือ **grah•dàrt chéht muue** paper towel

กระดาษทิชชู **grah•dàrt tíht•chôo** tissue

กระดาษฟอยล์ **grah•dàrt fory** aluminum [kitchen BE] foil

กระดุม **grah•duhm** button

กระดูก **grah•dòok** bone

กระท่อม **grah•tôhm** cottage

กระทะ **grah•táh** frying pan

กระทั่ง **grah•tâhng** until

กระเบื้อง **grah•bûeang** tile

กระป๋อง **grah•bpŏhng** n can

กระเป๋า **grah•bpŏu** luggage (baggage BE); handbag

กระเป๋าเงิน **grah•bpŏu ngern** wallet

กระเป๋าเดินทาง **grah•bpŏu dern•tarng** suitcase

กระเป๋าถือขึ้นเครื่อง **grah•bpŏu tûee kûen krûeang** carry-on [hand BE] luggage

กระเป๋ารถ **grah•bpŏu rót** (bus) fare collector

กระเป๋าสตางค์ **grah•bpŏu sah•tarng** purse

กระโปรง **gràh•bproeng** skirt

กระเพาะปัสสาวะ **grah•póh bpàht•sah•wáh** bladder

กรัม **grahm** gram

กรุณา **gah•rúh•nar** please

กลม **glom** adj round

กล่อง **glòhng** box

กล้องถ่ายรูป **glôhng tìe•rôop** camera

กล้องส่องทางไกล **glôhng sòhng tarng gli** binoculars

กลับ **glàhp** return (come back)

กลางคืน **glarng•kuuern** night

กลางแจ้ง **glarng•jâeng** outdoor

กล้าม **glârm** muscle

กลิ่น **glìhn** n smell

กลืน **glueen** swallow

กลุ่ม **glùhm** group

กว้าง **gwârng** wide

กวาด **gwàrt** sweep

ก๊อกน้ำ **góhk•nárm** faucet

กอด **gòrt** hug

ก่อน **gòrn** before

กอล์ฟ **górp** golf

กัด **gàht** bite

กันน้ำ **gahn•nárm** waterproof

กับ **gàhp** with

กางเกงขายาว **garng•geng kâr•yow** pants [trousers BE]

กางเกงขาสั้น **garng•geng kâr•sâhn** shorts

กางเกงว่ายน้ำ **garng•geng wìe•nárm** swimming trunks

ก๊าซบิวเทน **gárt bihw•ten** butane gas

การขนส่ง **garn kŏn•sòng** n transport

การเคลมประกัน **garn klem bprah•gahn** insurance claim

การจราจร **garn jah•rar•jorn** traffic

การจอง **garn jorng** reservation

การจ่ายเงิน **garn joe•ngern** payment

การเชื่อมต่อ **garn chûeam•dtòr** connection

การใช้ยา **garn chí yar** medication

การดูแล **garn doo•lae** supervision

การเดินทาง **garn dern•tarng** journey; trip

การติดเชื้อ **garn dtìht•chúea** infection

การติดต่อ **garn dtìht•dtòr** n contact

การทำร้าย **garn tahm•rie** n attack

การประชุม **garn bprah•chuhm** meeting

การประชุมเป็นทางการ **garn bprah•chuhm bpehn tarng•garn** convention

การประชุมสัมมนา **garn bprah•chuhm sǎhm•mah•nar** conference

การปล้น **karn bplôn** robbery

การรักษา **garn ráhk•sǎr** treatment

การวัด **garn wáht** measurement

การส่ง **garn sòng** delivery

การสอบ **garn sòrp** examination

การแสดง **garn sah•daeng** performance; n show

ทำกับ **gahm•gàhp** v direct

ทำแพง **gahm•paeng** wall

กิน **gihn** eat

กินอาหาร **gihn ar•hârn** dine

กิโลกรัม **gih•loe•grahm**

kilogram
กิโลเมตร **gih•loe•mét** kilometer
กีตาร์ **gee•dtâr** guitar
กีฬา **gee•lar** sport
กุญแจ **guhn•jae** key; padlock
เก็บ **gèhp** keep
เก็บรักษา **gèhp ráhk•sǎr** save
แก้ม **gęm** gume
เกษียณ **gah•sěan** retired
เกสต์เฮาส์ **gét•hóu** guesthouse
เก่า **gòu** old
เก้าอี้เด็ก **gôu•ee dèhk** highchair
เก้าอี้ผ้าใบ **gôu•ee pâr•bi** deck chair
เกิด **gèrt** born
เกินไป **gern bpi** too (much)
เกียร์ **gear** gear
เกือบจะ **gùeap•jah** almost
แก้ไข **gâe•kǐ** alter (a garment)
แก่ง **gàng** rapids
แก้ว **gâew** glass
โกนหนวด **goen•nòart** shave (beard)
ใกล้ **glî** near
ใกล้ๆ **glî•glî** nearby
ไกด์(ทัวร์) **gí (toar)** n (tour) guide
ไกล **gli** far

ข
ขนส่ง **kǒn•sòng** v transport
ขนาด **kah•nàrt** size; portion
ขนาดรับประทาน **kah•nàrt ráhp•bprah•tarn** dosage (medicine)

ขนาดสำหรับเด็ก **kah•nàrt sǎhm•ràhp dèhk** children's portion
ข่มขืน **kòm•kǔeen** rape
ขโมย **kah•moey** v steal; n theft, thief
ขยะ **kah•yàh** trash
ขยับ **kah•yàhp** move
ขวด **kòart** bottle; jar
ขวดนมเด็ก **kòart•nom dèhk** baby bottle
ขวา **kwǎr** right (direction)
ขอโทษ **kǒr•tôet** apologize; sorry
ขอแสดงความยินดี **kǒr sah•daeng kwarm•yihn•dee** congratulations
ข้อกำหนดในการแต่งกาย **kôr gahm•nòt ni garn dtàeng•gie** dress code
ข้อความ **kôr•kwarm** message
ข้อผิดพลาด **kôr piht•plàrt** error
ข้อมูล **kôr•moon** information
ของเก่า **kǒrng•gòu** antique
ของขวัญ **kǒrng•kwǎhn** n present
ของที่ระลึก **kǒrng•têe•rah•lúek** souvenir
ของแท้ **kǒrng táe** authenticity
ของฝาก **kǒrng fàrk** gift
ของเล่น **kǒrng•lên** toy
ของเลียนแบบ **kǒrng lean•bàep** imitation
ขอบคุณ **kòrp•kuhn** thank
ขับ **kàhp** drive
ขา **kǎr** leg

ขากรรไกร **kâr•gahn•gri** jaw
ขาเข้า **kâr•kôu** arrivals
ขาออก **kâr•òrk** departures
ข้างนอก **kârng•nôrk** outside
ข้างใน **kârng•ni** inside
ข้ามคืน **kârm kueen** overnight
ขาย **kǎi** sell
ขายหมด **kǐe mòt** sold out
ข่าว **kòw** news
ขี่ม้า **kèe már** horseback riding
ขึ้นเงิน **kûen•ngern** v cash
เขต **kèt** region
เขตคนเดินถนน **kèt kon dern tah•nǒn** pedestrian zone (precinct BE)
เขตอนุรักษ์ **kèt àh•núh•ráhk** conservation area
เขตอยู่อาศัย **kèt yòo•ar•sǐ** residential zone
เข็มขัด **kêhm•kàht** belt
เข็มขัดนิรภัย **kêhm•kàht níh•ráh•pi** seat belt
เขา **kǒu** horn (animal)
เข่า **kòu** knee
เข้า **kôu** v enter
เข้าใจ **kôu•ji** understand
เข้าถึง **kôu•tǔeng** v access
เข้าระบบ **kôu rah•bòp** log on
เขียน **kěan** write
แข็ง **kǎng** hard (solid)
แข็งแรง **kǎng•raeng** strong (physical)
แข่งม้า **kàng már** horse racing

แขน **kǎen** arm
แขนเสื้อ **kǎen sûea** sleeve
ไขควง **kǐ•koarng** screwdriver
ไข่มุก **kì•múhk** pearl
ไข้ **kì** fever
ไข้หวัด **kì•wàht** n cold
ไข้หวัดใหญ่ **kì•wàht•yì** n flu

ค
คงที่ **kong•têe** constant
คน **kon** person
คนขับ **kon kàhp** driver
คนไข้ **kon kì** patient
คนเดินถนน **kon dern tah•nǒn** pedestrian
คนตรวจตั๋ว **kon dtròart dtǒar** ticket inspector
คนเป็นโรคเบาหวาน **kon bpehn rôek•bou•wǎrn** n diabetic
คนพิการ **kon píh•garn** disabled (person)
คนยกกระเป๋า **kon yók grah•bpǒu** porter
คนอังกฤษ **kon ahng•griht** British (person)
คม **kom** sharp
ครอบครัว **krôrp•kroar** family
ครับ? **kráhp?** yes
คริสตัล **krihs•dtâhn** crystal
ครีมกันแดด **kreem gahn•dàet** sunblock; sunscreen
ครีมแก้อักเสบ **kreem gâe àhk•sèp** antiseptic cream
ครีมโกนหนวด **kreem goen•nòart** shaving cream

ครีมนวดผม **kreem nôart•pôm** conditioner (hair)

ครึ่ง **krûeng** half

คลอง **klorng** canal

คลับ **klàhp** club

คลับเต้นรำ **klàhp dtêhn•rahm** dance club

คลาสสิก **klárt•sihk** classical

คลีนิก **klee•nihk** clinic

คลื่น **klûen** wave

คลื่นไส้ **klûeen•sî** nausea

ควบคุม **kôarp•kuhm** control

ควบคุมอาหาร **kôarp•kuhm ar•hârn** diet

ความช่วยเหลือ **kwarm chôary•lûea** assistance; help

ความดันเลือด **kwarm•dahn lûeat** blood pressure

ความปลอดภัย **kwarm bplòrt•pi** safety

ความยาว **kwarm yarw** length

ความร้อน **kwarm rórn** heat

ความรับผิดชอบ **kwarm ráhp•piht•chôrp** responsibility

ความเร็ว **kwarm•rehw** n speed

ความสนใจ **kwarm sŏn•ji** interest (hobby)

ความสัมพันธ์ **kwarm săhm•pahn** relationship

ความสูง **kwarm•sŏong** height

คอ **kor** neck

คอกเด็กเลน **kôrk dèhk•lêhn** playpen

คอนแท็คเลนส์ **kohn•tàk•lehn** contact lens

คอนเสิร์ต **kohn•sèrt** concert

คอมพิวเตอร์ **kohm•pihw•dtêr** computer

คอร์สภาษา **kórt par•sâr** language course

ค่ะ/ **kâh**/ yes

คัน **kahn** itch

คับ **káhp** tight

คาเข้า **kâr kôu** admission charge

ค่าใช้จ่าย **kâr chi•jìe** allowance; n cost

ค่าบริการ **kâr bor•rih•garn** service charge; commission

ค่าบริการต่อหัว **kâr bor•rih•garn dtòr•hŭa** cover charge

ค่าผ่านทาง **kâr pàrn•tarng** toll

ค่าผ่านประตู **kâr pàrn bprah•dtoo** entrance fee

ค่าแสตมป์ **kâr sah•dtaem** postage

คาสิโน **kar•sih•noe** casino

คำเตือน **kahm•dtuean** warning

คำแปล **kahm•bplae** translation

คำสั่ง **kahm•sàhng** instructions

คิดเงิน **kiht•ngern** v charge

คิดเงินเกิน **kiht•ngern gern** overcharge

คิดว่า **kiht wâr** think

คิว **kihw** n line [queue BE]

คิ้ว **kihw** eyebrow

คีม **keem** clamp

คีย์การ์ด **kee•gárt** key card

คืน **kueen** return; give back

คืนเงิน **kueen ngern** v refund

คืนนี้ **kueen•née** tonight

คือ **kuee** be

คุก **kúhk** prison

คุณ **kuhn** you

คุณภาพ **kuhn•nah•pârp** quality

คุมกำเนิด **kuhm gahm•nèrt** contraceptive

คู่ **kôo** double; pair

คู่มือของที่ระลึก **kôo•muee kŏrng•têe•rah•lúek** souvenir guide

คู่มือแหล่งบันเทิง **kôo•muea làng bahn•terng** entertainment guide

คู่สมรส **kôo sŏm•rót** spouse

คู่หมั้น **kôo•mâhn** fiancé

เครือข่าย **kruea•kìe** network

เครื่องโกนหนวดไฟฟ้า **krûeang goen•nòart fi•fár** electric shaver

เครื่องคิดเงิน **krûeang kít•ngern** cash register

เครื่องช่วยฟัง **krûeang chôary•fahng** hearing aid

เครื่องซักผ้า **krûeang sáhk•pâr** washing machine

เครื่องดับเพลิง **krûeang dàhp•plerng** fire extinguisher

เครื่องดื่ม **krûeang•dùeem** n drink

เครื่องดูดฝุ่น **krûeang dòot•fùhn** vacuum cleaner

เครื่องนอน **krûeang•norn** bedding

เครื่องบิน **krûeang bihn** plane

เครื่องประดับ **krûeang bprah•dàhp** jewelry

เครื่องปั้นดินเผา **krûeang•bpâhn dihn•pŏu** pottery

เครื่องแฟกซ์ **krûeang fáhk•fáw** machine

เครื่องมือ **krûeang• muee** equipment

เครื่องยนต์ **krûeang•yon** motor

เครื่องล้างจาน **krûeang lárng•jarn** dishwasher

เครื่องลายคราม **krûeang lie•krarm** porcelain

เครื่องเล่นซีดี **krûeang lêhn see•dee** CD player

เครื่องสำอาง **krûeang săhm•arng** cosmetic

เคาน์เตอร์ **kóu•dtêr** counter

เคาะ **kóh** knock

แคชเชียร์ **káet•chea** cashier

แคลอรี่ **kae•lor•rêe** calorie

โคเชอร์ **koe•chêr** kosher

โคมไฟ **koem•fi** lamp

ใคร **kri** anyone; who

ฆ

ฆ้อน **kórn** hammer

ง

งดงามมาก **ngót•ngarm mârk** magnificent

ง่วง **ngôarng** drowsy

งาน **ngarn** job

งานแต่งงาน **ngarn**

dtàng•ngarn wedding

งานทำถนน **ngarn tahm tah•nŏn** roadwork

งานปาร์ตี้ **ngarn bpar•dtêe** party

งานฝีมือ **ngarn fĕe•muee** crafts

ง่าย **ngîe** easy

เงิน **ngern** money; silver (metal)

เงินคืน **ngern•kueen** n refund

เงินบริจาค **ngern bor•rih•jàrk** donation

เงินปอนด์ **ngern•bporn** pound sterling

เงินมัดจำ **ngern máht•jahm** n deposit

เงินสด **ngern•sòt** n cash

เงินสเตอร์ลิง **ngern sah•dter•lihng** sterling silver

เงียบ **ngêap** quiet

จดหมาย **jòt•mîe** n mail [post BE]; letter

จบ **jòp** v end

จมน้ำ **jom•nárm** drown

จมูก **jah•mòok** nose

จริง **jihng** true

จริงจัง **jihng•jahng** serious

จอง **jorng** reserve

จอด **jòrt** v stop

จอดรถ **jòrt•rót** v park

จักรยาน **jàhk•grah•yarn** bicycle

จักรยานยนต์ **jàhk•grah•yarn yon** motorcycle

จัดระบบ **jàht rah•bòp** organize

จับ **jàhp** catch

จาก **jàrk** depart; from

จาน **jarn** dish; plate

จ่าย **jie** pay

จำกัดความเร็ว **jahm•gàht kwarm•rehw** speed limit

จำได้ **jahm•dîe** remember

จำนวน **jahm•narn** amount

จำเป็น **jahm•bpehn** essential; necessary

จี้ **jêe** mugging

จุกนม **jùhk•nom** pacifier [dummy BE]

จุด **jùht** spot (place; site)

จุดชมวิว **jùht chom wihw** viewpoint

จุดไฟ **jùht•fi** v light

จูบ **jòop** kiss

เจ **je** vegan

เจ็ทแล็ก **jéht•làk** jet lag

เจ็ทสกี **jéht sah•gee** jet-ski

เจ็บ **jèhp** pain; hurt

เจ็บคอ **jèhp•kor** sore throat

เจ้าของ **jôu•kŏrng** owner

แจ้ง **jäeng** notify

แจ้งความ **jäeng•kwarm** report (to police)

แจ๊ส **jáet** jazz

ใจดี **ji•dee** adj kind

ฉีก **chèek** torn

ฉีดยา **chèet•yar** inject

ฉุกเฉิน **chùhk•chĕrn** emergency

ชกมวย **chók•moary** boxing

ชนิด **chah•níht** type

ช่วงออฟพีค **chôarng órp•péek** off-peak (ticket)

ช่วย **chôary** v help

ช่วยด้วย **chôary dôay** help (command)

ช็อก **chóhk** shock

ช่องคลอด **chông•klôrt** vagina

ช่องทำน้ำแข็ง **chôhng tahm náhm•kăeng** freezer

ช้อน **chórn** spoon

ชอบ **chôrp** like

ช็อปปิ้ง **chóp•bpîhng** shopping

ชั่งน้ำหนัก **châhng náhm•nàhk** weigh

ชัน **chahn** steep

ชั้น **chahn** floor (level)

ชั้นใต้ดิน **cháhn tîe•dihn** basement

ชั้นธุรกิจ **cháhn túh•ráh•giht** business class

ชั้นบน **cháhn bon** upstairs

ชั้นประหยัด **cháhn bp-rah•yàht** economy class

ชั้นหนึ่ง **cháhn nùeng** first class

ชั่วโมง **chôar•moeng** hour

ช้า **chár** delay; slow

ช่าง **chârng** mechanic

ช่างตัดผม **chârng tàht•pŏm** barber

ช่างทำผม **chârng tahm•pŏm** hairdresser

ช่างทำแว่น **chârng tahm wân** optician

ชานชาลา **charn char•lar** platform

ชาม **charm** bowl

ชายฝั่ง **chie•fàhng** coast

ชายหาด **chie•hàrt** beach

ชิ้น **chíhn** piece

ชิม **chihm** v taste

ชีวิต **chee•wiht** life

ชื่อ **chûee** name

ชื่อผู้ใช้ **chûee pôo•chí** username

ชุดกระโปรง **chúht grah•bproeng** dress

ชุดเป็นทางการ **chúht bpehn tarng•garn** formal dress

ชุดนอน **chúht•norn** pajamas

ชุดว่ายน้ำ **chúht wîe•nárm** swimsuit

ชุดสูท **chúht sòot** suit

ชุน **chuhn** mend (clothes)

เช็ค **chékh** n check [cheque BE]

เช็คเดินทาง **chékh dern•tarng** traveller's check [traveller's cheque BE]

เช็คอิน **chékh•ihn** check in

เช็คเอาท์ **chékh•óu** check out

เช็ด **chéht** wipe

เช่า **chôu** hire; rent

เช้า **chów** morning

เชิญ **chern** invite

เชื่อถือได้ **chûea•tŭee•dîe** reliable

เชือก **chûeak** rope

เชื่อมต่อ **chûeam•dtòr** connect

แชมพู **chaem•poo** shampoo

ใช้ **chí** use

ใช้จ่าย **chí•jie** spend

ใช้ได้ **chí•dîe** valid

ใช้แล้วทิ้ง **chí láew tíhng** disposable

ซ

ซองจดหมาย **sorng jòt•mîe** envelope

ซ่อม **sôhm** repair

ซ่อมรองเท้า **sôhm rorng• tów** shoe repair

ซักแห้ง **sàhk•hâeng** dry clean

ซ้าย **sie** left

ซ้ำอีกที **sáhm èek•tee** repeat

ซิการ์ **síh•gâr** cigar

ซิป **síhp** zipper

ซีดี **see•dee** CD

ซื้อ **súee** buy

ซุปเปอร์ **súhp•bpêr** premium (fuel)

ซุปเปอร์มาร์เก็ต **súhp• bpêr•mar•gêht** supermarket

เซ็กซ์ **séhk** sex (activity)

เซ็นชื่อ **sehn•chûee** v sign

เซรามิก **se•rar•mìhk** ceramics

ด

ดนตรี **don•dtree** music

ด่วน **dòarn** urgent; express

ดอกไม้ **dòrk•míe** flower

ดอลลาร์ **dohn•lâr** dollar

ดัง **dahng** loud (noise); famous

ดั้งเดิม **dâhng•derm** original

ด่านเก็บค่าผ่านทาง **dàrn gèhp kâr•pàrn•tarng** toll booth

ด้านหน้า **dârn•nâr** front

ดำน้ำ **dahm•nárm** dive

ดิจิตอล **dih•jih•dtohn** digital

ดี **dee** nice; good

ดีเซล **dee•sen** diesel

ดีมาก **dee mârk** great; very good

ดึง **dueng** pull

ดื่ม **dùeem** v drink

ดู **doo** look

เด็ก **dèhk** child

เด็กผู้ชาย **dèhk•pôo•chie** boy

เด็กผู้หญิง **dèhk•pôo• yĭhng** girl

เด็กอ่อน **dèhk•òrn** baby

เดิน **dern** walk

เดินป่า **dern bpàr** hike

เดินรถทางเดียว **dern•rót tarng deaw (wahn•we)** one-way (traffic)

เดือน **duean** month

แดด **dàet** sun (light)

แดดเผา **dàet pŏu** sunburn

โดย **doey** by

โดยประมาณ **doey bprah•marn** approximately

ได้กลิ่น **dî•glìhn** v smell

ได้รับ **dî•ráhp** receive

ได้ยิน **dî•yihn** hear

ต

ตกแต่ง **dtòk•dtàng** decorative

ตกปลา **dtòk•bplar** fishing

ต้นขา **dtôn•kâr** thigh

ต้นไม้ **dtôn•míe** tree

ตรง **dtrong** adj direct

ตรงข้าม **dtrong•kârm** across; opposite

ตรงไป **dtrong•bpi** straight (ahead)

ตรวจ **dtròart** v check

ตรวจสอบ **dtròart•sòrp** examine

ตลก **dtah•lòk** funny

ตลาด **dtah•làrt** market

ตลาดนัด **dtah•làrt náht** flea market

ต่อราคา **tòr rar•kar** bargain

ต่อสู้ **dtòr•sôo** fight

ต้อง **dtôhng** must

ต้องการ **dtôhng•garn** want

ตอนเข้า **dtorn•chów** morning

ตอนนี้ **dtorn•née** now

ตอนบ่าย **dtorn•bìe** afternoon

ตอนเย็น **dtorn•yehn** evening

ตะกร้า **dtah•grâr** basket

ตะกร้าช็อปปิ้ง **dtah• grâr chóhp•bpîhng** shopping basket

ตะคริว **dtah•krihw** cramp (sports)

ตะขัดเล็บ **dtah•bi kàht léhp** nail file

ตะหลิว **dtah•lĭhw** spatula

ตั้งแคมป์ **dtâhng•káem** v camp

ตั้งท้อง **dtâhng•tórng** pregnant

ตัด **dtàht** v cut

ติดการเชื่อมต่อ **dtàht garn chûeam•dtòr** disconnect

ตัวกรอง **dtoar grong** filter

ตัวต่อ **dtoar•dtòr** wasp

ตั๋ว **dtŏar** ticket

ตั๋วขากลับ **dtŏar kâr• glàhp** return ticket

ตั๋วขึ้นเครื่อง **dtŏar kûen krûeang** boarding card

ตั๋วเที่ยวเดียว **dtŏar**

ตรวจสอบ **dtròart•sòrp** examine

เถ้าเดียว **têaw•deaw** one-way ticket

ตั๋วไปกลับ **dtŏar bpi• glàhp** round-trip ticket

ตั๋วรถเมล์ **dtŏar rót•me** bus ticket

ตั๋วดู **dtŏar rúe•doo** season ticket

ตั๋วสำรอง **dtŏar sâhm• rorng** standby ticket

ตั๋วอิเล็กทรอนิกส์ **ee•léhk•tror•nihk** e-ticket

ตา **dtar** eye

ตาชั่ง **dtar•châhng** scale

ตารางเดินรถ **dtar•rarng** schedule [timetable BE] (bus)

ต่างชาติ **dtàrng•chârt** foreign

ต่างประเทศ **dtàrng• bprah•têt** foreign; abroad

ต่างหู **dtàrng•hŏo** earrings

ตาม **dtarm** follow

ตาย **dtie** dead

ต่ำ **dtàhm** low

ตำรวจ **dtahm•ròart** police

ติดกับ **dtit•gàhp** next to

ติดต่อ **dtìht•dtòr** v contact

ติดต่อกันได้ **dtìht•dtòr gàhn dîe** contagious (disease)

ติดทะเล **dtìht tah•le** seafront

ตื้น **dtûeen** shallow

ตุ๊กตา **dtúhk•gah•dtar** doll

ตู้จดหมาย **dtôo jòt•mîe** mailbox [postbox BE]

ตู้เซฟ **dtôo•séf** n safe

ตู้โทรศัพท์ **dtôo toe•rah•sàhp** telephone booth

ตู้นอน **dtôo•norn** sleeping car

ตู้เย็น **dtôo•yehn** refrigerator

เต้นรำ **dtêhn•rahm** dance

เต็มที่ **dtehm lȗut**

เต็ม **dtehm** full

เตา **dtou** stove

เตารีด **dtou•rêet** n iron

เตาอบ **dtou•òp** oven

เติม **dterm** fill

เติมให้เต็ม **dterm hî dtehm** fill up

เตียง **dteang** bed

แต่ **dtàe** but

แตก **dtàek** break

แต่งงาน **dtàng•ngarn** marry

แต่งหน้า **dtàng•nâr** v make-up

แตร **dtrae** horn (car)

โต๊ะ **dtó** table

โต๊ะเช็คอิน **dtó chéhk• ihn** check-in desk

ใต้ **dtîe** under

ไต **dti** kidney

ถ

ถนน **tah•nǒn** road; street

ถ้วย **tôary** cup

ถอน **tǒrn** withdrawal

ถอนเงิน **tǒrn•ngern** withdraw (bank)

ถัง **tǎhng** bucket

ถังขยะ **tǎhng kah•yàh** trash can

ถังน้ำมัน **tǎhng náhm• mahn** fuel tank

ถัดไป **tàht•bpi** next

ถ่าน **tàrn** charcoal

ถาม **tǎrm** ask

ถ่ายเอกสาร **tìe èk•gah•**

สำเนา **sǎrn** photocopy

ถ้ำ **tâhm** cave

ถึง **tǔeng** to (place)

ถือ **tǔee** hold

ถุงขยะ **tǔhng kah•yàh** garbage bag

ถุงเท้า **tǔhng•tów** socks

ถุงน่อง **tǔhng•nôhng** nylon tights

ถุงนอน **tǔhng•norn** sleeping bag

ถุงมือ **tǔhng•muee** gloves

ถุงยางอนามัย **tǔhng•yarng ah•nar•mi** condom

ถูก **tòok** cheap; right (correct)

ถูกกฎหมาย **tòok gòt•mǐe** legal

ถูกขโมย **tòok kah•moey** stolen

ถูกต้อง **tòok•dtôhng** correct

แถว **tǎew** n row

ท

ทนายความ **tah•nie• kwarm** lawyer

ทราย **sie** sand

ทอง **torng** gold

ทองแดง **torng•daeng** copper

ท่องเที่ยว **tôhng•têaw** travel

ท้อง **tórng** stomach

ท้องกิน **tórng•tihn** local

ท้องร่วง **tórng•rôarng** diarrhea

ทะเล **tah•le** sea

ทะเลสาบ **tah•le•sàrp** lake

ทั้งหมด **táhng•mòt** all

ทัวร์ชมเมือง **toar chom mueang**

sightseeing tour

ทัวร์เดินนำเที่ยว **toar dern nahm têaw** guided walk

ทัวร์ทางเรือ **toar tarng ruea** boat trip

ทัวร์นำเที่ยว **toar nahm• têaw** guided tour

ทัวร์ระยะสั้น **toar rah•yáh sôhn**

excursion

ทัวร์วันเดียว **toar wahn•deaw** day trip

ท่าเรือ **târ•ruea** harbor

ทาง **tarng** way

ทางขึ้นสำหรับรถเข็นคน พิการ **tarng kûen sǎhm•ràhp rót kěhn kon píh•garn** wheelchair ramp

ทางจักรยาน **tarng jàhk•grah•yarn** bike path; cycle route

ทางเดินชมธรรมชาติ **tarng dern chom tahm•mah•chárt** nature trail

ทางตัน **tarng•tahn** dead end

ทางเท้า **tarng•tów** sidewalk [pavement BE]

ทางเบี่ยง **tarng•bèang** detour

ทางม้าลาย **tarng•már• lie** pedestrian cross- ing [zebra crossing BE]

ทางหนีไฟ **tarng něe fi** fire escape; fire exit

ทางหลวง **tarng•lǒarng** highway [motorway BE]

ทางออก **tarng•òrk** n exit

ทางออกฉุกเฉิน **tarng• òrk chùhk•chěrn** emergency exit

ทำ **tahm** do

ทำความสะอาด **tahm kwarm•sah•àrt** v clean

ทำงาน **tahm•ngarn** work

ทำไม **tahm•mi** why

ทำร้าย **tahm•ríe** v attack

ทำเล็บ **tahm•léhp•muee** manicure

ทำสำเนา **tahm• sǎhm•nou** copy

ทำอาหาร **tahm ar•hǎrn** v cook

ทำเอง **tahm•eng** homemade

ทิศ **tiht** direction

ทิศตะวันตก **tíht dtah• wahn•dtòk** west

ทิศตะวันออก **tíht dtah• wahn•òrk** east

ทิศใต้ **tíht•dtîe** south

ที่เขี่ยบุหรี่ **têe kèar• buh•rèe** ashtray

ที่จอดรถ **têe•jòrt•rót** parking lot [car park BE]

ที่จอดรถแท็กซี่ **têe jòrt rót ták•sêe** taxi stand [rank BE]

ที่ชอบ **têe chôrp** favorite

ที่ดิน **têe•dihn** land

ที่ดูดส้วม **têe dòot•sôarm** plunger

ที่ตั้งแคมป์ **têe dtâhng• káem** campsite

ที่ทำการไปรษณีย์ **têe•tahm•garn bpri•sah•nee** post office

ที่ทำงาน **têe•tahm• ngarn** office

ที่นอน **têe•norn** mattress

ที่นอนอัดลม **têe•norn àht•lom** air mattress

ที่นั่ง **têe•nâhng** seat (on train, etc.)

ที่นั่งเด็ก **têe•nâhng dèhk** child seat

ที่นั่งริมหน้าต่าง **têe• nâhng rihm nâr• dtarng** window seat

ที่นั่น **têe•nâhn** there

ที่นี่ **têe•nêe** here

ที่ปิคนิค **têe bpíhk•níhk** picnic area

ที่เปิดกระป๋อง **têe bpèrt grah•bpŏhng** can [tin BE] opener

ที่เปิดขวด **têe bpèrt kòart** bottle opener

ที่เปิดจุกก๊อก **têe bpèr jùhk•gó hk** corkscrew

ที่พัก **têe•páhk** accommodation

ที่พักเยาวชน **têe•páhk you•wah•chon** youth hostel

ที่พักริมทาง **têe•páhk rihm tarng** rest area

ที่รับกระเป๋า **têe ráhp grah•bpŏu** baggage claim

ที่รับฝากเสื้อโค้ท **têe ráhp•fàrk sûea•kóet** coat check

ที่รับแลกเงิน **têe ráhp lâek•ngern** currency exchange office

ที่แล้ว **têe•láew** last (previous)

ที่ว่าง **têe•wârng** space; room

ที่สูบบุหรี่ **têe sòob• buh•rèe** smoking area

ที่สูบลม **têe•sòob•lôm** air pump

ที่ใส่ของ **têe sì kŏrng** compartment

ที่หนึ่ง **têe•nùeng** first

ที่ไหน **têe•nĭ** where

ที่อยู่ **têe•yòo** address

ที่อุดฟัน **têe•ùht•fahn** filling (dental)

ทีม **teem** team

ทีวี **tee•wee** TV

ทุก **túhk** every

ทุ่งนา **túhng** field

เทนนิส **tehn•níht** tennis

เทปนำเที่ยว **tép nahm• têaw** audio guide

เทอร์มินอล **ter•mih• nôrn** terminal

เท่านั้น **tôu•náhn** only

เท่าไหร่ **tôu•rì** how much; how many

เท้า **tów** foot

เที่ยง **têang** noon [midday BE]

เที่ยงคืน **têang•kueen** midnight

เทียน **tean** candle

เที่ยว **têaw** tour

เที่ยวเดียว **têaw•deaw** one way

เที่ยวบิน **têaw•bihn** flight

เที่ยวบินตรง **têaw•bihn trong** non-stop flight

เที่ยวบินที่ **têaw•bhin têe** flight number

แท้ **táe** authentic; real; pure

แท็กซี่ **ták•sêe** taxi

แทนที่ **taen•têe** instead; replace

แทรก **sâek** insert

โทร **toe** v telephone

โทรศัพท์ **toe•rah•sàhp** call (phone); phone; phone call

โทรศัพท์มือถือ **toe• rah•sàhp muee• tŭee** cell [mobile BE] phone

โทรศัพท์สาธารณะ **toe• rah•sàhp sâr•tar• rah•náh** pay phone

ไทย **ti** Thai

ธ

ธนาคาร **tah•nar•karn** bank

ธนาณัติ **tah•nar•náht** money order

ธรรมชาติ **tahm•mah• chârt** nature

ธรรมดา **tahm•mah• dar** normal; regular; typical

ธุรกิจ **túh•ráh•gìht** business

น

นก **nók** bird

นมผง (เด็ก) **nom•pŏng (dèhk)** formula (baby)

นวด **nôart** massage

นอน **norn** sleep

นอนไม่หลับ **norn mî làhp** insomnia

น้อย **nóry** little; few

น้อยกว่า **nóry•gwàr** less

นักท่องเที่ยว **náhk• tôhng•têaw** tourist

นักศึกษา **náhk• sùek•sâr** student

นั่ง **nâhng** sit

นัด **náht** appointment

นั้น **nân** that

นา **nar** rice field

น่าเกลียด **nâr•glèat** ugly

นาง **narng** Mrs.

นาที **nar•tee** minute

นามบัตร **narm•bàht** business card

นาย **nie** Mr.

นาฬิกา **nar•lih•gar** clock

นาฬิกาข้อมือ **nar• lih•gar kôr•muee** watch

นาฬิกาปลุก **nar•li•gar bplùhk** alarm clock

นำ **nahm** lead

นำเนา ปลม นาร์ luhy lulug

น้ำ **nárm** water

น้ำตก **náhm•dtòk** waterfall

น้ำพุ **náhm•púh** fountain

น้ำมัน **náhm•mahn** fuel

น้ำยาคอนแท็ค เลนส์ **náhm•yar kohn•tàk•len** contact lens solution

น้ำยาล้างจาน **náhm•yar lárng•jarn** dishwashing liquid

น้ำหนัก **náhm•nàhk** weight

นิตยสาร **níht•tah• yah•sârn** magazine

นิ้ว **níhw** finger

นิ้วเท้า **níhw•tów** toe

นิ้วหัวแม่มือ **nihw hŏar• mâe•muee** thumb

นี่ **nêe** this

เนคไท **néhk•tie** tie

เนินเขา **nern•kŏu** hill

เนื้องอก **núea•ngôrk** tumor

เนื้อผ้า **núea•pâr** fabric

แน่นอน **nâe•norn** exact; sure

แนะนำ **ná•nahm** introduce; recommend; suggest

ใน **ni** in

ในประเทศ **ni bprah•têt** domestic

ในไม่ช้า **ni•mî•chár** soon

ในที่กลับ **ní•klàp** night club

ในลอน **ni•lôhn** nylon

บ
บกพร่อง **bok•prôhng** faulty

บทเรียน **bòt•rean** lesson

บน **bon** on

บริการ **bor•rih•garn** service (work)

บริการฉุกเฉิน **bor•rih• garn chùk•chêrn** emergency service

บริการซักรีด **bor•rih• garn sáhk•rêet** laundry service

บริการตนเอง **bor•rih• garn dton•eng** self-service

บริการโทรปลุก **bor• rih•garn toe bplùhk** wake-up call

บริการรับจอดรถ **bor• rih•garn jòrt rót** valet service

บริการลูกค้า **bor•rih• garn lôok•kár** customer service

บริการอินเตอร์เน็ต **bor•rih•garn ihn•dter•nèht** internet service

บริษัท **bor•rih•sàht** company

บริษัททัวร์ **bor•rih•sàht toar** travel agency

บริสุทธิ์ **bor•rih•sùht** innocent; pure

บวม **boarm** swelling

บ่อน้ำ **bòr•nárm** pond

บอก **bòrk** tell

บ่อย **bòhy** frequent; often

บ๋อย **bŏhy** waiter

บังคับ **bahng•káhp** mandatory

บัญชีกระแสรายวัน **bahn•chee grah•sâe rie•wahn** checking account

บัญชีออมทรัพย์ **bahn• chee orm•sáhp** savings account

บัตร **bàht** card

บัตรเครดิต **bàht kre•dìht** credit card

บัตรจอดรถ **bàht jòrt• rót** parking ticket

บัตรโทรศัพท์ **bàht toe• rah•sàhp** phone card

บัตรโทรศัพท์แบบเติมเงิน **bàht toe•rah•sàhp bàep dterm•ngern** prepaid phone card

บัตรนักศึกษาสากล **bàht náhk•sùek•sâr• sâr•gon** International Student Card

บัตรประจำตัว **bàht• bprah•jahm•dtoar** identification

บัตรประจำตัวผู้เอา ประกัน **bàht•bprah• jahm•dtoar pôo• ou•bprah•gahn** insurance card

บันได **bahn•di** ladder; stairs

บันไดเลื่อน **bahn•di• lûean** escalator

บัลเล่ต์ **bahn•lê** ballet

บาง **barng** some; thin

บางคน **barng•kon** someone

บางครั้ง **barng•kráhng** sometimes

บางที **barng•tee**

perhaps

บางที่ **barng•têe** somewhere

บางอย่าง **barng•yàrng** something

บาดเจ็บ **bàrt•jèhp** injure

บาดแผล **bàrt•plâe** *n* cut

บ้าน **bârn** house

บาร์ **bar** bar

บาสเก็ตบอล **bàrt•sah• gêht bohn** basketball

บิกินี **bih gìh nêe** bikini

บิด **biht** twist

บิน **bihn** fly

บิล **bihn** bill

บุหรี่ **buh•rèe** cigarette

เบนซิน **ben•sihn** gas [petrol BE]

เบรก **brèk** n brake

เบรคฉุกเฉิน **brèk chùhk•chêrn** emergency brake

เบอร์ต่อ **ber dtòr** extension (phone)

เบอร์โทรศัพท์ **ber toe•rah•sàhp** phone number

เบอร์แฟกซ์ **ber fàk** fax number

เบา **bou** *adj* light (weight)

เบาหวาน **bou•wârn** *n* diabetic

แบบเดียวกัน **bàep deaw•gahn** same

แบบฟอร์ม **bàep•form** form

โบสถ์ **bòet** church

ใบขับขี่ **bi kàhp•kèe** driver's license

ใบแจ้งความ **bi jâeng• kwarm** police report

ใบมีดโกน **bi mêet•goen** razor blade

ใบรับรอง **bi ráhp•rorng**

certificate

ใบสั่งยา **bi sàhng•yar** prescription

ใบเสร็จ(รับเงิน) **bi•sèht (ráhp•ngern)** receipt

ป
ปฏิกิริยา **bpah•dtih• nih•rih•yar** reaction

ปฏิทิน **bpah•dtih•tihn** calendar

ปรอท **bpah•ròrt** thermometer

ประกันภัย **bprah• gahn•pi** insurance

ประกันสุขภาพ **bprah•gahn sùhk• kah•pârp** health insurance

ประจำเดือน **bpràh• jahm•duean** period (menstrual)

ประชาสัมพันธ์ **bprah• char•sâhm•pahn** information desk

ประตู **bprah•dtoo** gate; door

ประตูขาออกขึ้นเครื่อง **bprah•dtoo tarng• òrk kûen krûeang** departure gate

ประเทศ **bprah•têt** country

ประภาคาร **bprah• par•karn** lighthouse

ประเภท **bprah•pêt** kind (type)

ประมาณ **bprah•marn** about

ประหลาด **bprah•làrt** bizarre

ปรับปรุง **bpràhp• bpruhng** improve

ปรับปรุงใหม่ **bpràhp• bpruhng mì** renovation

ปรึกษา bprúek•sǎr consult

ปลอดภัย bplòrt•pi *adj* safe

ปล้อก bplòhy let

ปลั๊กแปลงไฟฟ้า bpláhk bplaeng fi•fár adapter

ปลาย bplie n end

ปลายทาง bplie•tarng destination

ปลุก bplùhk wake

ปลด bprod ???

ปวดท้อง bpòart•tórng stomachache

ปวดประจำเดือน bpòart bprah•jahm•duean menstrual cramps

ปวดฟัน bpòart•fahn toothache

ปวดหลัง bpòart•lǎhng backache

ปวดหัว bpòart•hǔa headache

ปวดหู bpòart•hǒo earache

ปอด bpòrt lung

ปอดบวม bpòrt•boarm pneumonia

ป้อน bpórn feed

ปอนด์ bporn pound (weight)

ปัจจุบัน bpàht•juh•bahn present (time)

ปัญหา bpahn•hǒr problem

ปั๊ม bpáhm pump

ปั๊มน้ำมัน bpáhm náhm•mahn gas [petrol BE] station

ป่า bpàr forest

ปาก bpàrk mouth

ปากกา bpàrk•gar pen

ป้าย bpîe label; n sign

ป้ายรถเมล์ bpîe rót•me bus stop

ปิคนิค bpíhk•níhk picnic

ปิด bpìht v close; turn off; shut

ปี bpee year

เป้สะพายหลัง bpê sah•pie lǎhng backpack

เป็น bpehn be

เป็นของ bpehn•kǒhng belong

เป็นเจ้าของ bpehn jôw•kǒhng own

เป็นนิยม bpehm tee•níh•yom popular

เป็นผื่นคัน bpehn pǔeen•kahn rash

เป็นลม bpehn•lom faint

เป็นโสด bpehn•sòet single (unmarried)

เป็นหนี้ bpehn•nêe owe

เปรี้ยว bprêaw sour

เปลเด็ก bple•dèhk crib

เปลี่ยน bplèan v change

เปิด bpèrt turn on; open

เปิดดู bpèrt•doo browse

แปรงแปรงผม bpraeng bpraeng•pǒm hairbrush

แปรงสีฟัน bpraeng sěe•fahn toothbrush

แปล bplae translate

โปรแกรม bproe•graem program

โปรแกรมส่งข้อความว่า bproe•graem sòng kôr•kwarm instant messenger

โปสการ์ด bpóet•sah•gárt postcard

ไป bpi go

ไปรษณีย์ด่วน bpri•sah•nee dòarn express mail

ไปรษณีย์อากาศ bpri•

สห•นี ar•gàrt airmail

ฝ

ผงซักฟอก pǒng sáhk•fôrk detergent

ผม pǒm hair

ผลข้างเคียง pǒn•kârng•keang side effect

ผลัก plàhk push

ผ่าตัด pàr•dtàht operation

ผ้าก๊อซ pâr•górt gauze

ผ้าซาติน pâr sar•dtin satin

ผ้าปูที่นอน pâr bpoo têe•norn sheet (bed)

ผ้าฝ้าย pâr•fîe cotton

ผ้าพันคอ pâr•pahn•kor scarf

ผ้าพันแผล pâr•pahn•plǎe bandage [plaster BE]

ผ้าม่าน pâr•mârn curtain

ผ้าลูกไม้ pâr lôok•mí lace

ผ้าห่ม pâr•hòm blanket

ผ้าอนามัยแบบสอด pâr ah•nar•mi bàep•sòrt tampon

ผ้าอ้อม pâr•ôrm diaper [nappy BE]

ผ่าน pàrn through

ผิด piht wrong

ผิดกฎหมาย piht gòt•mǐe illegal

ผิดพลาด piht•plârt mistake

ผิวหนัง pǐhw•nǎhng skin

ผู้จัดการ pôo•jàht•garn manager

ผู้ชาย pôo•chie man

ผู้โดยสาร pôo•doey•sǎrn passenger

ผู้นำ pôo•nahm leader (group)

ผู้แปล poo•bplae translator

ผู้สอน pôo•sǒrn instructor

ผู้สูงอายุ pôo•sǒong•ar•yúh senior citizen

ผู้ใหญ่ pôo•yì adult

ผู้อำนวยการ pôo•ahm•noary•garn director (company)

ผ้าเช็ดตัว pâr•chéht•dtoar towel

ผ้ายีนส์ pâr•yeen denim

ผ้าวูล pâr woon wool

ผ้าไหม pâr•mǐ silk

ผ่อนอนามัย pâr ah•nar•mi sanitary napkin [pad BE]

ผ่าน pàrn v pass (drive)

เผ็ด pèht hot (spicy)

แผงขายหนังสือพิมพ์ pâeng kǐe nǎhng•sǔee•pihm newsstand

แผน pâen plan

แผนที่ pâen•tée map

แผนที่ถนน pâen•tée tah•nǒn road map

แผนที่รถไฟใต้ดิน pâen•tée rót•fi tí•dihn subway [underground BE] map

แผ่นพับ pâen•páhp brochure

แผนกของหาย pah•nàek kǒrng hǐe lost and found [lost-property office BE]

แผนกจำหน่ายตั๋ว pah•nàek jahm•nìe dtǒar ticket office

แผนกต้อนรับ pah•nàek dtôrn•ráhp reception (desk)

แผนกรับจอง **pah•naek ráhp•jorng** reservation desk

แผลพุพอง **plae púh•porng** blister

ฝ

ฝน **fön** n rain

ฝนตก **fön•dtòk** v rain

ฝังเข็ม **fâhng•kĕm** acupuncture

ฝาครอบเลนส์ **fâr•krórp•lehn** lens cap

ฝากกระเป๋า **fàrk grah•bpŏw** v check (luggage)

ฝากเงิน **fàrk•ngern** v deposit (bank)

ฝากไว้ **fàrk•wí** leave (deposit)

ฝาน **fârn** v slice

ฝึก **fùek** practice

ฝูงคนเดินตล **föong•kon** crowd

พ

พจนานุกรม **pót•jah•nar•núh•grom** dictionary

พนักงาน **pah•náhk•ngarn** staff

พนักงานขาย **pah•náhk•ngarn kĭe** shop assistant

พนักงานดับเพลิง **pah•náhk•ngarn dàhp•plerng** fire department [brigade BE]

พนักงานต้อนรับ **pah•náhk•ngarn dtôrn•ráhp** receptionist

พนักงานต้อนรับบนเครื่องบิน **pah•náhk•ngarn dtôrn•ráhp bon krûeang bihn** flight attendant

พนัน **pah•nahn** bet

พบ **póp** meet

พยากรณ์อากาศ **pah•yar•gorn ar•gàrt** weather forecast

พยาน **pah•yarn** witness

พยาบาล **pah•yar•barn** nurse

พรม **prom** carpet

พร้อม **prórm** ready

พระพุทธรูป **práh•puh•tah•rôop** Buddha image

พลั่ว **plôar** shovel

พลาสติก **plárt•sah•dtihk** plastic

พวงกุญแจ **poarng guhn•jae** key ring

พอ **por** enough

พอดี **por•dee** fit

พ่อแม่ **pôr•mâe** parents

พัก **páhk** v rest; stay

พัฒนา **páht•tah•nar** develop

พัดลม **páht•lom** fan

พัสดุ **páht•sah•dùh** package [parcel BE]

พาโนรามา **par•noe•rar•mâr** panorama

พาราเซตตามอล **par•rar•séht•dtar•môhn** acetaminophen [paracetamol BE]

พาย **pie** v row

พาสปอร์ต **párs•sàh•bpòrt** passport

พิการ **píh•garn** adj handicapped

พิการทางสายตา **píh•garn tarng sãry•dtar** visually impaired

พิการทางหู **píh•garn tarng hŏo** hearing impaired

พิพิธภัณฑ์ **píh•píht•tah•pahn** museum

พิมพ์ **pihm** print

พิเศษ **píh•sèt** special

พิวเตอร์ **pihw•dtĕr** pewter

พี่เลี้ยงเด็ก **pêe•léang dèhk** babysitter

พื้นเมือง **púeen•mueang** native

พูด **pôot** talk; say; speak

เพชร **péht** diamond

เพนิซิลลิน **pe•níh•sih•lihn** penicillin

เพราะว่า **próh•wâr** because

เพศชาย **pêt•chie** male

เพศหญิง **pêt•yĭhng** female

เพิ่ม **pêrm** extra

เพิ่มเติม **pêrm•dterm** additional

เพื่อ **pêua** for

เพื่อน **pûean** friend

เพื่อนร่วมงาน **pûean•rôarm•ngarn** colleague

แพง **paeng** expensive

แพลง **plaeng** sprain

แพลตตินั่ม **pláet•dtih•nâhm** platinum

โพลีเยสเตอร์ **poe•lee•yét•dtĕr** polyester

ฟ

ฟองน้ำ **forng•nárm** sponge

ฟัน **fahn** tooth

ฟันปลอม **fahn•bplorm** denture

ฟิล์มถนอมอาหาร **feem tah•nŏrm ar•hârn** plastic wrap [cling film BE]

ฟุตบอล **fúht•bohn** soccer [football BE]

เฟอร์นิเจอร์ **fer•nih•jêr** furniture

แฟกซ์ **fàk** fax

แฟลต **flàt** apartment [flat BE]

ไฟ **fi** fire; n light

ไฟฉาย **fi•chĭe** flashlight

ไฟแช็ก **fi•chák** lighter

ไฟฟ้า **fi•fár** electronic

ภ

ภรรยา **pahn•rah•yar** wife

ภาพวาด **pârp•wârt** painting (picture)

ภาษาไทย **par•sãr ti** Thai (language)

ภาษาอังกฤษ **par•sãr ahng•grìht** English (language)

ภาษีมูลค่าเพิ่ม **par•sĕe moon•kâr pêrm** sales tax [VAT BE]

ภาษีศุลกากร **par•sĕe sŭhn•lah•gar•gorn** duty (tax)

ภูเขา **poo•kŏu** mountain

ภูมิแพ้ **poom•páe** allergy

ม

มรกต **mor•rah•gòt** emerald

มรสุม **mor•rah•sŭhm** monsoon

มอเตอร์ไซค์ **mor•dter•si** moped; motorcycle

มะเร็ง **mah•rehng** cancer

มังสวิรัติ **mahng•sàh•wih•ráht** vegetarian

มัสยิด **máht•sah•yìht** mosque

มา **mar** come

มาถึง **mar•tĕung** arrive

มาเยี่ยม **mar•yêam** v visit

ม้า **már** horse

มาก **mârk** much; very

มากกว่า **mârk•gwàr** over (more than); more

มาตรฐาน **mârt•dtah•târn** standard

มาสคารา **márs•kar•rârr** mascara

มินิบาร์ **míh•níh bar** minibar

มิสซา **míh•sar** mass (church)

มี **mee** have; contain

มีความสุข **mee kwarm•sùhk** happy

มีค่า **mee•kâr** valuable

มีชื่อเสียง **mee chùee•sêang** famous

มีซับไตเติล **mee sáhp•dti•dtern** subtitled

มีเสน่ห์ **mee sah•nè** attractive

มีด **mêet** knife

มีดโกน **mêet•goen** razor

มืด **mûeet** dark

มือ **muee** hand

มือสอง **muee•sŏrng** secondhand

มุม **muhm** corner

มูลค่า **moon•kâr** value

เมนู **me•noo** menu

เมนูเด็ก **me•noo dèhk** children's menu

เมโมรีการ์ด **mem•moe•rêe gárt** memory card

เมาเครื่องบิน **mou krûeang•bihn** airsickness

เมารถ **mou rót** motion sickness

เมาเรือ **mou ruea** seasickness

เมื่อวาน **mûea•warn** yesterday

เมื่อไหร่ **mûea•ri** when

เมือง **mueang** town

เมื่อย **mûeay** stiff (muscle)

แม่น้ำ **mâe•nárm** river

แมลง **mah•laeng** bug; insect

แมลงกัดต่อย **mah•laeng gàht•dtòry** insect bite

แมลงสาบ **mah•laeng•sàrp** cockroach

โมง **moeng** o'clock

ไม่ **mî** no; not

ไม่กี่ **mi•gèe** a few

ไม่เคย **mi•kery** never

ไม่แพง **mî paeng** inexpensive

ไม่มีอะไร **mî mee ah•ri** nothing

ไม่สบาย **mî sah•bie** sick [ill BE]

ไม่ใส่ **mî sì** without

ไม้ **míe** wood (material)

ไม้กวาด **míe•gwart** broom

ไม้กอล์ฟ **míe•górf** golf club

ไม้แขวนเสื้อ **míe•kwâen•sûea** hanger; coat hanger

ไม้ถูพื้น **míe tŏo•púeen** mop

ไม้เทนนิส **míe tehn•níht** racket (tennis)

ไมเกรน **mi•gren** migraine

ไมโครเวฟ **mi•kroe•wép** microwave (oven)

ย

ยกเลิก **yók•lêrk** cancel

ยกเว้น **yók•wéhn** except

ยอมรับ **yorm•ráhp** accept; approve

ย่อยนมไม่ได้ **yôry nom mi•dîe** lactose intolerant

ยังไง **yahng•ngi** how

ยา **yar** medicine

ยากันแมลง **yar gahn mah•laeng** insect repellent

ยาชา **yar•char** anesthetic

ยานอนหลับ **yar norn•làhp** sleeping pill

ยาปฏิชีวนะ **yar bpah•dtih•chee•wah•náh** antibiotics

ยาพิษ **yar•píht** poison

ยาระงับกลิ่นตัว **yar rah•ngáhp glìhn•dtoar** deodorant

ยาระงับประสาท **yar rah•ngáhp bprah•sàrt** sedative

ยาระบาย **yar rah•bie** laxative

ยาลดกรด **yar lót•gròt** antacid

ยาสีฟัน **yar sĕe•fahn** toothpaste

ยาเส้น **yar•sên** tobacco

ยาเหน็บ **yar•nèhp** suppository

ยาก **yârk** difficult

ยาง **yarng** tire

ย่านใจกลางเมือง **yârn ji•glarng mueang** downtown

ย่านช็อปปิ้ง **yârn chóhp•bpîhng** shopping area

ย่านธุรกิจ **yârn túh•ráh•gìht** business district

ยาม **yarm** lifeguard / ยามไลฟ์การ์ด **yarm li•gàrt** lifeguard

ยาว **yow** long

ยินดีต้อนรับ **yihn•dee**

ดีต้อนรับ **dtôrn•ráhp** welcome

ยีนส์ **yeen** jeans

ยืน **yueen** stand

ยืนกราน **yueen•grarn** insist

ยืนยัน **yueen•yahn** confirm

ยืม **yueem** borrow

ยุงกัด **yuhng•gàht** mosquito bite

ยุ่ง **yûhng** busy

ยูโรเช็ค **yoo•roe ++ chéhk** Eurocheque

เย็น **yehn** cool

เย็บ **yéhp** sew

เยี่ยมมาก **yêam•mârk** superb

แยก **yâek** separate

แยกกันอยู่ **yâek gahn yòo** separated (marital status)

แยกตามรายการ **yâek dtarm rie•garn** itemized

ร

รถ **rót** vehicle

รถเข็น **rót•kêhn** cart [trolley BE]

รถเข็นกระเป๋า **rót•kêhn grah•bpŏu** luggage cart [trolley BE]

รถเข็นคนพิการ **rót•kêhn kon píh•garn** wheelchair

รถเข็นเด็ก **rót•kêhn dèhk** stroller [push-chair BE]

รถเช่า **rót•chôu** car rental [hire BE]

รถบรรทุก **rót bahn•túhk** truck [lorry BE]

รถบัสทางไกล **rót báht tarng gli** long-distance bus

รถพยาบาล **rót pah•yar•barn** ambulance

รถห่วง **rót•pôarng** trailer

รถไฟ **rót•fi** train

รถไฟใต้ดิน **rót•fi tíe•dihn** subway [underground BE]

รถเมล์ **rót•me** bus

รถยนต์ **rót•yon** car

รถราง **rót•rarng** tram

รถบรรทุก **rót•bàn•túk** tow truck

รถเสบียง **rót sah•beang** dining car

รบกวน **róp•goarn** bother; disturb

ร่ม **rôm** umbrella

รวม **roarm** merge; include

รวมค่าบริการ **roarm kâr•bor•rih•garn** service included

รสชาติ **rót•chârt** flavor; taste

รหัส **rah•hàht** code; password

รหัสประเทศ **rah•hàht bprah•têt** country code

รหัสพื้นที่ **rah•hàht púeen•têe** area code

รอ **ror** wait

รองเท้า **rorng•tów** shoe

รองเท้าแตะ **rorng•tów dtà** slippers; sandals

รองเท้าบูท **rorng•tów bóot** boots

รองเท้าผ้าใบ **rorng•tów pâr•bi** sneakers

ร้อน **rórn** adj hot

รอบ **rôrp** n round (golf)

รอบ ๆ **rôrp•rôrp** around

รอบกลางวัน **rôrp glarng•wahn** matinée

รอยฟกช้ำ **rory fók•chárm** bruise

ระเบียง **rah•beang** balcony

ระมัดระวัง **rah•máht•rah•wahng** caution

ระยะทาง **rah•yáh•tarng** distance

ระวัง **rah•wahng** beware; careful

ระหว่าง **rah•wàrng** between; during

ระหว่างประเทศ **rah•wàrng bprah•têt** international

รัก **ráhk** love

รับ **ráhp** pick up

รับประกัน **ráhp•bprah•gahn** guarantee

ราคา **rar•kar** price; v cost

ร้านกาแฟ **rárn gar•fae** cafe

ร้านกิฟต์ช็อป **rárn gíp•chòhp** gift store

ร้านขายขนม **rárn kíe kah•nŏm** candy store

ร้านขายของชำ **rárn kíe kŏrng•chahm** grocery store

ร้านขายของที่ระลึก **rárn kíe kŏrng têe•rah•lúehk** souvenir store

ร้านขายของเล่น **rárn kíe kŏrng•lên** toy store

ร้านขายเครื่อง กีฬา **rárn kíe krúeang•gee•lar** sporting goods store

ร้านขายเครื่องมือ อุปกรณ์ **rárn kíe krúeang•muee ùhp•bpah•gorn** hardware store

ร้านขายงานฝีมือ **rárn kíe**

ngan•fĕe•muee craft shop

ร้านขายดอกไม้ **rárn kíe dòrk•míe** florist

ร้านขายผักผลไม้ **rárn kíe pàkk pŏn•lah•míe** produce store

ร้านขายยา **rárn kíe yar** pharmacy [chemist BE]

ร้านขายยาเปิด 24 ชั่วโมง **rárn kíe yar bpèrt yêe•sìhp•sèe chôar•moeng** all-night pharmacy [chemist BE]

ร้านขายรองเท้า **rárn kíe rorng•tów** shoe store

ร้านขายเสื้อผ้า **rárn kíe sûea•pâr** clothing store [clothes shop BE]

ร้านขายเหล้า **rárn kíe lôu** liquor store

ร้านขายอาหารสุขภาพ **rárn kíe ar•hârn sùhk•kah•pârp** health food store

ร้านค้า **rárn•kár** store

ร้านค้าปลอดภาษี **rárn•kár bplòrt par•sĕe** duty-free

ร้านเครื่องประดับ **rárn krûeang bprah•dàhp** jeweler

ร้านซักรีด **rárn sáhk•rêet** laundromat [launderette BE]

ร้านซักแห้ง **rárn sáhk•hâeng** dry cleaner

ร้านทำเล็บ **rárn tahm•léhp** nail salon

ร้านเบเกอรี่ **rárn be•ger•rêe** bakery

ร้านหนังสือ **rárn nâhng•sŭee** bookstore

ร้านอาหาร **rárn ar•hârn** restaurant

รายการ **rie•garn** n list

รายการร้านค้า **rie•garn rárn•kár** store guide [directory BE]

รายละเอียด **rie•lah•èat** detail

รายวัน **rle•walm** daily

ร้าว **róarw** fracture

ริมฝีปาก **rihm•fĕe•bpàrk** lip

รีด **rêet** v iron

รีบ **rêep** hurry

รู **roo** hole

รู้จัก **róo•jàhk** know

รู้สึก **róo•sùek** feel

รู้สึกตัว **róo•sùek•dtoar** conscious

รู้สึกสนุก **róo•sùek sah•nùhk** enjoy

รูป **rôop** photograph

รูปแบบ **rôop•bàep** feature

รูปปั้น **rôop•bpâhn** statue

รูปร่าง **rôop•rârng** shape

รูมเซอร์วิส **room ser•wìht** room service

เร่ง **rêhng** rush

เร่งความเร็ว **rêhng kwarm•rehw** v speed

เร็ว **rehw** quick; fast

เริ่ม **rêrm** start; begin

เรียก **rêak** call (summon)

เรียนรู้ **rean•róo** learn

เรือข้ามฟาก **ruea kârm•fârk** ferry

เรือแคนู **ruea kae•noo** canoe

เรือชูชีพ **ruea choo•chêep** life boat

เรือเดินทะเล **ruea dern tah•le** ship

เรือพาย **ruea•pie** rowboat

เรือยนต์ **ruea•yon** motorboat

เรือยอทช์ **ruea•yórt** yacht

เรื่องตลก **rûeang dtah•lòk** joke

โรคไขข้อเสื่อม **rôek kî•kôr sŭeam** arthritis

โรคเบาหวาน **... bou•wărn** diabetes

โรคแพ้อากาศ **rôek páe ar•gàrt** hay fever

โรคโลหิตจาง **rôek loe•hìht jarng** anemia

โรคหอบหืด **rôek hòrp•hùeet** asthma

โรคหัวใจ **rôek hŏar•ji** heart condition

โรงพยาบาล **roeng pah•yar•barn** hospital

โรงยิม **roeng yihm** gym

โรงรถ **roeng•rót** garage

โรงแรม **roeng•raem** hotel

โรงละคร **roeng lah•korn** theater (play)

โรงหนัง **roeng•năhng** movie theater (cinema BE)

โรแมนติก **roe•maen•dtihk** romantic

ไร่องุ่น **rî àh•ngùhn** vineyard

ไร้สาย **rí•sĭe** wireless

ล

ลง **long** get off (bus, etc.)

ลด **lót** reduce

ลดราคา **lót rar•kar** clearance; sale

ลบ **lóp** delete

ลม **lom** air (tire); wind

ลมแดด **lom•dàet** sunstroke

ลมแรง **lom raeng** windy

ล้มลง **lóm•long** collapse

ล็อค **lóhk** lock

ล่องเรือ **lôhng•ruea** cruise

ล็อตเตอรี่ **lóht•dter•rêe** lottery

ล็อบบี้ **láhp•bêe** lobby (theater, hotel)

ละคร **lah•korn** n play

ละลาย **lah•lie** dissolve

ล่า **lâr** hunt

ล่าม **lârm** interpreter

ลำคอ **lahm•kor** throat

ลำธาร **lahm•tarn** stream

ลำไส้ **lahm•sî** bowel

ลิตร **líht** liter

ลิ้น **líhn** tongue

ลินิน **lih•nihn** linen

ลิปสติก **líhp•sah•dtihk** lipstick

ลิฟต์ **líhp** elevator (lift BE)

ลึก **lúek** deep

ลืม **lueem** forget

ลู่ม้าวิ่ง **lôo már wîhng** horsetrack

ลู่วิ่ง **lôo wîhng** racetrack

ลูกเต๋า **lôok•dtŏu** n dice

ลูกบอล **lôok•bohn** ball

เล็ก **léhk** small

เลน **len** lane

เล่น **lêhn** v play

เล่นวินด์เซิร์ฟ **lêhn wihn•sérp** windsurfing

เลนส์ **lehn** lens

เล็บ **léhp** nail

เล็ม **lehm** trim

เลว **lew** bad

เลี้ยว **léaw** turn

เลือก **lûeak** choose

เลือด **lûeat** blood

เลือดออก **lûeat•òrk** bleed

แลกเงิน **lâek•ngern** v/n change (money)

แลกเปลี่ยน **lâek•bplèan** exchange

แล้ว **láew** already

แล้วก็ **láew•gôr** then (afterwards)

และ **láe** and

โลชั่นหลังโกนหนวด **loe•chăhn lăhng goen•nòart** aftershave

โลชั่นอาบแดด **loe•chăhn àrp•dàet** suntan lotion

โลหะ **loe•hàh** metal

ว

วง (ดนตรี) **wong (don dtree)** band (music)

วลี **wah•lee** phrase

วอร์ดคนไข้ **wôrt kon•kî** ward (hospital)

วอลเลย์บอล **wohn•lê•bohn** volleyball

วัง **wahng** palace

วัดขนาด **wáht kah•nàrt** v measure

วัตถุประสงค์ **wáht•tùh bprah•sŏng** purpose

วัน **wahn** day

วันเกิด **wahn•gèrt** birthday

วันธรรมดา **wahn tahm•mah•dar** weekday

วันนี้ **wahn•née** today

วันพรุ่งนี้ **wahn prûhng•née** tomorrow

วันสุดสัปดาห์ **wahn sùht•sàhp•dar** weekend

วันหยุด **wahn•yùht** vacation (holiday BE)

ว่าง **wârng** available; empty, free, vacant

วาดภาพ **wârt•pârp** v paint (picture)

ว่ายน้ำ **wîe•nárm** swim

วาล์ว **wow** valve

วิชา **wih•char** course

วิดีโอเกม **wih•dee•oe•gem** video game

วิว **wihw** view

วีซ่า **wee•sàh** visa

วีซ่าเข้าประเทศ **wee•sàh kôu bprah•têt** entry visa

เว็ทสูท **wéht•sòot** wetsuit

เวลา **we•lar** time

เวลาทำการ **we•lar tahm•garn** opening hours

เวลาเยี่ยม **we•lar yêam** visiting hours

เวียนศีรษะ **wean sĕe•sàh** dizzy

แว่นกันแดด **wân gahn•dàet** sunglasses

แว่นตา **wân•dtar** glasses (optical)

ศ

ศาสนา **sàrt•sa•nâr** religion

ศึกษา **sùek•sâr** study

ศุลกากร **sŭhn•lah•gar•gorn** customs

ศูนย์การค้า **sŏon•garn•kár** shopping mall (centre BE)

ศูนย์บริการทางธุรกิจ **sŏon bor•rih•garn tarng túh•rá•gìht** business center

ส

สกปรก **sòk•grah•bpròk** dirty

สกีน้ำ **sah•gee nárm** water skis

ส่ง **sòng** deliver; drop off; send

ส่งข้อความ **sòng kôr• kwarm** v text (SMS)

ส่งจดหมาย **sòng jòt• mĭe** v mail [post BE]

สด **sòt** fresh

เหล็กไม่เป็นสนิม **sah•dtien lòt** stainless steel

สไตล์ **sah•dtie** style

สถานที่ **sah•tärn•têe** site; place

สถานที่ท่องเที่ยว **sah• tärn•têe tôhng• têaw** sight (attraction)

สถานที่นัดพบ **sah•tärn•têe náht• póp** meeting place

สถานทูต **sah•tärn•tôot** embassy

สถานีรถเมล์ **sah•tär• nee kön•sòng** bus station

สถานีตำรวจ **sah•tär• nee dtahm•ròart** police station

สถานีรถไฟ **sah•tär• nee rót•fi** train [railway BE] station

สถานีรถไฟใต้ดิน **sah•tär•nee rót•fi tîe dihn** subway [underground BE] station

ส้น **sôn** heels

สนอร์กเกิล **sah•nórk• gêrn** snorkel

สนามกอล์ฟ **sah•nârm górp** golf course

สนามกีฬา **sah•nârm gee•lar** stadium

สนามเด็กเล่น **sah•nârm dèhk lên** playground

สนามเทนนิส **sah•nârm** tehn•níht tennis court

สนามบิน **sah•nârm• bihn** airport

สนุก **sah•nùhk** fun

สแน็คบาร์ **sah•nák bar** snack bar

สบายดี **sah•bie dee** fine (health)

สปอร์ตคลับ **sah•bpòrt• kláhp** sports club

สปา **sah•bpar** spa

สมรภูมิ **sah•mŏr•rah• poom** battleground

สมาชิก **sah•mar•chíhk** member

สมุดโทรศัพท์ **sah•mùht toe•rah•sàhp** phone directory

สร้อยข้อมือ **sôry kôr•muee** bracelet

สร้อยคอ **sôry kor** necklace

สระกลางแจ้ง **sàh glarng•jäeng** outdoor pool

สระเด็ก **sàh dèhk** kiddie [paddling BE] pool

สระว่ายน้ำ **sàh wîe• nárm** swimming pool

สระว่ายน้ำในร่ม **sàh wîe•nárm ni rôm** indoor pool

สลัก **sah•làhk** engrave

สวดมนต์ **sòart•mon** prayer

สวน **sŏarn** garden

สวนพฤกษศาสตร์ **sŏarn prúek•sah•sàrt** botanical garden

สวนสนุก **sŏarn sah•nùhk** amusement park; theme park

สวนสัตว์ **sŏarn sàht** zoo

สวนสาธารณะ **sùan sâr•tar•rah•náh** n park

ส่วนตัว **sòarn•dtoar** private

ส่วนลด **sòarn•lót** discount; (price) reduction

สวม **sŏarm** wear

ห้องน้ำเคมี **sŏarm ke•mee** chemical toilet

สวย **sŏary** beautiful

สหรัฐอเมริกา **sah•hàh•ráht ah•me•rih•gar** United States

สหราชอาณาจักร **sah•hàh rârt•chah• ar•nar•jàhk** United Kingdom

ส้อม **sôrm** fork

สะกด **sah•gòt** spell

สะพาน **sah•parn** bridge

สะอาด **sah•àrt** adj clean

สั่ง **sàhng** order

สังเคราะห์ **sâhng•króh** synthetic

สัญชาติ **sân•chârt** nationality

สัญญาณไฟไหม้ **sâhn•yarn fi•mî** fire alarm

สัญลักษณ์ **sâhn•yah• làhk** symbol

สัตว์ **sàht** animal

สัตว์ป่า **sàht•bpàr** wildlife

สัปดาห์ **sàhp•dar** week

สัมมนา **sâhm•mah•nar** seminar

สาธารณะ **sâr•tar• rah•náh** public

สามี **sâr•mee** husband

สาย **sĭe** late

สายการบิน **sĭe•garn• bihn** airline

สายตายาว **sĭe•dtar• yow** far-sighted [long-sighted BE]

สายตาสั้น **sĭe•dtar sâhn** near-sighted [short-sighted BE]

สำคัญ **sâhm•kahn** important; main

สำนักงานท่องเที่ยว **sâhm•náhk•ngarn tôhng•têaw** tourist office

สำรอง **sâhm•rorng** spare

สำหรับขาย **sâhm•ràhp kĭe** for sale

สิ่งของ **sihng•kŏrng** thing

สี **sĕe** color; paint

สี่แยก **sèe•yâek** intersection

สุขภาพ **sùhk•kah•pârp** health

สุดท้าย **sùht•tíe** last

สุนัข **suh•náhk** dog

สุนัขนำทาง **suh•náhk nahm•tarng** guide dog

สุสาน **sùh•sârn** cemetery

สุเหร่า **suh•ròu** mosque

สุเหร่ายิว **suh•ròu yihw** synagogue

สูง **sŏong** tall; high

สูตินรีแพทย์ **sŏo•dtih• nah•ree•pâet** gynecologist

สูบบุหรี่ **sòop buh•rèe** smoke

เส้น **sêhn** line

เส้นทาง **sêhn•tarng** route

เส้นทางเดินป่า **sêhn• tarng dern•bpàr** trail

เสาเต็นท์ **sǎo dtéhn** tent pole

เสิร์ฟ **sèrp** serve

เสีย **sêa** break down; broken

เสียหาย **sêa•hǐe** damage

เสียงดัง **sěarng dahng** noisy

เสื้อกันฝน **sûea gahn fǒn** raincoat

เสื้อกันลม **sûea gahn lom** windbreaker

เสื้อกันหนาว **sûea gahn nǒw** sweater

เสื้อโค้ท **sûea•kóet** coat

เสื้อแจ็กเก็ต **sûea ják•gèht** jacket

เสื้อชูชีพ **sûea choo•chêep** lifejacket

เสื้อผู้หญิง **sûea pôo•yǐhng** blouse

เสื้อยกทรง **sûea yók•song** bra

เสื้อยืด **sûea yûeet** T-shirt

แสดง **sah•daeng** v show

แสดงรายการสิ่งของ **sah•daeng rie•garn sǐhng•kǒrng** declare

แสตมป์ **sah•dtaem** stamp

ใส่ **sì** put

ห

หญ้า **yâr** grass

หน่วย **nòary** units

หนัก **nàhk** heavy

หนัง **nǎhng** movie [film BE]; leather, skin

หนังสือ **nǎhng•sǔee** book

หนังสือนำเที่ยว **nǎhng•sǔee nahm•têaw** guide book

หนังสือพิมพ์ **nǎhng•sǔee•pihm** newspaper

หนา **nǎr** thick

หน้า **nâr** face

หน้ากาก **nâr•gàrk** mask

หน้าต่าง **nâr•dtàrng** window

หน้าผา **nâr•pǎr** cliff

หน้าอก **nâr•òk** breast; chest

หนทาง **hǒn** v cold

หมดแรง **mòt•raeng** exhausted

หมดสติ **mòt sah•dtìh** unconscious

หมวก **mòark** hat

หมวกแก๊ป **mòark gáp** cap

หมวกนิรภัย **mòark níh•ráh•pi** helmet

หมอ **mǒr** doctor

หมอเฉพาะทาง **mǒr chah•póh•tarng** specialist (doctor)

หมอเด็ก **mǒr dèhk** pediatrician

หมอฟัน **mǒr•fahn** dentist

หมอก **mòrk** fog

หมอน **mǒrn** pillow

หมั้น **mâhn** engaged

หมุด **mùht** peg

หมุดปักเต็นท์ **mùht bpàhk dtéhn** tent peg

หมู่บ้าน **mòo•bârn** village

หยด **yòt** drip

หย่า **yàr** divorce

หยาบคาย **yàrp•kie** rude

หยุด **yùht** v brake; stop

หรือ **rǔee** or

หลงทาง **lǒng•tarng** lost

หลวม **lǒarm** loose

หลอดไฟ **lòrt•fi** lightbulb

หลัง **lǎhng** back; behind

หลังคา **lǎhng•kar** roof

หลังจาก **lǎhng•jàrk** after

หลาย **lǐe** many

หวัด **wàht** n cold

หวาน **wǎrn** adj sweet

หวี **wěe** comb

หอศิลป์ **hǒr•sǐhn** gallery

หอ **hǒr** pack; wrap

หอไป **hǒr bpi** to go [take away BE] (food)

ห้อง **hôhng** room

ห้องครัว **hôhng•kroar** kitchen

ห้องคอนเวนชั่น **hôhng kohn•wehn•châhn** convention hall

ห้องคู่ **hôhng•kôo** double room

ห้องเดี่ยว **hôhng•dèaw** single room

ห้องนอน **hôhng•norn** bedroom

ห้องน้ำ **hôhng•nárm** bathroom; restroom [toilet BE]

ห้องประชุม **hôhng bprah•chuhm** meeting room

ห้องพักผู้โดยสาร **hôhng páhk pôo•doey•sârn** waiting room

ห้องพักผู้โดยสารขาออก **hôhng páhk pôo•doey•sârn kâr•òrk** departure lounge

ห้องลองเสื้อผ้า **hôhng lorng sûea•pâr** fitting room

ห้องสมุด **sah•mùht** library

ห้องอาบน้ำ **hôhng àrp•nárm** n shower

ห้องอาหาร **hôhng ar•hǎrn** dining room

หัตถกรรม **hàht•tah•gahm** handicraft

หั่น **hàhn** v dice

หัว **hǔa** head

หัวใจ **hǔa•ji** heart

หัวใจวาย **hǔa•ji wie** heart attack

หา **hǎr** find

ทาง **hàrng** away

ห้างสรรพสินค้า **hârng sàhp•pah•sǐhn•kár** department store

ห้าม **hârm** prohibited

ห้ามสูบบุหรี่ **hârm sòop buh•rèe** no smoking

หาย **hǐe** missing; lose (item)

หายใจ **hǎi•ji** breathe

หิมะ **hìh•máh** snow

หิว **hǐw** hungry

หิวน้ำ **hǐw•nárm** thirsty

หุ้นส่วน **hûhn •sòarn** partner

หู **hǒo** ear

หูหนวก **hǒo•nòark** deaf

เหตุการณ์ **hèt•garn** event

เห็น **hěhn** see

เห็นด้วย **hěhn•dôary** agree

เหนียว **nêaw** tough (texture)

เหนือ **nêua** north

เหนื่อย **nùeay** tired

เหมาะสม **mòh•sǒm** suitable

เหมือนกัน **mǔean•gahn** also; too

เหมือนกับ **mǔean•gàhp**

v like (same)

เหรียญ **rêan** coin

เหล็ก **lèhk** iron (metal)

เหล็กกล้า **lèhk•glâr** steel

แห้ง **hâeng** *adj* dry (clothes)

แหนบ **nàep** tweezers

อวยพร **oary•porn** v wish (bless)

แหวน **wâen** *n* ring (jewelry)

โหล **lŏe** dozen

ให้ **hî** give

ให้นม **hî•nom** breastfeed

ให้ยืม **hî yueem** lend

ใหญ่ **yì** big; large

ใหม่ **mì** new

ไหมขัดฟัน **mǐ kàht•fahn** dental floss

ไหม้ **mî** burn

ไหล่ **lì** shoulder

อ

องศา **ong•sâr** degree (weather)

อธิบาย **ah•tíh•bie** describe

อนุญาต **ah•núh•yârt** allow

อนุสาวรีย์ **ah•núh•sâr•wah•ree** memorial

อนุสาวรีย์สงคราม **ah•núh•sâr•wah•ree sŏng•krarm** war memorial

อบซาวน่า **òp sow•nâr** v sauna

อพาร์ตเมนต์ **ah•párt•méhn** apartment

อเมริกัน **ah•me•rih•gahn** American

อยากได้ **yàrk•dîe** want

อย่างไม่เป็นทางการ **yàrng mî•bpehn tarng•garn** informal

อยู่ **yòo** stay; live

อร่อย **ah•ròhy** delicious

อโรมาเทราปี **ah•roe•mâr te•rar•pêe** aromatherapy

ออก **òrk** out

ออกเดิน **òrk•jàrk** v leave

ออกจากระบบ **òrk•jark rah•bòp** log off

ออกเสียง **òrk•sĕang** pronounce

ออกซิเจน **óhk•sih•jên** oxygen

ออเคสตรา **or•két•trâr** orchestra

อ่อน **òrn** light (color)

อะไร **ah•ri** what

อะไหล่ **ah•lì** replacement part

อัตโนมัติ **àht•tah•noe•máht** automatic

อัตราแลกเปลี่ยน **àht•dtrar lâek•bplèarn** exchange rate

อันตราย **ahn•dtah•rie** dangerous

อาการ **ar•garn** symptom

อาการท้องผูก **ar•garn tórng•pòok** constipation

อาการอักเสบ **ar•garn àhk•sèp** inflammation

อากาศ **ar•gàrt** weather

อาคาร **ar•karn** building

อาคารจอดรถ **ar•karn jòrt•rót** parking garage

อ่างล้างน้ำ **àrng** sink

อ่างเก็บน้ำ **àrng•gèhp•**

นาร์ม **nárm** reservoir

อาจจะ **àrt•jah** maybe

อาเจียน **ar•jean** vomit

อาชีพ **ar•chêep** profession

อ่าน **àrn** read

อาบแดด **àrp•dàet** sunbathe

อาบน้ำ **àrp•nárm** v bath

อาบน้ำฝักบัว **àrp•narm fàhk•boar** v shower

อาหาร **ar•hârn** food; meal

อาหารกลางวัน **ar•hârn glarng•wahn** lunch

อาหารจานด่วน **ar•hârn jarn•dòarn** fast food

อาหารชุด **ar•hârn chúht** set menu

อาหารเช้า **ar•hârn chóu** breakfast

อาหารเด็ก **ar•hârn dèhk** baby food

อาหารเป็นพิษ **ar•hârn bpehn•píht** food poisoning

อาหารไม่ย่อย **ar•hârn mî yôry** indigestion

อาหารเย็น **ar•hârn yehn** dinner

อาหารว่าง **ar•hârn wârng** snack

อินซูลิน **ihn•soo•lihn** insulin

อินเตอร์เน็ต **ihn•dter•nèht** internet

อินเตอร์เน็ตคาเฟ่ **ihn•dter•nèht kar•fê** internet cafe

อีบูโปรเฟน **ee•boo•bproe•fen** ibuprofen

อีเมล **ee•mew** e-mail

อีเมลแอดเดรส **ee•mew át•drèt** e-mail address

อุณหภูมิ **uhn•hah•poom** temperature

อุดฟัน **ùht•fahn** filling (dental)

อุ่น **ùhn** warm

อุบัติเหตุ **uh•bàht•tih•hèt** accident

อุปกรณ์ดำน้ำ **ùhp•bpah•gorn dahm•nárm** diving equipment

อุปกรณ์เดินป่า **ùhp•bpah•gorn dern•bpàr** hiking gear

อุปรากร **ùhp•bpah•rar•gorn** opera

อุโมงค์ **uh•moeng** tunnel

อู่เรือ **òo ruea** dock

เอ็กซเรย์ **éhk•sah•re** x-ray

เอกอัครราชทูต **èk•àhk•kah•rârt•chah•tôot** ambassador

เอทีเอ็ม **e•tee•ehm** ATM

แอร์ **ae** air conditioning

แอสไพริน **áes•pi•rihn** aspirin

เอา **ou** take

เอาออก **ou òrk** remove

เอื้อม **ûeam** reach

โอเค **oe•ke** OK

โอนเงิน **oen•ngern** transfer (finance)

ไอ **i** cough

ไอโอดีน **i•oe•deen** iodine

ฮี

ฮันนีมูน **hahn•nee•moon** honeymoon

ฮัลโหล **hahn•lŏe** hello (phone)

ฮาลาล **har•larn** halal

INDEX

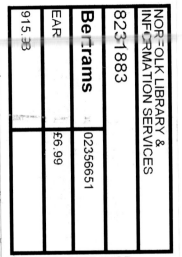

Berlitz pocket guide

THAILAND

Seventh Edition 2018

Editor: Sian Marsh
Author: Ben Davies and Paul Stafford
Head of Production: Rebeka Davies
Picture Editor: Tom Smyth
Cartography Update: Carte
Update Production: Apa Digital
Photography Credits: Alamy 5MC, 92;
Dreamstime 52, 54; Getty Images 1; Hans
Fonk 6R; iStock 4ML, 4TL, 5T, 5MC, 5M,
15, 36, 56, 59, 60, 63, 79, 89; John Ishii/
Apa Publications 77, 80, 82; Luca Invernizz
Tettoni 19; Mandarin Oriental 6L; Nikt Won
Apa Publications 94; Peter Stuckings/Apa
Publications 5M, 7, 7R, 11, 12, 17, 20, 24,
26, 29, 31, 32, 35, 37, 38, 40, 42, 45, 47, 48,
50, 64, 65, 66, 68, 70, 71, 72, 75, 84, 86, 90,
91, 99, 100, 103, 104, 106; Shutterstock 4T
4MC, 5TC, 53
Cover Picture: Shutterstock

Distribution
UK, Ireland and Europe: Apa Publications
(UK) Ltd; sales@insightguides.com
United States and Canada: Ingram
Publisher Services; ips@ingramcontent.com
Australia and New Zealand: Woodslane;
info@woodslane.com.au
Southeast Asia: Apa Publications (SN) Pte;
singaporeoffice@insightguides.com
Worldwide: Apa Publications (UK) Ltd;
sales@insightguides.com

welcome your suggestions; please contact
us at: berlitz@apaguide.co.uk
www.insightguides.com/berlitz

Berlitz Trademark Reg. U.S. Patent Office
and other countries. Marca Registrada.
Used under licence from the Berlitz
Investment Corporation